**FORESIGHT BOOKS IN PSYCHOLOGY**
*David F. Ricks, General Editor*


SCIENCE, PSYCHOLOGY, AND COMMUNICATION
Essays Honoring William Stephenson
*Steven E. Brown and Donald J. Brenner, Editors*

TRUE AMERICANISM: GREEN BERETS AND
WAR RESISTERS
A Study of Commitment
*David Mark Mantell*

VARIETIES OF PSYCHOTHERAPEUTIC EXPERIENCE
Multivariate Analyses of Patients' and Therapists' Reports
*David E. Orlinsky and Kenneth I. Howard*

# Varieties of Psychotherapeutic Experience

## Multivariate Analyses of Patients' and Therapists' Reports

### DAVID E. ORLINSKY

*The University of Chicago*
*and the Institute for Juvenile Research*

### KENNETH I. HOWARD

*Northwestern University*
*and the Institute for Juvenile Research*

**TEACHERS COLLEGE PRESS**
*Teachers College, Columbia University*
*New York and London*

*Library of Congress Cataloging in Publication Data:*

Orlinsky, David E.
    Varieties of psychotherapeutic experience.

    (Foresight books in psychology)
    1. Psychiatric Research.    2. Psychotherapy.
I. Howard, Kenneth Irwin, 1932-    joint author.
II. Title. [DNLM: 1. Psychotherapy. WM420 071v]
RC337.074      616.8'914      74-22011

"Thirteen Ways of Looking at a Blackbird," © 1923, 1951 by Wallace
Stevens. Reprinted from *The Collected Poems of Wallace Stevens* by per-
mission of Alfred A. Knopf, Inc.

Cover drawing by Deborah Howard
Cover design by Angela Foote

*Manufactured in the United States of America*

To Our Parents
*Max and Gertrude Orlinsky*
*Simon and Florence Howard*
With Loving Appreciation for
The Gift of Education

# Series Editor's Foreword

An intelligent reader who wants to find out what goes on in psychotherapy is faced with a bewildering variety of theories. Books by practicing therapists usually tell more about what the therapist thinks than about what actually happens in therapy. Reports by patients are often moving human stories, but one is left wondering about how general or typical each experience might have been. At best, a person who reads a series of books by patients and by therapists will emerge from his study with an awareness of some of the profoundly important things that can occur in psychotherapy. At worst, he will find his enthusiasm withering as he meets evidence of faddishness, hucksterism, narrow orthodoxy, stuffed shirts, and mediocre minds.

Until recently, there was no way out of this dilemma. Psychotherapy was still seen as a field in which scientific inquiry was either impractical or irrelevant. Belief and practice were based on the inadequate foundation of self-proclaimed or tradition-sanctioned authority. A fresh spirit of inquiry has come into therapy, however, and in the work of Bergin, Beck, Lerner, Luborsky, Strupp, and the present authors we see a new willingness to observe and to ask questions rather than to proclaim premature answers.

*Varieties of Psychotherapeutic Experience* seems to me to be one of the finest examples of this new empirical approach. Its authors knew psychotherapy as participants before they studied it as scientists. Their study takes its questions and methods from the actual practice of therapy. Information on the developing process of therapy is gathered from both patients and therapists. In a remarkable series of analyses, the two perspectives are combined into patterns that are statistically clear and clinically important.

The book offers evidence for a belief, long held by many psychotherapists, that there are productive and unproductive matches between particular types of therapists and particular types of patients. It also documents some of the differences between periods of movement and periods of stagnation, and it offers the thoughtful practitioner clues to routes out of situations of therapeutic impasse.

This is not an easy book. It is a complex analysis of a complicated process, and its results merit careful thought. It can be read as an introduction to, and an overview of, the phenomena of psychotherapeutic experience. It will prove informative and instructive to serious students entering the field of psychotherapy, and it will also reward experienced therapists who want to expand their awareness of the dynamics of human interaction.

This is the third Foresight Book. Like the first two, it presents innovative research on problems of practical importance. It is not the definitive study that might be produced in a world in which therapists and patients were available in unlimited numbers and were always cooperative. Rather, it opens a gate, points us toward the garden, and hands us the tools with which to cultivate our own intellectual growth.

David F. Ricks

# A Foreword on
# the Clinical Setting

The material contained in this study of therapeutic experience should be of interest to all therapists who share a concern for documenting what they do and how they do it. The study was conducted at the Katharine Wright Psychiatric Clinic in Chicago, which in several respects was and is a distinctive clinical setting. A brief note on the clinic and its history may help the reader to a better appreciation of the research reported in this volume.

The clinic was established in 1947 as the mental hygiene clinic of the Women and Children's Hospital under the leadership of Dr. Katharine Wright, the chief psychiatrist. Women and Children's Hospital (since renamed Mary Thompson Hospital) had been founded in 1865 as the first hospital for women in Chicago—at that time the only facility in the city where women physicians could take their patients.

The aims and purposes of the clinic, at the outset, were: (1) to provide treatment for emotionally disturbed women and to attain for them a more acceptable vocational, social, or family adjustment, or a combination of these three; (2) to provide low-cost treatment on such a basis that the self-respect of the individual was maintained and her budget also considered; and (3) to provide evening hours so that treatment would not interfere with duties at work or at home.

The original staff (all women) consisted of three part-time psychiatrists, two part-time psychologists, and a full-time psychiatric social worker. Currently there are some 40 professionals on the staff, most in part-time affiliations while continuing their primary activities in nearby major hospitals, universities, medical schools, and private practices. This arrangement permits an unusual mix of therapists, many of whom would simply be unavailable to such a clinic were attempts made to hire them on a full-time basis.

The services provided by the mental hygiene clinic during evening hours continued to expand over the years. In 1963 the clinic reached a peak load in its use of facilities at Mary Thompson Hospital, and a decision was taken to seek larger quarters. On January 1, 1964, the clinic moved to the Michigan Avenue Hospital (later known as the Stone-Brandel Center), and was renamed to honor its founder, who remained an active practitioner on its staff. Most of the data presented in this book were gathered while the clinic was at this location. In 1970, the clinic was once more ready for a new home, and accepted an invitation to become the psychiatric outpatient facility of the Illinois Masonic Medical Center. Since then, the services provided to the community have been substantially increased, with longer hours and more types of treatment offered to a broader range of patients in need of therapeutic help.

Katharine W. Wright, M.D.
S. Dale Loomis, M.D.

# Preface

Over the past decade, we have pursued a single line of research into the experiences of patients and therapists in psychotherapy. We have shared equally in all phases of this work, and our contributions are inextricably blended in this book. Throughout, we have been animated by two beliefs: that the subjective involvement of persons in their activities and relationships is an important and enduring datum for psychology; and that rigorous quantitative analysis, when adapted to the data, offers the surest method for generating knowledge about a subject. Work in the field of psychotherapy has usually held to one or the other of these beliefs—yielding, on the one hand, a rich and intriguing clinical literature that (unhappily) has traded methodological rigor for practical and experiential relevance, and, on the other hand, an increasingly rigorous research literature that too often has sacrificed the substance and flavor of the phenomenon to the ideal (or idol) of objective science. We have sought in our own work to hold to both beliefs, out of a conviction that ultimately they will be seen as mutually enhancing rather than as necessarily antithetical principles.

This book is the fullest and most detailed report of results that have emerged from our research on psychotherapeutic experience. It provides an overview of our project and an account of some major analyses of data, but does not present a complete survey or summation of our work. Analyses of other aspects and specific segments of our data have been reported in various scientific journals (cited for the most part in Howard and Orlinsky, 1972), and more are currently in progress. Beyond these, new questions continue to arise for which relevant data already exist, or for which supplementary data can be gathered.

The most dramatic—and, admittedly, embarrassing—instance of questions that we did not anticipate is the concern about psychotherapy raised by the women's liberation movement. All the patients (and some of the therapists) discussed in this book are women, yet at the time that we formulated our research program this fact seemed incidental. The questions that were uppermost in our minds in 1964 concerned their experiences *qua* patients and therapists, not *qua* women. That was before most of the recent works on women had appeared, the same year in which Friedan's *The Feminine Mystique* was published, when hardly anyone's "consciousness" had yet been "raised." Consequently, there is regrettably little in this volume that speaks to the criticisms and concerns about psychotherapy that have been expressed in the women's movement. *An important exception may be found in Chapter 8, where patients who had women therapists were discovered to be more likely to have had a helpful experience in psychotherapy (see Table 42).* Our data have permitted us to explore this in greater detail, and we have already presented a preliminary report on "The Effects of Sex of Therapist on Women's Experiences in Psychotherapy" at the 1974 Annual Conference of the Society for Psychotherapy Research. Another, mainly stylistic, feature of this book that may grate on contemporary sensibilities is our consistent use of the pronouns "her" and "she" to refer to patients, and "him" and "he" to refer to therapists. Our aim was clarity, within the limits of current usage; no affront was intended—either way.

We owe a special and substantial debt of gratitude to the two institutions and several individuals whose collaboration and support made our work possible. The Research Program of the Illinois Institute for Juvenile Research, and the Katharine Wright Psychiatric Clinic of Chicago, provided us quite literally with all that we needed in pursuing our research.

Noël Jenkin, Ph.D., was responsible for bringing us to the Institute for Juvenile Research, and—as its Research Director until his untimely death in 1971—created an ideal environment for scientific inquiry. We hope this book will in some measure repay his encouragement and trust. Merton S. Krause, Ph.D., was the next Research Director. In his capacities as thoughtful administrator, stimulating colleague, and personal friend, he made the completion of our work an objective of his own. Anne M. Seiden, M.D., our current Research Director, has generously continued this support. James A. Hill, Ph.D., was our research associate and collaborator for several years, and assisted in nearly all phases of our research. Edward Barnes provided valuable help in the computer analysis of our data, and Donald Hlousek, M.D., was an esthusiastic and able research assistant—without their help, we would still be counting. The clerical staff of the Research Program, and especially Bettye Wharton and Joanne Brown, already know how much we needed and appreciate their help.

The research reported here also would have been impossible without the understanding and cooperation of Thaddeus Kostrubala, M.D., and S. Dale Loomis, M.D., who served as successive Directors of the Katharine Wright Clinic. Our work at Katharine Wright was made easier and more pleasant through the graces of Walter Miller and Angela Heisler, who served successively as Clinic Administrators. Perhaps most of all, we owe thanks to the necessarily anonymous therapists and patients who collaborated in this research, and shared their experiences with us through many hours and many questionnaires.

A number of distinguished colleagues served as consultants to our project during its formative years, and contributed much of merit. These were: John Butler, Ph.D., Rosalind Dymond Cartwright, Ph.D., Raymond B. Cattell, Ph.D., Irving D. Harris, M.D., Merton S. Krause, Ph.D., Maurice Lorr, Ph.D., Nancy Orlinsky, Ph.D., Laura N. Rice, Ph.D., and Hans Strupp, Ph.D. We have also benefited from the comments and advice of our colleagues in the Society for Multivariate Experimental Psychology.

Our editors, David F. Ricks, Ph.D., and Janet M. Simons of Teachers College Press, have helped to make this book more readable and more digestible; for this feat the reader ought to join us in thanking them. Marcia Bourland and Carol Howard assisted in the onerous task of proofreading, and had the yet more difficult task of maintaining loving relationships under the pressure of our work.

Finally, there are two intangibles of unfathomable value to acknowledge: our own friendship, which has survived the chafing harness of collaboration and has been strengthened by it; and the experience of psychotherapy, which we have scrutinized at so many levels from so many angles, and with which our lives have been so variously involved. Wallace Stevens stated this latter aspect of research as well as can be in "Thirteen Ways of Looking at a Blackbird":

> I know noble accents
> And lucid, inescapable rhythms;
> But I know, too,
> That the blackbird is involved
> In what I know.

David E. Orlinsky, Ph.D.
Kenneth I. Howard, Ph.D.

Chicago, Illinois
September 1974

# *Contents*

## Part I

### *Introduction*

# Part II

## *The Psychotherapy Session Project*

# Part III

## *The Average and the Ideal: Composite Patterns of Psychotherapeutic Experience*

## Part IV

## *Differential Patterns of Psychotherapeutic Experience: Patients, Therapists, and Relationships*

12 / Types of Psychotherapeutic Relationships
and their Correlates                          177

## Part V

## *The Functioning of the Psychotherapist: Some Implications for Clinical Practice*

13 / The Therapist as an Instrument of Observation    193

# List of Tables

# Part I
# *Introduction*

# Chapter 1

# The Study of
# Psychotherapeutic
# Experience

Psychotherapy is an experience of special interest to many people. Most directly, it is of interest to those who come to it as patients—in a mood of hope or anguish, puzzlement or despair. It may represent the beginning of a spiritual quest, like Dante's journey through Hell and Purgatory. It may represent another round in the seemingly endless labor to raise oneself, like Sisyphus, after having fallen down in life. It may represent, too, the end of the line in an individual's deviant moral career, a more or less humane form of punishment cast in the form of "correction" or "rehabilitation" (Szasz, 1963; Goffman, 1961). There are as many meanings to the experience of psychotherapy as there are types of persons who undertake the role of patient in it, or types of circumstances under which it is entered. Whatever the particular circumstances may be, it is fairly certain that for a greater or shorter period of time the experience of psychotherapy will have a special place in the life of the patient.

Psychotherapy is also a special experience for its practitioner, the psychotherapist. Psychotherapy is a craft in which the therapist is both the craftsman and the tool, a performing art that is played for no audience but is played "for keeps," a personal relationship that is engaged in to earn a livelihood. Although his work with patients and his training for it are constituted as a profession (Henry, Sims, & Spray, 1971), this profession will often entail intense involvement in the personal lives of other people. The feelings generated and the degree of intimacy achieved

3

in the therapeutic relationship may even exceed in dramatic force those comparable elements in the therapist's own day-to-day personal life.

Finally, psychotherapy is an experience of special interest to the social scientist. It is a unique source of data about personality, virtually the only relationship in which individuals reveal events and reactions of their personal or private lives to trained observers. Erikson (1959) has noted that the patient "participates in becoming a *case*," and in the process opens himself to professional therapeutic and scientific scrutiny. As a result of this, the most important and influential theories of personality have been based primarily on data drawn from psychotherapeutic experience. The normatively simple and standard format of individual psychotherapy also makes it a natural laboratory for the social psychological study of interpersonal relations.

This book is about the experience of psychotherapy, and about the different forms it takes for different people. This is a book *about* the experiences of patients and therapists, but a book primarily *for* therapists and researchers.

For the practicing therapist, this book offers a systematic and empirical view of the variety of experiences had in psychotherapy by a number of his colleagues, against which he might wish to compare his own impressions. Therapists in training often have a special need to make such comparisons, and will find in this volume a record of the pitfalls encountered as well as exemplary progress made by a group of experienced therapists. More seasoned therapists will find this a useful means for sharpening their own formulations of psychotherapy.

Therapists will also find a systematic and empirical view of the variety of experiences had in psychotherapy by a substantial number of patients, *based on the patients' own reports.* As Mendelsohn and Geller (1965) have remarked: "Reviews of the literature indicate that while self-report has been used extensively . . . the client has not often been asked about his view of his counseling experience. . . . We have very little information on how the client reacts to and structures what he encounters in his interaction with the world of [psychotherapy], or on the variables which influence his reaction" (pp. 63-64). The plain fact is that almost all [1] of the formulations that have been made about psychotherapy are based on therapists' experiences, or on observations by external observers. There has been a general neglect of the patient's perspective as a source of valid or valuable data, *despite* the fact that the therapist in practice tries to listen empathically and to understand the patient's experiences from the patient's point of view. The therapist's sensitivity

---

[1] The principal exceptions are Snyder (1961) and the retrospective studies of Strupp, Wallach, and Wogan (1964), Feifel and Eells (1963), and Kamin and Caughlan (1963).

to what the patient experiences in psychotherapy can be importantly enhanced by research focused on those experiences.

Further, this book offers a view of the *patterns of connection between the patient's experiences and the therapist's experiences,* which yields a new perspective on *the relationship as a whole.* This perspective focuses on the inter-subjective structure of the involvement and represents a study of what Laing (1967) has aptly called "social phenomenology," a study of inter-experience to complement the more frequent studies of inter-action.[2]

To the researcher interested in psychotherapy, this book offers new instruments for studying experiential qualities of the psychotherapeutic process. By using these instruments, we have given empirical definition to a number of quantitative variables. These variables correspond directly to salient aspects of clinical experience and provide an effective link between research findings and their possible applications in the therapeutic context. We present a body of empirical results relating these variables to one another and to objective characteristics of patients and therapists.

## STUDYING THE PSYCHOTHERAPEUTIC EXPERIENCE

Our principal reason for focusing on the experience of psychotherapy, in contrast to its overt public aspects or its physically measurable properties, is our belief that subjective experience is the primary locus of action and impact in *psycho*therapy. We make no claim that this is the only effective or interesting way to view psychotherapy, but it does seem to us to be a most relevant way. The specific words used, and how they are spoken, seem less germane than the meanings that are intended and conveyed. Fluctuations in autonomic responsiveness seem less directly pertinent than the feelings the participants perceive in themselves and in each other. The impressions the participants have of how they relate to each other are at least as important as are the impressions *any* number of external observers might form of them. The study of psychotherapeutic experience has the greatest manifest validity among these different approaches, since the patients and therapists themselves deal chiefly with the data of experience in their work together: with perceptions and thoughts, feelings and fantasies. The salience of "inner" or psychological reality in psychotherapy, in contrast to "outer" social reality, has been accepted by clinicians since Freud discovered that his patients' memories of childhood sexual traumas were

---

[2] As exemplified in Lennard and Bernstein (1960) and the work of Matarazzo and his associates (1968).

as often wishful fantasy as fact, yet were nevertheless etiologically significant in their neuroses.

Psychotherapeutic experience has been described many times, chiefly in the theories and case histories written by psychotherapists, but also in the form of diaries, solicited reports, and fictionalized narratives written by patients. Together these sources compose a rich clinical literature, abounding in striking suggestions and insights. As a body of systematic knowledge in any formal sense, however, it leaves much to be desired. Often, for instance, the primers and theoretical texts that describe psychotherapy state what is supposed to happen, not what actually does happen. These, as well as more factual case reports, suffer the additional limitation of being based on the impressions of a single observer whose idiosyncracies of interest, bias, and style are rarely specified. However deeply the writer may probe, there is no guarantee that his observations are typical of anyone else, or even representative of his own systematic experience. A third limitation of the clinical literature is that almost uniformly the formulations in it are made in qualitative, impressionistic terms that make systematic comparison difficult if not impossible. As a result, one is left to study his favorite authorities much as he chooses his favorite novelists, according to which of them "speak to him." The fact that there are many theoretical schools or orientations in the field of psychotherapy derives, at least in part, from this situation.

A more reliable but also more limited source of information can be found in the scientific studies of psychotherapy that have been made in the past twenty or thirty years. These have been more precise, systematic, and quantitative than are corresponding reports in the clinical literature, but this research literature tells us surprisingly little about the experience of psychotherapy. Many studies have concentrated on evaluating the outcome of therapy without observing the actual process. When they have focused on therapeutic process, they have typically done so *via* the media of sound recordings or motion picture films, from the perspective of an external non-participant observer who is, in effect, on the outside looking in. Such studies [3] have yielded valuable knowledge, but little basic information about what the patients and therapists who are the primary participants see, hear, and feel during their sessions; what

[3] We have chosen not to include a general review of either the clinical or the research literature on psychotherapy—the former because it is too vast to be dealt with in less than a separate volume (e.g., Ford & Urban, 1963), and the latter because it is amply covered in the *Annual Review of Psychology* (e.g., Howard & Orlinsky, 1972), and in several recent volumes (e.g., Bergin & Garfield, 1971; Meltzoff & Kornreich, 1970). Directly pertinent studies will be cited where relevant.

they want and get from them; what *they* think about the psychotherapeutic process.

An important exception to this criticism of research is the work
reported by William Snyder in *The Psychotherapy Relationship* (1961).
Snyder developed two questionnaires to be answered after each therapy
session, one by the therapist and one by the client. The Client's Post
Interview Attitudes Toward Therapy questionnaire surveyed the client's
feelings and reactions to the therapist and to himself. The Therapist's
Personal Reaction Questionnaire covered the therapist's post-interview
affect toward the client, the therapist's estimate of the client's feelings
toward the therapist, and the therapist's ratings of the client's progress
in therapy and emotional maturity. Snyder used these questionnaires,
each of which consisted of 200 true-false statements, with 20 of his own
clients. From analyses of the data collected, he developed a "positive
affect scale" and a "negative affect scale" for measuring client and
therapist affect within each therapy session. He then studied changes
in the level of positive and negative affect over the course of therapy with
his 20 clients, and related these to his estimates of outcome.

A somewhat similar study was carried out by Meyer, Borgatta, and
Fanshel (1964). These investigators used a 20-item questionnaire, the
Casework Interview Check Sheet, to obtain ratings from caseworkers
(but not from clients) on interviews with clients. The areas surveyed
were actions by the caseworker, actions of the client, the general level
of interaction, and the caseworker's assessment of the interview. Although more limited than Snyder's study, theirs was based on a larger
(but unspecified) number of therapists—all or most of the caseworkers
at a metropolitan social work agency—who rated from one to ten interviews with 355 different clients. Ratings on the initial sessions with
these cases were analyzed to determine the structure of the casework
interview (as experienced by the therapist). The several dimensions
discovered in the first session were used to score subsequent interviews
so that sequential analyses could be made for the continuing cases.

These two pioneering efforts at studying the experience of the participants in therapeutic or quasi-therapeutic relationships have certain
features in common with our approach. All necessarily follow an adaptation of the method of participant observation. That is, the patients or
the therapists themselves—or both, as in Snyder's study and ours—are
asked to report on their experiences in therapy sessions. No one but the
actual subjects can say what they experienced. Also, the participants are
"expert" judges who, by virtue of prolonged familiarity with the events,
are in a better position to describe them more fully and meaningfully
than is the detached and occasional external observer. As immediate
participants, they have greater access to the full range of cues. As

observers, they may perceive these cues differently from the way a non-participant would, but in this type of study, interest is focused precisely on how the participants perceive psychotherapy.[1] To make the reports from patients and therapists comparable and accessible to quantitative analysis, each of the studies developed objective questionnaire instruments. To ensure a degree of stability in the reports that were made, each of the studies employed a longitudinal design.

In terms of providing a full understanding of psychotherapeutic experience, however, these two pioneering efforts have some important limitations. In Snyder's study, the fact that only one therapist participated limits the generalizability of the findings. One cannot tell how similarly or how differently other therapists might have experienced psychotherapy, nor can one tell how similarly or how differently the clients of other therapists would have experienced therapy with them. In addition, Snyder's reduction of his questionnaires for analytic purposes to two "affect" scales resulted in a restriction of the participants' reports to a global characterization of the session. With this restriction, there was no possibility of capturing the finer structure of psychotherapeutic experiences, or of representing the significant nuances in the reports of patients and therapists.

The study by Meyer, Borgatta, and Fanshel suffers the complementary limitation of not including the experiences of clients. Further, only a limited number of aspects of experience could be reported with the brief questionnaire that was used. One may also question the representativeness of the initial interview in a casework agency—the only one actually analyzed—as a typical example of therapeutic experience.

The present study was designed to provide a more finely textured and more representative picture of patients' and therapists' experiences, and to investigate both their significant relationships and their determinants. The means to this enterprise were the Therapy Session Report (TSR) questionnaires. The TSR is, metaphorically but in effect, the photographic plate on which these experiences were recorded. The results of any study are shaped before data are ever collected by the thought that is embodied in the study's design, much as the picture that can be developed is predetermined by the design of the camera and the sensitivities of the photographic plate. Thus once we decided to study the experience of psychotherapy, we immediately had to decide *what* questions to ask the participants and *how to ask them*.

The first phase of our research required articulation of the salient dimensions of patients' and therapists' experiences into an array of

---

[1] The qualms about "objectivity" some readers may feel at this point will be dealt with in Chapter 3.

measurable variables. The procedure that we followed in this task involved imagining that we could approach participants immediately after each therapy session to ask, "What went on in there?" A number of more specific questions were devised to focus the "interview," and the imaginary interviewer was replaced operationally with a questionnaire. Since the time that could be given by each participant was limited, our questions were designed to be as concise and as descriptive as possible—that is, directly answerable without lengthy inference or deliberation.

A necessary preliminary to construction of questionnaire items involved analyzing the *possible* experiences of patients and therapists into descriptively distinct components or facets. In this enterprise we were guided by the available clinical and research literature, discussions with colleagues and consultants, reports of patients, and our own experiences as therapists and as patients.

In a most general sense, a therapy session can be viewed as both an interpersonal system and a social occasion.[5] The interpersonal system in which individuals participate involves each person's instrumental and relational conduct, and each person's perceptions of himself and of his partner.[6] Thus, the description of an interpersonal system would require attention to such features as the motives and satisfactions, the attitudes and manners, and the actions and feelings of the participants.

The social occasion is a concrete embodiment of an interpersonal system in a specific time and situation. The social occasion has a logic of its own, however. It proceeds from the anticipations of each participant, takes shape according to the perceptions and performance of each participant, and results in a variable degree of closure or consummation for each participant. This analysis of the social occasion in terms of anticipation, perception, performance, and consummation is derived from the scheme proposed by G. H. Mead in his analysis of stages in the *act* (Mead, 1956). The combination of these two general schemes, analyzing the interpersonal system and the social occasion respectively, served as the organizing principles of the TSR questionnaires.

This will be seen more clearly in what follows. Dealing first with the idea of instrumental conduct, we were led to ask, "What actually happened?" We assumed that most of the behavior in therapy consists in talking and listening, i.e., in *dialogue*. Therefore, the questionnaires were designed to find out what was talked about during the session.

The manner in which patient and therapist conduct themselves in

[5] This distinction is analogous to that between "synchronic" and "diachronic" studies of culture drawn by anthropologists; the former view abstracts process from time, highlighting its systemic character, whereas the latter view focuses on temporal sequences in process, highlighting its evolutionary character.

[6] This conception is discussed at greater length in Howard and Orlinsky (1972).

relation to one another is also a matter of primary interest. In addition to knowing what was said and done by the participants, we wanted to know how they did it, i.e., to gain a view of therapy as a patterned *relationship*.

Behavior has an affective component as well as instrumental and relational aspects, however, and in therapy particularly the affective component is usually given much prominence. Assuming that therapy is essentially also a *feeling process,* we wanted to know what each participant felt during the session, and what each perceived the other as feeling.

Finally, therapist and patient come together for some purpose. The patient comes seeking certain gains, and the therapist comes with certain expectations concerning what he intends to give to, or to do for, the patient. Therapy involves a process of *exchange*. We therefore wanted to know something of the patient's hopes, the therapist's intentions, and the resulting satisfactions that accrue to the patient.[7]

Our analysis of therapy as an interpersonal system thus entailed four facets of potential therapeutic experience: dialogue, relationship, feeling process, and exchange. Analysis of the therapy session as a social occasion showed us another facet of potential therapeutic experience: therapy as an interpersonal act developing, through mutual role implementation, toward a common goal. We wanted to know about the *development of the therapy session,* as it is affected by the anticipations, perceptions, and responses of each participant.

The Therapy Session Reports [8] thus inquire into a broad spectrum of potential experiences. The TSRs are intended to be filled out as soon as possible after each therapy session while the experiences are still fresh in mind. Our choice of the session as the basic unit of observation seemed natural in view of the fact that the session is an inherent rather than an imposed segment of psychotherapy, and is of relatively short duration. It also has a certain unity of form as a single occasion of interaction.

There are clearly many subjectively discriminable moments in a therapy session, however, and the character of experience typically does change somewhat—and may change dramatically—over the span of these subjective moments. Returning to the analogy of photographic plates to the TSRs, we might say that the pictures we obtained were really time exposures rather than instantaneous snapshots. The quicker changes and fluctuations appeared somewhat blurred and some informa-

---

[7] The complementary part of the exchange cycle—what the therapist seeks and what the patient provides—was not included. Normally, this part of the therapeutic contract is covered by the therapist's fee.

[8] The actual TSR forms are presented in Appendices B and C.

tion was inevitably lost, but we have found that the main features of experience showed forth clearly enough. The TSR instructions directed the respondent to indicate all of the experiences (e.g., feelings) he had during the session, without regard to sequence or consistency. This results, as with a time exposure, in an overlapping of traces, some of which may be intelligibly separated through their differential patterning in correlational and factor analyses. The alternative would have been some form of interruption of the session, and with it an intrusive disruption of the flow of experience. That alternative seemed to us considerably less desirable than the loss of some information through the use of the whole therapy session as the unit of experience.

At this point some readers might feel inclined to ask, "How is it possible to study *experience* with a questionnaire?" The underlying difficulty felt by some who have actually raised this question is the disparity they sense between the fixed, verbal, objective character of a questionnaire and the fluid, nonverbal, subjective character of experience. A satisfactory answer to this very legitimate question requires that we consider, first, how one can study experience at all, and then what is meant by the term "experience." This is not a mere semantic exercise, but a necessary step in specifying the meaning of our research operations.

If by "experience" we meant only the immediate sensed-and-felt stuff of awareness, the elemental there-ness of consciousness, then it would seem somewhat farfetched to employ questionnaires in its study. Experience in that sense is formed and meaningful, but its forms are wholly concrete and its meanings are wholly implicit. It is, in other words, incommunicable to others and unavailable to study even by means of introspective reflection. Although psychotherapists sometimes use the word in this sense, to emphasize to patients its difference from verbalization about experience, this definition is too restrictive from a scientific point of view. The limitation of "experience" to nonverbal and nonsymbolic referents may correspond to what we imagine as the subjective state of lower animals, but it does not correspond to what we know of ourselves as human beings. What we know of ourselves is precisely that symbols are part and parcel of the flux of experience. Words and images come to mind as well as, and along with, feelings and urges. *Experience, after infancy, is always a compound of concrete form and symbolic formulation, of immediate presentation and mediatory representation, of implicit meaning and expressed significance.*

It is the symbolic, representational, expressive aspect that makes it possible to communicate our experiences to others and to reflect on them ourselves—not totally or perfectly, but at all! The symbolic, representational, expressive elements also make it possible for us to investigate experience by giving formulation to our own and others' experiences. We do this through a process of responding to statements and questions, deliberately as in interview or introspection, or spontaneously as in free association and artistic composition. We understand a questionnaire to be a standardized body of such statements and questions, designed to elicit formulations of some area of a person's experience. The area surveyed may be his attitudes and opinions, his tastes and preferences, or his perceptions, feelings, and beliefs.

The real problem attending the use of a questionnaire arises when we consider that the questions and statements it contains may be more or less effective in eliciting adequate or fitting formulations. The questions may be poorly phrased or beside the point, and they may be offered in a leading, threatening, or tendentious way. The content of the questionnaire or the circumstances of its administration may incite the respondent to answer untruthfully. Thus, either the questionnaire or the respondent may figure as a source of distortion in the formulation of experience.

Our basic protection against the former danger is the respondent's sense of fit between the form of his experience and the formulations offered for its encoding in the questionnaire. This sense of fit is ultimately an esthetic judgment. We took considerable time and effort (the better part of a year) to draft, pre-test, revise, and further pre-test the TSR questionnaires by consulting our patients and therapeutic colleagues. Our basic safeguard against the second type of danger, deliberate misrepresentation, lay in removing or neutralizing as much as possible the respondent's reasons for being untruthful. We took special care in designing the circumstances under which the TSR questionnaires were administered, and in controlling access to the information provided us in confidence by patients and therapists.

We hope the reader will concede that, in principle, it is possible to study experience by means of a questionnaire. Whether ours was designed with sufficient artistry, presented with sufficient candor, and analyzed with sufficient skill, he may judge for himself from the results of our research.

## A GUIDE TO THE READER

Readers who are primarily interested in the practice of psychotherapy and readers who are primarily interested in research may wish to follow different paths in exploring the contents of this book. The next chapter offers a synoptic view of the design, subjects, and major results of the Psychotherapy Session Project. It is a logical sequel to this chapter and should be read as part of the Introduction.

Beyond that, the interests of researchers and of psychotherapists may diverge. The researcher, having a summary of our findings, is likely to want to know more about the methodological aspects of our study before examining the results presented in Chapters 5 through 12. Methods of data collection and methods of data analysis are reported and discussed in Chapters 3 and 4. The psychotherapist, having a summary of our findings, may want to know what these have taught us about the nature and problems of therapeutic practice. Part V focuses on the therapist's functioning and offers some practical reflections about the conduct of psychotherapy, such as identified signs of progress and suggestions for dealing with different types of impasse. From this point, the therapist may wish to return to the fuller report of our findings in Chapters 5 through 12, to assess for himself what justification there is for our interpretations.

In Chapters 1 and 2 we offer the reader a sample of what is contained in this volume, and an invitation to read on. If students of psychotherapy following primarily practical or research interests approach this book from different directions, they will nevertheless find within it many points of productive and meaningful contact.

# Chapter 2

# Summary of
# Major Findings

The Psychotherapy Session Project [1] was conducted at the Katharine Wright Mental Health Clinic in Chicago. This clinic was established originally as an out-patient facility for lower- and middle-income working women, and operated as an evening clinic offering individual and group psychotherapy on a reduced-fee basis. The Clinic received referrals from other community agencies, from private physicians and therapists, and through current and former patients. The population served was essentially urban and preponderantly female in character, although husbands were seen conjointly in cases where marital difficulties were focally involved.

The 60 patients [2] included in our sample were predominantly single, employed, neurotic, young adult women in individual psychotherapy. They were generally between 20 and 40 years of age, more than four out of five were gainfully employed, and nearly two-thirds had attended college. About one-third of the patients were currently married. Neurotic reactions accounted for 60% of the clinical diagnoses, personality disorders for 25%, and schizophrenia for 15%. The sample of patients seems in several respects typical of the patients encountered in private

---

[1] The data reported in this volume represent the first in a series of coordinated studies in the Psychotherapy Session Project.

[2] See Chapter 3 for a more detailed description of the patients and therapists in this study.

psychotherapeutic practice in the major metropolitan centers (Ryan, 1969).

The therapists in our sample included both men and women trained in psychiatry, clinical psychology, or psychiatric social work. An unusual feature for our therapist sample is the length of therapeutic practice; the median for the group was 6 years. Nearly two-thirds had also undergone personal psychotherapy. The therapists' theoretical orientations might best be described as "dynamic-eclectic," influenced in varying degrees by psychoanalytic principles but not rigidly adhering to them. All of the therapists worked at the Katharine Wright Clinic on a part-time basis, and were otherwise established either in private practice or in responsible positions at institutions in the community. They were fairly representative of therapists practicing in a large urban center (Henry, Sims, & Spray, 1971).

Since our initial interest was to develop a reliable depiction of the qualities and types of therapeutic experience, we set a minimum limit of 8 sessions per participant as a criterion for inclusion in the patient or therapist sample. As most therapy sessions were scheduled at weekly intervals, a minimum of two months of therapy were studied for each individual. For statistical analyses, the responses of each individual to each of the items on the TSR were averaged across all of the sessions on which he or she reported. The patients contributed a total of 890 sessions (an average of 15 per patient) over a six-month period. Seventeen therapists contributed a total of 470 sessions. Several of the therapists reported on more than one case, making a total of 31 different therapist-cases available for study (an average of 15 per therapist-case).

## THE LEVELS OF DATA ANALYSIS [3]

A proper understanding of the results summarized in this chapter requires a brief introduction to the analyses that were performed on the data. Four distinct levels of analysis were involved. First, we examined the responses made by patients and therapists to the individual *items* of the TSRs. Group averages for each item provided an idea of the frequency of specific experiences. By noting the most frequently reported experiences, we derived composite portraits of the typical experiences of patients and therapists. Through correlational analyses at the item level, we derived composite portraits of their ideal experiences.

The second level of analysis involved the intercorrelation and factor analysis of the specific items within each of the facets of therapeutic

---

[3] See Chapter 4 for a more detailed account of the strategy and methods of data analysis.

experience (dialogue, relationship, etc.). The factorial dimensions for each facet delineated the structure of that area of experience. This analysis also provided a smaller number of independent variables for further analysis, each such variable constituting a cluster of individual items.

The third level involved the intercorrelation and factor analysis of the facet dimension scores previously derived. This yielded inter-facet or *global* dimensions of experience: one set derived from the patient TSRs, and another set from the therapist TSRs, representing dimensions of individual differences. A further analysis conducted at this level involved the determination of different types of experience on the basis of profiles of scores on these global experience factors. We then compared the individual and social characteristics of patients and therapists representing each type.

The fourth level of analysis involved the intercorrelation and factor analysis of both patient and therapist global experience dimensions across the 28 patient-therapist pairs from whom we had matching TSRs. This process allowed us to examine relationships between the patient's and the therapist's experiences within the therapeutic dyad, and to determine dimensions of *conjoint* experience. Further analysis enabled us to construct dyadic experience types and to investigate their determinants.

The levels of data analysis may be more easily understood through the use of an analogy. One may compare each of the *items* on the TSRs to a musical note or tone. The *facet* dimensions or item-clusters found at the second level would then be comparable to musical chords. The *global* experience dimensions at the third level would resemble themes or melodies, and the types of experience could then be likened to compositions made by the differential combination of these themes. Finally, the *conjoint* experience dimensions represent patterns of harmony or counterpoint in the therapeutic relationship.

## COMPOSITE PORTRAITS OF TYPICAL AND IDEAL EXPERIENCES

Composite portraits of typical experiences [4] were drawn from the most frequently endorsed items in the patient and therapist TSRs. In the typical session, patients reported seeking better self-understanding, help from the therapist in discussing difficult matters, problem resolution, and personal collaboration with the therapist. In doing so, these women tended to focus their discussion with the therapist on feelings and atti-

---

[4] A full report of typical experiences is given in Chapter 5.

tudes toward themselves, on their social activities, and on their personal involvements with men. The most frequent feelings accompanying these topics, for patients, were feeling anxious, tense, and frustrated, but also interested and accepted. Patients typically saw their style of relating in therapy as taking initiative but sharing control with the therapist, as being friendly or respectful, and emotionally involved. The satisfactions most frequently found by patients in their exchanges with their therapists were a sense of honest collaboration, help in discussing difficult matters, and deeper self-understanding.

The aims most frequently pursued by therapists, according to their reports, were the deepening of their patients' insight and capacity for genuine feeling, and the maintenance of an effective collaborative relationship in therapy. Typical therapist feelings were interested, calm, involved, alert, confident, and sympathetic. Typical therapist modes of relating to the patient included interacting cooperatively with the patient's initiative, sharing control, being warm and friendly, and being emotionally responsive.

Comparison of these composite pictures suggests that patients and therapists tended to seek and to realize the same goals, and related to each other with similar and complementary modes of conduct. Patients tended to feel involved and distressed, whereas therapists felt concerned but calm. If this highly condensed summary sounds quite familiar, the very fact that it does lends support to the validity of our approach to the study of psychotherapy.

Composite projections of ideal experiences [5] were drawn from the items of the TSRs by correlating each item with the participant's evaluations of the overall quality of sessions. The typical experience and the ideal experience were found to have many features in common, suggesting that by and large the average experience is positively valued. In some respects, what was found to be present in the typical experience was found to be present more intensely in the ideal. This was true in general of the goals sought by patients, and their therapists' aims, and of the ways in which patients and therapists related to each other. Yet, some interesting differences between ideal and typical patterns did occur. In the projected ideal, patients did not focus discussion upon immediate attitudes toward themselves, but turned instead to their dreams, fantasies, and memories of childhood. Also, in the ideal experience, patients' feelings were predominantly positive and euphoric rather than distressed, and therapists' feelings evinced a distinctly more personal quality of involvement.

[5] A full report of ideal experiences is given in Chapter 6.

## PATTERNS OF PATIENT EXPERIENCE [6]

We were interested, too, in how the experiences of individual patients differed from one another. Factor analysis was utilized to define by empirical means the dimensions along which individual variation occurred. Using the facet factors defined at the second level of data analysis (dimensions of dialogue, feeling-process, etc.) as our component variables, we derived eleven global experience dimensions from the patients' TSRs.

One dimension [7] seemed to reflect the patient's basic attitude or approach to the patient role. It was a bipolar factor defined at one extreme by acceptance of the patient role, and at the other extreme by ambivalence.

Five dimensions reflected different patterns and degrees by which therapy emerged as a helpful experience for the patients. One emphasized the response of the patient, manifested in feelings of enthused satisfaction and acceptance. Another emphasized the patient's perception of the therapist as an emotionally responsive and effective helper. The third dimension of helpful experience reflected an attitude of autonomy and introspective openness, whereas the fourth revealed a problem-focused exploration by the patient of her involvements with significant others. The fifth focused on the mutual collaborative involvement of patient and therapist as the salient therapeutic element.

In contrast, two dimensions described distinctly threatening experiences for the patient. One was defined by a fearful negative response to a therapist perceived by the patient as being actively critical. In the other, the patient experienced associative blocking and embarrassing sexual arousal in the relationship. In the former case, it seems that the patient was frightened by what she perceived in the therapist; in the latter, the patient's own impulses were experienced as the source of threat.

Two other categories account for the remaining dimensions, dependency and manipulation. Dependent experience included two global dimensions: passive dependence with a therapist perceived as being directive, and the seeking of lenient acceptance or indulgence from a therapist perceived as rejecting. Manipulative experience included three dimensions: toying with the therapist, hostile provocation of a therapist perceived as noncommittal, and intrusive dependence with a therapist

---

[6] A full report of patient experience dimensions, experiential types, and their determinants is given in Chapters 7 and 8.

[7] Three of the eleven dimensions were bipolar, making a total of fourteen distinctive patterns of patient experience to be accounted for.

seen as embarrassed and tense. The three modes of patient manipulation represented here are seduction, provocation, and intrusion.

To explore the determinants of patients' experiences, we grouped patients according to experiential type and examined their individual and social characteristics. We also compared the characteristics of their therapists. These analyses indicated that helpful contact was more clearly related to the therapists' than the patients' characteristics. Another finding was that dependent contact was more frequent among patients who were older, married, or from larger families, and whose therapists too were from larger families and were themselves parents. On the other hand, patients who seemed prone to experiencing therapy as a stressful contact were disproportionately young and single, with therapists who had had personal psychotherapy.

### PATTERNS OF THERAPIST EXPERIENCE [8]

Eleven dimensions of global experience were also found in the therapist TSRs. These were grouped into four interpretive categories: helping the patient, coping with patient resistances, responding non-therapeutically, and experiencing distress.

The therapists' experience of helping the patient was reflected in eight of the dimensions,[9] indicating that this area was highly differentiated for therapists. Their helping influence was emphasized in four of the dimensions. One showed a supportive, educative involvement with a patient perceived as anxious but freely communicative. Another was manifested in intent warmth with a patient perceived as career-oriented but involved in therapy. The third was defined by a feeling of self-confident nurturant warmth toward a patient perceived as beset with feelings of inferiority. Two additional modes of helping were represented as opposite poles of a fourth dimension: nondirective restraint on the therapist's part, to permit cathartic relief, defined one pole; the other was defined by active interpretive confrontation aimed at stimulating experiential exploration and insight in the patient.

Two other dimensions emphasized the patient's participation in the helping contact. The first of these involved a sense of responsiveness with a patient perceived as feeling enthused, trusting, and happy. The second was defined by an attitude of responsive collaboration with a patient viewed as involved, collaborative, and therapeutically motivated.

Among the different modes of helping, another two dimensions empha-

---

[8] A full report of therapist experience dimensions, experiential types, and their determinants is given in Chapters 9 and 10.

[9] Seven of the eleven therapist global experience dimensions were bipolar, yielding a total of eighteen distinctive experience patterns to be considered.

sized qualities of the patient-therapist relationship. One of these was defined by the therapist's sense of expectation and rapport with a patient perceived as collaborative, progressing well in treatment, and functioning effectively. The other was manifested in an attitude of confident frankness with a patient who was perceived as feeling accepted and accepting.

The therapist's experience of coping with patient resistances was reflected in three dimensions: calm frank clarification with a patient perceived as hostile and withdrawing; reserve with a patient viewed as ambivalent, suspicious, and uncomfortable; and non-directive detachment with an aggressive, obstructive, narcissistic patient.

Therapists experienced themselves as responding non-therapeutically to patients by reacting with resignation to patients' narcissistic depression; by reacting with detachment to patients' intellectualization; by reacting with uneasy nurturance to patients' seductiveness; and by reacting with directiveness to patients' dependent passivity.

Finally, two dimensions went beyond a sense of professional ineffectiveness to a more painful or personally distressing experience for therapists. One was defined by feelings of disturbing sexual arousal toward a patient perceived as feeling angry and guilty. The other was manifested in a sense of failure with a patient who was seen as also feeling a failure and inferior.

Empirical analysis of therapists' profiles on the eleven global dimension scores revealed two clear types of experience, helping contact and distressing contact. Some interesting patient characteristics seemed to influence which type of experience a therapist had, although none of the therapist characteristics did so. Therapists whose experience was one of helping contact had patients who were disproportionately over 37 years old, mothers, and from broken homes. Therapists whose experience was one of distressing contact had patients all of whom were under 26 years old, not mothers, and disproportionately college graduates.

## PATTERNS OF CONJOINT EXPERIENCE [10]

The preceding analyses focused on therapeutic experience as a function of individual patients or therapists. What happens to each participant in a relationship is also a function of the emergent properties of their combination, however. At the fourth level of data analysis, we investigated therapeutic experience as a function of the *dyad*. Through factor analysis of the correlations among patients' and therapists' global experi-

---

[10] A full report of the conjoint experience dimensions, experiential types, and their determinants is given in Chapters 11 and 12.

ence scores, we were able to examine patterns that extended across the subjective experiences of both participants. This resulted in the empirical definition of seven dimensions of conjoint experience,[11] which we interpretively classified as normative, therapeutic, or conflictual patterns.

Normative patterns included dimensions of experience defined by adaptation of the patient and the therapist to his own and to the other's role. The basic functions of the patient and therapist roles in the therapeutic relationship are help-taking and help-giving. The dimension reflecting the patient's approach to the help-taking role was defined by the opposite poles of passive contact-waiting and intrusive contact-seeking. The therapist's approach to the help-giving role was also reflected in a bipolar dimension. At one extreme, the therapist viewed himself as a catalyst of change, a relatively impersonal and unchanging facilitator of processes within the patient. At the other extreme, the therapist saw himself and his interventions as active ingredients producing change, involved in a process capable of affecting him as well as his patient. A third normative pattern focused on each participant's view of the other's behavior, as congruent with or discrepant from his expectations about how the other *should* behave. One pole of this conjoint dimension reflected a basic congruence and rapport between the two participants, whereas the opposite pole revealed a mutually critical and unhappy reaction to disappointment in the other's behavior.

Therapeutic patterns included three dimensions of experienced benefit in the patient-therapist relationship. One entailed a state of positive transference in the patient. Another was defined as effective problem-solving in a working, interpretively oriented therapeutic alliance. The third showed a more existentially oriented, self-disclosing, mutual involvement between patient and therapist.

The last category of conjoint experience showed the therapeutic relationship as an arena of intrapersonal and interpersonal conflict. Three conflictual patterns were identified: an impasse of stalemated resistance and mutually projected hostility; a situation in which therapist and patient found themselves unhappily trapped in a frustrating, directive-dependent interaction; and an uncomfortable, erotic transference-counter-transference. These patterns reflect difficulties experienced by the patient-therapist pair in coping with mutual aggression, fears of rejection, and sexuality.

Analysis of the profiles of each of the patient-therapist pairs on the seven dimensions revealed two distinct types of conjoint experience, collaborative movement and dependency impasse. The two types repre-

---

[11] Each of the seven conjoint dimensions was bipolar, producing fourteen distinctive patterns to be considered.

sent patient-therapist dyads differentiated by their progressive or static experiential qualities. Several patient characteristics, but no therapist characteristics, distinguished pairs experiencing collaborative movement. Patients in such pairs tended to be young, unmarried, without children, college educated, and gainfully employed. They also tended to be the first-born children in their families, and in therapy for more than a year. These same patients, interestingly, were also those who tended to find therapy a subjectively stressful experience, and with whom therapists were likely to experience personal distress. Patients in pairs experiencing the dependency impasse, on the other hand, tended to be older married women, with children, not gainfully employed, and not college educated. They also tended to be the youngest children in their families. The therapists in these pairs tended to be the oldest children in large families, parents themselves, and less experienced than were other therapists in the sample.

## CONCLUDING COMMENT

In Chapter 1 we indicated the importance of psychotherapeutic experience as a subject for empirical inquiry, and argued that methods can be found to make such inquiry scientifically feasible. The findings summarized in Chapter 2 give evidence of the validity and the significance of these contentions. Readers who wish to examine the design and methods of our study more closely should continue with Chapters 3 and 4. Those who wish to examine the substantive findings in greater detail at this time should turn to Chapters 5 through 12. Readers wanting to explore clinical and theoretical implications of our findings will find these discussed in Part V.

# Part II
# *The Psychotherapy Session Project*

# Chapter 3

# Methods of
# Data Collection

Our data on the experience of psychotherapy were obtained through the use of the Therapy Session Report (TSR) questionnaires by patients and therapists at the Katharine Wright Mental Health Clinic in Chicago. In this chapter, we present a detailed description of the TSR instruments, the way in which they were used, and the people who used them. We also consider two methodological questions: Did the research instruments and procedures significantly affect the experiences they were designed to study? How representative were the patients and therapists at this clinic of patients and therapists in general?

## THE THERAPY SESSION REPORT QUESTIONNAIRES

The questionnaires were designed to survey the range of potential experiences in psychotherapy, by viewing the therapy session in five conceptually and phenomenologically distinct perspectives. Questions were directed at the experience of psychotherapy construed as (1) a *dialogue* between patient and therapist, (2) a *feeling process* or affective involvement between patient and therapist, (3) a behavioral *relationship* or pattern of interaction between patient and therapist, (4) a process of *exchange* in which patient and therapist strive to realize their wishes and intentions, and (5) the *development* or unfolding of a sequential interpersonal act.

Parallel forms of the TSR were constructed for use by patients (form P) and by therapists (form T). In each, questions assessed the behavior and experiences of the patient, the behavior and experiences of the therapist, and particular qualities of the patient-therapist interaction. Thus, each participant answered questions about himself, about the other, and about their relationship.

Form P of the TSR contained 167 items; form T contained 166. A structured response format allowed the participant to respond quickly and simply to each item, so that the TSR could be completed in less than ten minutes by most people, despite its apparent length. The items included in the two forms were extensively pilot-tested and revised in the light of item response characteristics and comments of patients and therapists who used the instrument.[1]

The items [2] in the patient form of the TSR (presented in Appendix B) were organized under the heading of sixteen questions about the therapy session, as shown in Table 1. The therapist form of the TSR (presented in Appendix C) was organized under the heading of seventeen general questions, as shown in Table 2. The only significant differences between form P and form T were in the facets of exchange and session development. Under exchange, the therapist was asked about his goals during the session, whereas the patient was asked about her satisfactions. Under session development, the questions on form P were more directly oriented to the patient's frame of reference, whereas on form T they were oriented to the therapist's perspective.

## THE RESEARCH PROCEDURES AND THEIR IMPACT

The design of the Psychotherapy Session Project called for the repeated use of TSR questionnaires by a panel of patients and therapists immediately following each of a series of consecutive therapy sessions. Sixty patients and seventeen therapists engaged in individual psychotherapy completed TSRs after a minimum of eight and as many as 26 sessions. Sessions were 45 minutes in length and were generally scheduled at weekly intervals. The segment of therapeutic experience represented in this block of sessions varied. For those who entered therapy during the study period, it was the initial segment; for others, we have segments covering periods within the second six months, second year, or third year of treatment.

Following each session, the patient went to a research room in a

---

[1] The TSR questionnaires were revised in light of the results of this study. Published versions of the revised forms are now available (Orlinsky & Howard, 1966).

[2] The rationales for the particular items under each facet are presented in Chapter 5 along with the basic item response data.

TABLE 1

## Summary of Items in the Patient Form of the
## Therapy Session Report

1. *How do you feel about the therapy session which you have just completed?* (This item, answered on a 6-point scale, was a global evaluation related to the facet of session development.)

2. *What did you talk about during this session?* (This 18-item checklist surveyed the facet of dialogue.)

3. *What did you want or hope to get out of this therapy session?* (This 20-item checklist surveyed part of the facet of exchange.)

4. *How did you act toward your therapist during this session?* (This 16-item checklist surveyed part of the facet of relationship.)

5. *How did you feel during this session?* (This 45-item checklist surveyed part of the facet of feeling process.)

6. *To what extent were you looking forward to coming this session?* (This item, answered on a 6-point scale, together with questions 7 through 11 and 14, surveyed the facet of session development.)

7. *How freely were you able to talk with your therapist during this session?* (Answered on a 4-point scale; part of session development.)

8. *How clearly did you know what you wanted to talk about during this session?* (Answered on a 4-point scale; part of session development.)

9. *How well did your therapist seem to understand how you were feeling and what was really on your mind during this session?* (Answered on a 4-point scale; part of session development.)

10. *Do you feel that what your therapist said and did this session was helpful to you?* (A 5-point scale; part of session development.)

11. *Do you feel that you made progress in this session in dealing with the problems for which you are in therapy?* (A 4-point scale; part of session development.)

12. *How well do you feel that you are getting along, emotionally and psychologically, at this time?* (Answered on a 5-point scale; designed as a subjective estimate of adjustment, related to the facet of session development.)

13. *What do you feel that you got out of this session?* (This 9-item checklist surveyed part of the facet of exchange.)

14. *To what extent are you looking forward to your next session?* (Answered on a 4-point scale; part of the facet of session development.)

15. *How did your therapist act toward you during this session?* (This 16-item checklist surveyed part of the facet of relationship.)

16. *How did your therapist seem to feel during this session?* (This 34-item checklist surveyed part of the facet of feeling process.)

TABLE 2

Summary of Items in the Therapist Form of the
Therapy Session Report

---

1. *How do you feel about the session which you have just completed?*
2. *What did your patient talk about during this session?*
3. *What did your patient seem to want out of this session?*
4. *How did your patient act toward you during this session?*
5. *How did your patient seem to feel during this session?*
6. *To what extent were you looking forward to seeing your patient this session?*
7. *How well motivated for coming to therapy was your patient this session?*
8. *How freely did your patient express herself (himself) in this session?*
9. *To what extent did your patient bring out the thoughts and feelings which really seemed to concern her (him) during this session?*
10. *To what extent did you feel in rapport or empathically "in touch" with what your patient was experiencing during this session?*
11. *How well do you feel you understood the meaning of what your patient said and did during this session (in whatever conceptual terms you find most useful for describing personality)?*
12. *How helpful do you feel that you were to your patient during this session?*
13. *To what extent did your patient seem to make progress during this session in dealing with the problems for which she (he) is in therapy?*
14. *At what level of effectiveness and integration (emotionally and psychologically) did your patient seem to be during this session?*
15. *In what direction were you working with your patient during this session?*
16. *How did you act toward your patient during this session?*
17. *How did you feel during this session?*

---

separate part of the Clinic, where she was given a copy of the TSR by a research assistant. Patients had been assured (see Appendix A) that their responses would be kept in the strictest confidence and would not be available either to their therapists or to other Clinic staff. They were informed that they were not doing this for their therapists, but rather as a standard Clinic procedure. Each patient was given a code number that she used, instead of her name, to identify her forms. After the questionnaires had been completed, they were returned to the research assistant and taken to the Institute for Juvenile Research, where the responses were recorded on IBM cards.

The same assurance of confidentiality was given to the therapists who participated in the study, and the same procedures were followed in the handling of data identification. Therapists usually completed the forms in their offices after each session with a selected patient. Since, on a clinic night, each therapist saw three patients with little break between sessions, he was requested to complete a TSR for only one of his patients.

The methodological question that most naturally arises concerning our research procedures is: To what extent, and in what ways, did filling out the TSR questionnaire after every session alter the nature of the experience that was reported? This question, often raised by colleagues when hearing of the study, may be taken in two ways. First, it inquires as to whether the mere fact of reporting on the confidential experience of therapy does not in some way alter the nature of that experience, presumably by introducing a new factor into the therapeutic relationship. The second point implicit in the question is whether patients and therapists, in completing the TSR questionnaire, can and will make an accurate representation of whatever they did experience.

It is now a generally accepted principle that the observation of a phenomenon in some ways alters the nature of that phenomenon. This is as true of any method used in studying psychotherapy as it is of research in general. The presence of tape recorders and/or cameras or observers behind a one-way window represents intrusions—in fact, far livelier intrusions than the TSR—upon the confidential experience of psychotherapy. The only alternative to intruding in some fashion is the rejection of research altogether. Since some perturbations are necessary, the only course is to make these explicit.

Some possible consequences of our research intervention are (1) the TSR might focus the attention of the patient and/or the therapist on phenomena that had not been considered in their endeavor; (2) the patient might use the TSR as a "third party" in which to confide, thus eliminating the necessity of discussing certain issues in the session itself; (3) anticipation of completing the TSR might serve to focus the session in a manner that would facilitate answering the questions; and (4) the TSR could provoke irritations and resentments that interfere with the therapeutic relationship. Countering these concerns are the routine nature of the TSR and its comprehensiveness and length. The TSR was introduced as a regular clinic requirement and apparently accepted as such by the patients. The length of the TSR tends to mitigate against its having a specific focusing effect on the therapy. The relatively even and descriptive sampling of facets should also mitigate against remembering particular issues from week to week.

It is also germane to ask whether the impact made by the method of study is consistent with the nature of the process being studied, or is disruptive to it. If the impact of completing the TSR questionnaire immediately after each therapy session is consonant with the aims of psychotherapy, then it may be counted as an acceptable form of research intervention on both professional and scientific grounds. In a very general sense, we may say that it is the aim of psychotherapeutic intervention to cause the patient to reflect upon his experience, in the expectation that such reflection will lead to beneficial changes in the quality of his experience. The procedure of having the patient take five to ten minutes after each session to reflect on the experience of that session, through the medium of a structured "self-interview" (the TSR), should have an effect that in most cases would be congruent with the intended impact of therapy itself. In support of this assertion, we can cite only anecdotal evidence: patients' positive remarks about the experience of filling out the questionnaire; their reflections on it as a source of insight; their requests to have copies for friends who were in treatment elsewhere; and their regular cooperation in completing the questionnaire. Needless to say, all the remarks patients made were not positive. The procedure constitutes a repetitious chore, may become boring in time, and may become the object of displaced irritation whose source is the therapist or the clinic itself. Every attempt was made to disassociate the research procedure from the therapeutic relationship itself in the patients' minds. Only rarely did patients refuse to participate, or did they or their therapists remark on the deleterious or disruptive impact of the research procedure. It seems safe to say that the research procedure interferes no more, and probably less, than other methods of study that have been used.

The second point under consideration involves the accuracy of the representations that patients and therapists made of their experiences. Were the participants honest in completing the TSR? To support the impulse to be honest, we arranged that neither the patient nor the therapist place his name on the form, and that these forms be dealt with in the strictest professional confidence, including the debarring of clinic personnel from access to them. The participants were probably as honest as people ever are in answering questionnaires when there is no obvious incentive for faking. The repetitive and routine administration of the TSRs should also have served to reduce tendencies to distort (Howard, 1964). Further, the results that have been reported here are not derived directly from the manifest statements of patients and therapists, but rather constitute the end products of analyses that significantly transform the raw data. Neither the patients nor the therapists could have had any idea of the dimensions that would emerge from the responses they made, nor could they have any idea of how these dimensions would be scored from the raw data. The dimensions that were obtained, in fact, went far beyond what could probably have been directly reported by either the patients or the therapists as present in awareness. The patterns that emerge through factor analysis must have included much that was unconscious to the participants, if our interpretations of them have been correct.

## SAMPLE CHARACTERISTICS AND THE PROBLEM OF GENERALIZATION

One aim of the Psychotherapy Session Project was to discover what *kinds of experience* people have in psychotherapy. Another aim was to find out which *kinds of people* have what kinds of experience in psychotherapy. In line with the second aim, we hoped to gain a deeper understanding of how the personal and social characteristics of patients and therapists influence the quality of their experience.

To implement this second aim, we required demographic and other background data from participants. These additional data were collected from patients and therapists by means of brief questionnaires (see Appendices D and E), and are summarized here to give a fuller depiction of the individuals who participated in this study.

Four general categories of information were sought from the participants: current life status, sociocultural status, family background, and therapeutic or professional status. The current life status variables were age, marital status, parental status, and (for patients) employment status. These define some of the more important conditions determining the individual's current experience outside of psychotherapy, and influence the types of needs, satisfactions, and concerns that are likely to be salient for him.

The variables included under sociocultural status—social class of origin, religion, and education—are generally acknowledged to be important influences in shaping the individual's attitudes, life goals, and value orientations.

Family background data included family size, birth order, and (for the patient sample) age at family disruption, if there had been any. The structure and stability of an individual's early family life are commonly found to have important effects on personality, and on typical patterns of interpersonal behavior.

Therapeutic or professional status information was obtained to assess the nature and extent of the individual's previous participation in psychotherapy. The therapeutic status variables for patients included clinical diagnosis, previous psychotherapy, and length of time in the current therapeutic involvement. The professional status variables for therapists included professional discipline in which training was received, length of time in therapeutic practice, and whether the therapist had undergone psychotherapy.

Table 3 shows the individual and social characteristics of the patient

TABLE 3

## Individual and Social Characteristics of Patient Sample

**Current Life Status**

|  |  |  |
|---|---|---|
| 1. Age | | |
| | 20-26 | 45% |
| | 27-36 | 31% |
| | 37-60 | 24% |
| 2. Marital status | | |
| | Single | 47% |
| | Married | 25% |
| | Other | 28% |
| 3. Parental status | | |
| | No children | 58% |
| | Children | 42% |
| 4. Employment | | |
| | Employed | 83% |
| | Not employed | 17% |

**Sociocultural Status**

|  |  |  |
|---|---|---|
| 5. Social class of origin [a] | | |
| | Upper middle and middle | 25% |
| | Lower middle | 25% |
| | Upper lower | 40% |
| | Lower and lower lower | 10% |
| 6. Education | | |
| | H.S. graduate or less | 35% |
| | Some college | 33% |
| | College graduate or more | 31% |
| 7. Religion | | |
| | Protestant | 43% |
| | Catholic | 35% |
| | Jewish | 15% |
| | Other or none | 7% |

**Family Background**

|  |  |  |
|---|---|---|
| 8. Family size | | |
| | Only child | 12% |
| | One sib | 18% |
| | Two or three sibs | 43% |
| | Four or more sibs | 27% |
| 9. Birth order | | |
| | Oldest | 45% |
| | Middle | 32% |
| | Youngest | 23% |

TABLE 3 (continued)

| | |
|---|---|
| 10. Age at family disruption | |
| Under 5 | 12% |
| 6-10 | 7% |
| 11-15 | 7% |
| 16+ or never | 75% |
| **Therapeutic Status** | |
| 11. Diagnosis | |
| Depressive reaction | 45% |
| Anxiety reaction | 15% |
| Personality disorder | 25% |
| Schizophrenia | 15% |
| 12. Previous psychotherapy | |
| Yes | 62% |
| No | 38% |
| 13. Weeks of current therapy | |
| 1-26 weeks | 45% |
| 27-52 weeks | 28% |
| 53 or more weeks | 27% |

[a] Based on father's occupation.

sample. 76% of the patients were between 20 and 36 years of age, although the sample included individuals as old as 60. The youthfulness of the patients is also reflected in the median age of the group, which was 28. Only 25% of the patients were then currently married and living with their spouses, but another 28% had been married. 42% were mothers, although only a small minority were housewives in the traditional sense of being married, mothers, and homemakers as a major occupational commitment. More than four-fifths of the patients were gainfully employed, indicating that most of the sample consisted of young working women, career women, and working mothers.

The outstanding feature of the patient sample in terms of sociocultural background was its high level of educational attainment. 90% had at least graduated high school, and 64% had done at least some college work. Most indices of social class or socioeconomic status would place these patients at middle-class levels by virtue of their educational attainments. This fact, contrasted with ratings of their social class of origin (based on father's occupation), indicates that the women in this sample have been upwardly mobile, by their own achievements rather than by marriage. Only 25% of the patients came from middle- or upper-middle-class homes; nearly two-thirds came from small business or working-class backgrounds.

The patients tended to come from relatively large families, 70% having three or more children in them. Controlling for family size, oldest children were overrepresented in our sample and middle children were underrepresented. Three-fourths of the patients came from families that were intact through childhood and early adolescence, although a significant minority did come from broken homes.

The most striking fact about the therapeutic status of the patients in our sample was that 62% had had some previous psychotherapy, although 73% of the patients were in the first year of their present course of therapy. The most frequently assigned clinical diagnosis at intake was depressive reaction. The patients diagnosed as schizophrenic (15%) constituted a somewhat special group, as they were able to maintain themselves sufficiently well in the community to be seen in outpatient therapy.

Table 4 shows the individual and social characteristics of the therapist sample. Nearly 60% of the therapists were over 35 years of age and none was younger than 29. In this respect, the therapists were considerably more mature than those samples of clinical psychology interns or psychiatric residents typically used in research on psychotherapy. 41% of the therapists were currently married, and another 24% had been married. 35% of the therapists were parents.

The vast majority of the therapists (94%) were of middle-class origin and thus came from higher status backgrounds than did their patients. The patients' current status level (by virtue of educational attainment), however, was not *too* greatly discrepant from that of the therapists, even though their income levels were markedly different. Another significant discrepancy in sociocultural status appeared in religious affiliations. Although 78% of the patients claimed some Christian affiliation, only 36% of the therapists did. In addition, 29% of the therapists claimed no formal religious affiliation. Thus, the therapist sample reflects a more secular, as well as a higher status, sociocultural milieu.

Therapists also tended to come from smaller families than did patients. Somewhat surprising in this context was the fact that the therapists tended to be younger rather than oldest children in their families.

The median length of therapeutic practice was six years. Only one therapist in the group had been in practice for less than four years, whereas some had been practicing for more than 20 years. This high level of practical experience is an uncommon and advantageous sample characteristic. Furthermore, nearly two-thirds of the therapists had undergone personal psychotherapy.

We must now consider the generalizability of the findings obtained from the characteristics of the patients and therapists studied. Generalizability of findings beyond the sample of individuals studied is usually determined by the degree to which the individuals included in the sample are representative of the larger population from which they were drawn. The best guarantee of representativeness is random sampling from the larger population. Neither the patients nor the therapists in our samples were randomly selected. We had an opportunity sample, that is, we took those participants who were convenient to us and would cooperate with us, with all of the potential biases or deviations from representativeness this implies. In addition, the nature of the clinic at which the study was pursued limited us to female patients, placing a further quite obvious restriction on the generalizability of the findings.

To evaluate this issue, we must define the populations from which our patients and therapists were presumably a sample. This in itself is not without difficulty. We might say that our patients were a sample of all *psychiatric* patients, of all adult psychiatric *outpatients,* of all adult *female* psychiatric outpatients, of all *urban* adult female psychiatric outpatients, and so on. The difficulty is in drawing a rational boundary for the parent population. People have too many attributes that may be crucial in the definition of a population; attributes, moreover, that shift in salience according to the purpose and context of inquiry. These attributes are also inevitable factors in determining where in the organization of our social institutions the persons might become available for inclusion in a study sample. To take examples from the field of psychotherapy alone, it is clear that patients are most likely to become available for inclusion in a study if they are being seen at an institutional facility rather than in private practice, and this fact is likely to set a basic limit on generalizability. Further, the nature of the institutional facility imposes other selective biases on the sample. The most frequently utilized sources of patients have been Veterans Administration clinics and hospitals, university counselling centers, and university-affiliated psychiatric facilities. Representativeness of some vaguely defined general psychotherapeutic population can hardly be a serious proposal under any of these circumstances.

A different approach to the problem of generalization seems to be indicated. This calls for the diversification of samples in cross-validating the findings of a study. Thus, if a certain set of findings is obtained with subjects of specific characteristics, the point of effective replication ought to be a study conducted with subjects of contrasting characteristics (Chassan, 1967; Roff & Ricks, 1972). To the extent that similar findings are obtained, one gains confidence in their generality along the dimensions of difference between the two samples. The repetition of this procedure is required until all those diverse types of people who are of interest have been studied, although clearly each successful extension of the findings to a new and different sort of sample increases one's overall

TABLE 4

**Individual and Social Characteristics of Therapist Sample**

**Current Life Status**

   1. Age
| | |
|---|---:|
| 29-35 | 41% |
| 36 or over | 59% |

   2. Marital status
| | |
|---|---:|
| Single | 35% |
| Married | 41% |
| Other | 24% |

   3. Parental status
| | |
|---|---:|
| No children | 65% |
| Children | 35% |

**Sociocultural Status**

   4. Social class of origin [a]
| | |
|---|---:|
| Upper middle and middle | 59% |
| Lower middle | 35% |
| Upper lower | 6% |

   5. Religion
| | |
|---|---:|
| Protestant | 24% |
| Catholic | 12% |
| Jewish | 35% |
| Other or none | 29% |

**Personal and Family Background**

   6. Sex
| | |
|---|---:|
| Male | 59% |
| Female | 41% |

   7. Family size
| | |
|---|---:|
| Only child | 18% |
| One sib | 24% |
| Two or three sibs | 53% |
| Four or more sibs | 6% |

   8. Birth order
| | |
|---|---:|
| Oldest | 35% |
| Middle | 29% |
| Youngest | 35% |

**Professional Status**

   9. Profession
| | |
|---|---:|
| Psychiatry | 59% |
| Psychology | 18% |
| Social Work | 24% |

**TABLE 4 (continued)**

| | |
|---|---|
| 10. Years of experience | |
|     0-5 years | 47% |
|     6 or more years | 53% |
| 11. Personal psychotherapy | |
|     Yes | 65% |
|     No | 35% |

[a] Based on father's occupation.

confidence in the generality of the findings. By such diversification of samples, the extent and limits of generalizability can be empirically established.

The determination of the limits of generalizability by this procedure calls for sharing research obligations. The person who initially makes a study and reports his findings is under obligation to state in adequate detail the characteristics of his subjects as particular kinds of people. Just which parameters are to be specified has not been established, although there are certain standard characteristics that it is more or less customary to report. To these standard characteristics must be added those others that the researcher believes are likely to be pertinent to the phenomena under study. Under these circumstances, if the study is well done, i.e., has internal validity (Campbell & Stanley, 1966), the findings may be presumed to apply to other persons who are *like* the persons studied in these specified characteristics, and to apply with decreasing confidence to persons who are increasingly dissimilar.

A second obligation devolves upon the person who wishes to apply findings to people who are different from the people studied. This person has the obligation to ascertain the characteristics of individuals in his target sample, and to *test* the applicability of the facts he wishes to utilize. This testing can be done formally in a designed study or informally by comparing the findings with, or attempting to fit them to, his own experience with other samples. The obligation to evaluate generalizability carefully naturally applies more forcibly to the extent that the target sample differs from the original study sample.

To whom, then, do the findings pertain? At the very minimum, the findings may apply only to the subjects of this study. This would be disappointing but not without interest or value, since the findings are exciting (if only in the case history tradition) and may stimulate research with other samples. At the maximum, the findings may apply to all varieties of dyadic psychotherapy, and some of the findings may even apply to all types of psychologically intense dyadic relationships. Within the range of possibilities defined by these limits, we must say what seems in our own judgment to be the warranted extent of generalization.

The safest course in defining the application of our findings should probably take account of the fact that the patients were all women in their adult years, able to maintain themselves in the general community, and to sustain themselves in weekly therapeutic contacts. They could all afford clinic fees, and thus represent neither the upper nor the lower socioeconomic levels of the community. They were generally well-educated and usually employed, although these limitations are of lesser moment, since we have been able to test variations in education and employment within the sample and have determined their association with certain patterns of therapeutic experience. This sample, if not representative of all patients in individual psychotherapy, probably resembles the major segment of the patient population in many ways.

Of direct relevance are the findings of a survey conducted by Ryan (1969) in the Boston area from 1960 to 1962. These findings indicated that patients in private psychotherapy constituted a:

. . . group of patients with the most clear-cut and distinguishable characteristics. These patients cover a relatively narrow age range, half of them falling between the ages of 22 and 36. About two-thirds are female; four out of five have gone to college or are now college students; occupations are generally consistent with education, reflecting a class level in the middle and upper ranges. Only about one patient in five is diagnosed by his psychiatrist as psychotic or even borderline psychotic, the great majority being seen as suffering from chronic neurosis or character disorder. Close to half of these patients have had previous psychiatric care. The average patient is described as a person with a chronic character disorder having symptoms reflecting anxiety, depression, or both (p. 19).

If Ryan's findings are typical of conditions in other metropolitan areas—and this seems indicated by the findings of Kadushin (1969) for New York City—it is clear that the sample employed in the Psychotherapy Session Project was representative of a significant patient population.

Other questions that come readily to mind about the varieties of therapeutic experience found among the patients in our sample are: How would these be different for male patients? How would these be different in private practice and inpatient settings? How would these be different for psychotherapy in which sessions are scheduled with greater frequency? How would these be different for therapies of markedly different theoretical and technical orientations? Each of these questions defines a research problem of considerable interest for the student of psychotherapy, and hopefully each will receive the attention it deserves.

To this point, we have concentrated on the patient sample. The limitations engendered by the sample of therapists studied also deserves consideration. Here we confront a slightly different problem in that a major source of dissatisfaction is the small number of therapists included in the sample. The sample of therapists, like the sample of patients, was an opportunity sample. In many important respects, this sample resembles the national samples of psychotherapists studied by Henry, Sims, and Spray (1971) and by Goldman and Mendelsohn (1969).

Most of the therapists in our sample would classify themselves as eclectic in theoretical and technical orientation. Their eclecticism makes them in some sense typical of the "average" psychotherapist, but it also makes them potentially unrepresentative of those who are stricter adherents to a particular school of thought. One of the questions raised in connection with the patient sample fits naturally here as well. We do not know—and we would certainly like to know—how the dimensions of therapeutic experience discovered in this study would be different for therapies of markedly different orientations. Here again, the strategy of divergent sampling seems to be a logical procedure in the development of cross-validating research.

*Chapter 4*

# Methods of
# Data Analysis

The data produced with the Therapy Session Reports consisted of responses indicating the presence or intensity of particular experiences in the therapy session. The questionnaires were numerically pre-coded, so that answers to the questions could be translated directly to IBM cards. The purpose of the data analysis was to transform these raw data into meaningful quantitative measures having both clinical and research importance. Four general types of statistical analysis were used in our work: item analysis, factor analysis, typal analysis, and group comparisons. Item analysis was utilized to delineate the frequencies and correlates of particular experiences. Factor analysis was applied to determine parsimonious sets of experiential dimensions. Typal analysis was used to define sets of patients, therapists, or patient-therapist pairs. Group comparisons were employed to discover the personal and social characteristics of the people who had each type of experience.

The Psychotherapy Session Project represents a type of scientific inquiry that can be characterized as naturalistic, exploratory, field, or survey research. This classification derives from the facts that no attempt was made to control independent variables (antecedent conditions), and the phenomena were studied in their natural context. After describing our analytic methods, we shall discuss the role of this type of research in the strategy of scientific inquiry and suggest how the Psychotherapy Session Project fits this context.

## ITEM ANALYSES

Two kinds of statistical analysis were applied directly to patients' and therapists' responses to the items in the TSR to delineate typical and ideal experiences. The analysis of *typical* experiences involved computation of the endorsement level for each item. For checklist items this was a percent endorsement; for multiple-alternative items this was an arithmetic mean. The responses of each participant to each item were averaged across the therapy sessions on which he reported. Then, the average response to each item was averaged across all patients and separately across all therapists. In other words, the view of typical experiences (presented in Chapter 5) was based on averages over sessions and participants.

The second mode of analysis applied to the TSR items was directed at delineating patients' and therapists' *ideal* experiences. The criterion of evaluation, or "dependent variable," in this analysis was the first question on each of the TSR forms: *"How do you feel about the therapy session which you have just completed?"* The participant's answer to this was marked on a 6-point scale that ranged from "one of the best sessions we have had" to "this was a really poor session." Items in the TSR that correlate highly with this criterion should indicate the kinds of experiences that embody patients' and therapists' implicit conceptions of the ideal session.

In determining the ideal experiences for patients and therapists, the data were analyzed in the following way. For each variable in the TSR, the product-moment correlation with the criterion was computed. This was done separately for each of the patients and therapists, the $N$ of the correlation being the number of sessions for which TSRs had been completed. With 60 patients, each relationship between the criterion and each other item in the TSR was thus estimated by 60 correlations. Statistical evaluation of the relationship between the criterion and each other item was made by taking a simple count of positive and negative correlations and evaluating the proportion observed against an expected 50-50 split, using a standard binomial table (MacKinnon, 1959). Zero correlations were eliminated whenever these were attributable to lack of variation in one variable, since our purpose was to estimate the degree of covariation.

The same procedure was followed in evaluating the relationships between the criterion and the other items for the 31 therapist-cases in our sample. Since a few therapists contributed more than one case, the independence of their cases was in question, but we found as much variation between the cases of one therapist as between the cases of different therapists, and consequently decided to utilize the full sample.

Finally, the presence in our sample of matched data from 28 patient-therapist pairs allowed us to follow the same procedure in comparing *patients'* reports with their *therapists'* post-session evaluations, and *vice versa*. We were thus able to examine both participants' views of what occurred in those therapy sessions that were rated as better or worse by each. Patients' and therapists' ideal therapy sessions are described in Chapter 6.

## FACTOR ANALYSES

The major reason for factor analyzing the data was to isolate the salient dimensions of patient and therapist experience tapped by the TSRs. Another purpose was to reduce the number of variables carried into subsequent analyses from the large number of items to a smaller number of composite variables. Composite variables so defined have higher reliability and potentially greater clinical meaning.

The general plan involved factor analyzing each checklist or group of scales in the TSR separately so that relatively independent scores could be computed for them, and then to factor analyze the entire TSR using these *facet* factor scores rather than item scores. By scoring on the basis of these facet factors, we attempted to minimize any artifactual impact of within-section (method) covariation. Factor analysis of the entire TSR yielded a set of *global* experience dimensions for patients and therapists, on the basis of which third level scores were computed. Scores for the global dimensions were used in the factor analysis of patient-therapist pairs that defined the *conjoint* experience dimensions. In sum, the general plan of factor analysis utilized item scores (first level) to derive facet dimensions, facet scores (second level) to derive global experience dimensions, and global experience scores (third level) to derive conjoint experience dimensions. Conjoint experience scores (fourth level) were used subsequently in group comparisons.

Although the results of the factor analyses are presented separately, the analyses all followed the same procedure. For each patient or therapist who had completed TSRs after at least eight consecutive sessions, each TSR item was averaged over the reported number of sessions (not including the first report).[1] These averages, representing a block of experience for the particular patient or therapist, constituted the basic data employed in the factor analyses. Patient and therapist forms were analyzed separately.

The procedure followed in the factor analysis of each section was as

---

[1] In the factor analyses of items within facets, first occasion TSR reports were excluded because of suspected atypicality (Howard, 1964).

follows. Product-moment correlations ($N=60$ patients; $N=31$ thera-pist-cases) were computed among the items within each section. Unities were placed in the major diagonal of each matrix. Principal components factor analysis was performed on each matrix, extracting as many fac-tors as the order of the matrix. Varimax rotations were performed for each problem on increasing numbers of factors until a solution contained a specific factor, i.e., a factor containing the salient loading of only one item. The immediately preceding solution was then retained for sub-sequent study except when there was a clearly "transitional" common factor. That is, that solution was retained for each section that gave the largest number of relatively stable common factors (Howard and Gordon, 1963). These analyses resulted in the definition of 45 facet factors for the patient form, and 43 facet factors for the therapist form.

In proceeding to the factor analyses of the entire patient and thera-pist forms, the following additional steps were taken. Item scores were standard scored for each item ($\overline{X}=10.00$, $s=2.00$). For each of the facet factors, salient items were assigned unit weight and summed for each patient or therapist. Items with no clear salient loadings were not scored. The 45 facet factor scores for each patient were intercorrelated over the patient sample ($N=60$) and the resulting matrix factor analyzed according to the procedures outlined above. The 43 facet factor scores for each therapist were intercorrelated over the therapist-case sample ($N=31$) and factor analyzed in the same fashion.[2] These analyses re-sulted in the definition of eleven dimensions of patient global experience and eleven dimensions of therapist global experience.

Factor scores for each patient and therapist-case were computed by combining standardized scores for salient facet factors. Correlations were computed between these global experience factor scores and the items not scored on the facet factors, and were used in the interpreta-tion of the global experience factors. Subsequently, these items were included in the scoring of the facet factors. The eleven patient and eleven therapist global experience factor scores were then standard scored.

In our sample there were 28 therapist-patient pairs who reported on their joint sessions. Each of the 28 pairs provided eleven patient and eleven therapist global experience scores. These 22 scores were inter-correlated ($N=28$) and the resulting matrix was factor analyzed as above. Seven dimensions of conjoint experience were defined. Factor

---

[2] Additional caution must be taken with the therapist results, since in some analyses there were more variables than subjects. This was particularly true of the analysis of global experience, where there were 43 scores and only 31 therapist-cases. The number of factors in any analysis never exceeded eleven, however, about one-third the number of subjects.

scores for these conjoint dimensions were computed by combining the global experience scores that were salient for each conjoint factor. Interpretations were augmented by correlating the facet factor scores that were not used in computing global experience scores with these conjoint dimensions. Finally, these seven conjoint factor scores were transformed to standard scores.

## TYPAL ANALYSIS

Once experiential dimensions were defined, the next step was to discover the configurations of experiences for patients and therapists. From a clinical point of view, the discrete dimensions are of less interest than the total pattern of experience for particular individuals or dyads. Only rarely would a person's experience in psychotherapy be characterized by the realization of a single predominant dimension. Rather, it is the profile of relevant scores that best represents the individual's psychotherapeutic experience. Although each person's profile was to some extent unique, clusters of patients (or therapists, or dyads) sharing a characteristic profile of scores could be defined by empirical means. Each characteristic profile would constitute a general type of therapeutic experience.

The procedure used in the derivation of empirical types was as follows. A measure of the "distance," or total difference, was computed between each profile and each other profile within its respective set: for each patient with each other patient; for each therapist with each other therapist; for each dyad with each other dyad. This distance measure was the sum of squared differences between the corresponding elements of each pair of profiles $(D^2)$. A profile-by-profile $D^2$ matrix was thus constructed for patient global experience, therapist global experience, and conjoint experience.

After this was done, a product-moment correlation was computed between each pair of profiles on the basis of the $D^2$ matrix; i.e., each column of the $D^2$ matrix was correlated with each other column.[3] This resulted in a correlation matrix of the same order as the $D^2$ matrix—a 60 x 60 patient matrix, a 31 x 31 therapist-case matrix, and a 28 x 28 dyad matrix. These correlations reflected the degree of similarity between two profiles in terms of the relation of each to the remaining profiles in the set. $D^2$ was employed here, instead of proceeding directly to a correlational analysis, because the direction of scoring of the dimensions was arbitrary. Profile correlations are very sensitive to direction

[3] The $N$ for these correlations was the number of profiles in the set minus 2. The two entries eliminated were the $D^2$'s between each profile and itself.

of scoring (Tellegen, 1965; Howard and Diesenhaus, 1967), whereas $D^2$ is completely insensitive to direction of scoring. The interposition of $D^2$ thus eliminated the production of artifactual types.

In each of the three analyses, the first type was derived from the correlation matrix by selecting that profile that had the largest number of correlations above .70. This profile defined the type and all other profiles correlating above .70 with it were classified as members of that type. The second type was defined by that profile not included in the first type that had the largest number of correlations exceeding .70 with the remaining profiles. These profiles were then classified as the second type. Each subsequent type was similarly derived. Profiles not correlating .70 or more with the defining profile of a type, but which had all of their correlations in excess of .70 with other members of that type, were also classified in that type. Any profile that correlated above .70 with members of more than one type was not classified.

The types reported in Chapters 8, 10, and 12 should not be thought of as singular categories within which no variation occurred. Rather, they represent modal points in a field of individual variations around which certain profiles of experience tended to cluster. There were, in addition, some individuals and patient-therapist pairs that lay part way between these modal points, sharing the characteristics of more than one, and individuals and pairs that did not approximate to any of the types. Most of the patients, therapists, and patient-therapist pairs were classifiable in one type or another according to the criteria stated above, however.

## GROUP COMPARISONS

The establishment of types made it possible to ask, "*Who* had what type of experience in psychotherapy?" This question could be answered by examining the differential personal and social characteristics of the individuals included in each type. Those characteristics that distinguished individuals having a given type of experience could be interpreted as possible determinants of that experience.

A number of objective patient and therapist characteristics were surveyed by questionnaire (see Appendices D and E). Summaries of these characteristics were presented in Tables 3 and 4. Cross-tabulations were made between each characteristic and the experience types within the patient, therapist, and matched-pair samples. Chi-squares were calculated to evaluate the statistical significance of these comparisons.

The samples of patients and therapists used in these analyses were too small to allow independent evaluation of all the different characteristics surveyed. Some of the characteristics were confounded, making it difficult to assess which of them was the effective variable influencing a pattern of therapeutic experience. We cross-tabulated the set of patient characteristics and the set of therapist characteristics to determine which among them were so confounded. The results of this tabulation are presented with the findings to which they pertain, as an aid to the interpretation of the personal patterning of psychotherapeutic experience.

## THE METHODOLOGY OF THE PSYCHOTHERAPY SESSION PROJECT

Methodology is properly distinguished (Kaplan, 1964) from the specific methods or techniques of observation and analysis employed in a study. "I mean by *methodology* [Kaplan writes] the study—the description, the explanation, and the justification—of methods and not the methods themselves" (p. 18). We have described our methods of observation and analysis in Chapter 3 and in the preceding sections of Chapter 4. Here we shall briefly comment on the more basic issues of scientific methodology that are relevant to an understanding of the Psychotherapy Session Project.

The fundamental issue to which methodology is addressed might arise in the reader's mind as the question, "Should I believe the results of this study?" Do the basic design, the research operations, and the statistical analyses employed in this study warrant the acceptance of its findings as reasonably established fact? Or may these findings be dismissed as instrumental, sampling, or statistical artifacts?

In practice, scientific investigation seeks evidence that bears on the credibility of propositions concerning the nature of the phenomena under study. To evaluate credibility, scientific methodology concerns itself with establishing rules of evidence, or maxims to guide the judgments of the "reasonable" person (scientist). These rules specify that the quality of evidence is a function of the relevance and representativeness (freedom from confounding) of the *data,* and the relevance and objectivity (replicability and immunity to subjective influence) of the *analyses.*

Given high quality evidence, the credibility of a proposition remains in part a function of the prior commitments of the audience, and the ability of a potential refuter to construct a more plausible alternative explanation (Campbell & Stanley, 1964). As Polya (1954) has said:

It is for the impersonal rules of plausible reasoning to decide which kind of evidence deserves consideration. Yet it is for your personal good sense to decide whether the particular piece of evidence just submitted has sufficient weight or not (p. 141).

For research to be successful—that is, for it to influence the state of knowledge—it must take into account the characteristics of its consumers. Each person operates in his particular field on the basis of what he believes, in terms of those propositions to which he attaches the highest credibility. The more necessary a particular belief is for his pursuit of the activities to which he is committed, the less likely it is that the person will be open to new evidence tending to decrease the credibility of that belief. For example, the practicing psychotherapist has as much difficulty accepting evidence that therapeutic treatment is ineffective, as the experimental psychologist has in accepting evidence that his biases influence the outcome of his research.

Assessment of the credibility of the Psychotherapy Session Project must be made with due regard for its two different (if overlapping) audiences. The practicing psychotherapist's and the scientific researcher's requirements of research in psychotherapy are inevitably somewhat different, as are their evaluative criteria. The therapist must understand and treat individuals rather than random samples of a specified population. He seeks understanding of human personality through intensive study of the individual. Since his concern is with the individual, he is not inclined to consider differences between persons as a product of random influences and sampling error. On the other hand, since the researcher's approach generally involves contrasts between differently treated groups, differences between persons *within* a group tend to be regarded as random phenomena, and are used as a criterion for judging the significance of the contrasts.

This difference has other important implications. The statistical model adopted by the researcher for the control of extraneous factors requires an evaluation of the events in terms of general trends in populations. Generalizations made from samples are taken to pertain to an idealized case—for example, the population mean—which may not have empirical existence (Chassan, 1967). This type of evidence is useful to the researcher in the evaluation of theoretical propositions. On the other hand, this type of information may be irrelevant to the therapist, who needs to apply his knowledge to the understanding and modification of individual behavior.

The model of inquiry adopted by the clinician involves an evaluation of events in terms of the behaviors of particular persons. Generalizations based on clinical observation pertain to the behaviors of a given person in different situations, and to propositions about the behavior of groups of similar people. Although this approach maximizes clinical relevance, it has often been impressionistic and susceptible to the influences of confounding variables.

The ideal in science is to maximize both relevance and freedom from confounding. In naturalistic or clinical research, relevance is given the most weight. Problems of inference come from an inability to specify which variables were operative in producing the observations. In experimental research, freedom from the influence of confounding variables is given the most weight. Here, the major problem of inference is one of limited generalizability to analogous situations outside the laboratory.

The best scientific evidence for both the clinical and scientific communities will come from clinical research in which it is possible to observe covariation between manipulable antecedent events and consequent responses (Bandura & Walters, 1963; Goldstein, Heller, & Sechrest, 1966). At present, however, this model has limited applicability to the study of psychotherapeutic process. We do not really know which antecedent events warrant systematic manipulation, and we do not know how to manipulate them reliably.

This state of affairs has led us to a naturalistic and non-manipulative approach. Two goals sought through such an approach were the isolation and definition of relevant variables, and the generation of hypotheses that could be more rigorously studied. The strategy of the Psychotherapy Session Project was to stay as close to the relevant phenomena as possible in observational method, and then to apply the most sophisticated techniques at our disposal to refine and analyze the data.

The quality of data can only be evaluated in the context of an empirical investigation. Our data were the reports of patients and therapists about their subjective experiences. These data are neither scientific nor unscientific, they are the object of study. The ultimate test of the quality of data produced by our instruments lies in the results of the analyses to which they were subjected. Although it involves several arbitrary decisions (communality estimates, number of factors extracted, type of rotation), factor analysis can be automatically (objectively) applied to a set of data. It is a sensitive method for abstracting underlying dimensions from the interrelationships among variables. For the analysis to be responsive to the influence of these underlying dimensions, care must be taken in sampling both attributes (behaviors or responses) and objects (persons)—each must be representative of its population or domain.

The influence of restrictive sampling of attributes is primarily relevant to theory. The definition of dimensions is clearly dependent on the selection of the variables that are to be intercorrelated and subjected to factor analysis. If a variable is not included in the study, it cannot contribute to the definition of a factor. In this study, we have attempted to exhaust a particular variable domain. To the extent that significant experiential variables were not included, the factor structures were biased. If the strategy of restricting attention to this particular collection of variables (the TSRs) is adopted, the issue of variable sampling is not relevant. We *can* specify the factor structure of the questionnaires.

Restriction in object (person) sampling is more serious, since it influences directly the obtained relationships among the variables. The results of an analysis that is restricted to a specific set of variables are still generalizable. An analysis that is restricted to a specific set of persons has limited utility. When person (object) sampling is not representative, generalizability of results can only be judged by each consumer or by replication of the study with other samples. It should be noted that whenever a population extends over time (e.g., the population of all persons who have ever been or ever will be in psychotherapy), demonstrably representative sampling is not possible. Since representative sampling of patients is not feasible in the current framework of research in psychotherapy, the clinical researcher can only define his samples as clearly as possible so that a useful patchwork of studies spanning the population can be accumulated.

Given the results of a particular factor analysis, the task remains to interpret or to give meaning to the dimensions. This task depends on the imagination and experience of the investigator. Factor analysis structures and details the linear relationships among the primary data. The investigator must study the structure and ask himself what he knows about nature that would lead to a particular configuration. He must discover a construct that encompasses the empirical relationships. There then remain several strategies for validating or refining these interpretations. One strategy would be to study the relationship of the factor to independent criteria, i.e., to conduct external construct validity studies. A different strategy would be to investigate the relationships among the dimensions in higher-order analyses, i.e., to conduct internal construct validity studies. In this volume, we have undertaken both strategies.

The results of our methodological emphases—staying close to common experience in observational technique, and applying objective analytical techniques—should offer a substantial measure of relevance to the clinician and a substantial measure of objectivity and rigor to the researcher. The clinician will find the observational technique and its results directly intelligible and applicable to his immediate experience in therapy. Some of the results will be familiar, whereas others will give him reason to probe unexpected aspects of his transactions with patients. The researcher will find a technique for studying an important aspect of psychotherapy. In addition to the characteristics of the questionnaires, he will find new variables defined, variables that invite further investigation into therapeutic processes. We trust that the researcher will be as intrigued with our methodology as the clinician will be with the substantive findings.

Part III

# The Average and the Ideal: Composite Patterns of Psychotherapeutic Experience

*Chapter 5*

# Typical Experiences
# in Psychotherapy

The Therapy Session Reports were designed to survey the whole range of experiences that patients and therapists might have. Yet, in fact, some of these experiences occur considerably more often than others. In this chapter we analyze the differential frequencies of therapeutic experiences, emphasizing the most common or typical experiences of our patients and therapists. Aside from the intrinsic interest of these facts, the reader may find it useful to compare his own or his patients' experiences with the normative baseline these data provide.

The findings are reported separately for each facet of therapeutic experience: dialogue, feeling process, relationship, exchange process, and session development. For each facet, we present the relevant items, the rationale for their inclusion, and their endorsement frequencies.[1] Finally, we summarize and compare the most typical experiences reported by patients and by therapists.

## THERAPY AS DIALOGUE

The purpose of investigating dialogue was to assess the content of verbal behavior in the therapy session. Eighteen topics of conversation, in

---

[1] Items are listed in the tables in the order of their endorsement frequencies. The number before each item indicates its order of presentation in the questionnaire (see Appendices B and C).

checklist format, were presented following the question, "What did you talk about during this session?" The categories were devised to give coverage to the major interpersonal and intrapersonal sectors of the patient's life-space or phenomenal world, as well as to common problematic concerns. Item selection and topical saturation were guided by clinical experience and pilot testing.

Tables 5 and 6 display the dialogue items and average frequencies of endorsement for the patient and therapist samples, respectively. Inspection of these tables reveals that patients most frequently talked about themselves and their current intimate relationships. The mean percentages of endorsement by patients and therapists for each topic of dialogue were compared statistically, using the *t*-test. Only four of the 18 com-

## TABLE 5

### Patient TSR:  Dialogue—"What did you talk about during this session?"

| "During this session, I talked about:" | Mean % Endorsement |
|---|---|
| 9. Feelings and attitudes toward myself. | 70 |
| 1. Social activities and relationships, friends and acquaintances. | 52 |
| 5. Relationship with spouse, boyfriend, or girlfriend. | 52 |
| 11. Inadequacies, fears, or successes in getting along personally and socially. | 45 |
| 2. Work, supervisors, associates on the job (or at school). | 43 |
| 14. Feelings about being close to or needing someone. | 40 |
| 13. Angry and aggressive feelings and experiences. | 38 |
| 4. Domestic and household responsibilities, concerns, and activities (finances, children, etc.). | 36 |
| 6. Current relations with parents, brothers, or sisters. | 32 |
| 16. Plans, hopes, and goals for the future. | 31 |
| 7. Childhood experiences with family members, and feelings about them. | 28 |
| 12. Sexual feelings and experiences. | 27 |
| 10. Body functions, health, physical symptoms. | 25 |
| 18. Therapy, the therapist, being a patient. | 25 |
| 3. Recreations, hobbies, interests. | 19 |
| 15. Dreams, fantasies. | 16 |
| 17. Strange or unusual ideas, feelings, or experiences. | 13 |
| 8. Childhood experiences in school, with friends and with other kids. | 8 |

TABLE 6

**Therapist TSR: Dialogue—"What did your patient talk about during this session?"**

| "During this session, my patient talked about:" | Mean % Endorsement |
|---|---|
| 9. Feelings and attitudes toward self. | 74 |
| 5. Relationship with spouse, boyfriend, or girlfriend. | 50 |
| 2. Work, supervisors, associates on the job (or at school). | 42 |
| 1. Social activities and relationships, friends and acquaintances. | 37 |
| 13. Angry and aggressive feelings and experiences. | 34 |
| 18. Therapy, the therapist, being a patient. | 34 |
| 11. Inadequacies, fears, or successes in getting along personally and socially. | 33 |
| 14. Feelings about being close to or needing someone. | 33 |
| 6. Current relations with parents, brothers, or sisters. | 31 |
| 12. Sexual feelings and experiences. | 30 |
| 4. Domestic and household responsibilities, concerns, and activities (finances, children, etc.). | 28 |
| 16. Plans, hopes and goals for the future. | 28 |
| 7. Childhood experiences with family members, and feelings about them. | 26 |
| 10. Body functions, health, and physical symptoms. | 22 |
| 15. Dreams, fantasies. | 15 |
| 3. Recreations, hobbies, interests. | 12 |
| 17. Strange or unusual ideas, feelings, or experiences. | 11 |
| 8. Childhood experiences in school, with friends and with other kids. | 5 |

parisons showed differences significant at or beyond the .05 level. In each case patients reported the topic of dialogue *more* frequently: domestic and household responsibilities, concerns, and activities (finances, children, etc.); social activities and relationships, friends and acquaintances; inadequacies, fears, or successes in getting along personally and socially; and childhood experiences in school, with friends and with other kids.

It is clear, both from their relative ranking and from their actual levels of endorsement, that the topics of dialogue reported for therapy sessions by patients and by therapists were essentially the same. The small differential results may be attributed plausibly to differences in the interest or salience of each topic for patients and therapists.

## THERAPY AS FEELING PROCESS

The content of verbal behavior is only one aspect of participation in psychotherapy. Another major category of response is affect. Moreover, feelings are not merely discussed in psychotherapy; they are evoked, experienced, and resolved—primarily, one supposes, in the patient, but inevitably in the therapist as well. Therefore, each participant was asked to report on his own feelings and on those of the other. Essentially identical feeling checklists were used to assess the patient's feelings and the therapist's feelings. The checklists differ in two main respects: first, the types of feelings included were somewhat different, since the patient's and therapist's participation in therapy constrain them toward different affective states; second, there were a few bodily sensations that the individual was asked to rate only for himself. In general, the actual feeling words were selected from established adjective checklists. Words were chosen that reflected affected states (rather than traits) and seemed relevant to therapeutic experience. Further selection resulted from pilot studies.

The items pertaining to the patient's feelings, together with the mean percent of endorsement for each, are shown in Tables 7 and 8. The predominant feelings indicate a high level of arousal and emotional involvement, although the modal feelings were dysphoric in tone. When the mean percentages of patients' and therapists' endorsements for each patient feeling were compared statistically, using the $t$-test, only two of the forty differences were significant at or beyond the .05 level. Therapists exceeded patients in rating patients as feeling suspicious, and patients exceeded therapists in rating themselves as feeling tired. Overall, there was a remarkable degree of agreement between the two samples in the levels of endorsement of each of the patient feelings in the checklist.

The items pertaining to the therapist's feelings and their average percent of endorsement are shown in Tables 9 and 10 for patients and therapists, respectively. The therapist feelings most frequently reported by patients contrasted sharply with the predominantly dysphoric affect of the patient, but they were similar to the modal patient feelings in reflecting a positive involvement in the therapeutic relationship. The feelings most frequently endorsed by therapists were essentially the same as those reported for therapists by patients, implying that the patients were as astute in perceiving their therapists' feelings as the therapists were in perceiving their patients' feelings.

The comparison of mean frequencies of endorsement for each of the 34 therapist feelings revealed that only four differences were significant at or beyond the .05 level. Patients exceeded therapists in rating the

TABLE 7

Patient TSR: Patient Feeling Process

| "How did you feel during this session?" | Mean % Endorsement | "How did you feel during this session?" | Mean % Endorsement |
|---|---|---|---|
| 1. Tense | 41 | 10. Effective | 12 |
| 2. Anxious | 41 | 32. Hurt | 12 |
| 13. Frustrated | 34 | 16. Satisfied | 12 |
| 28. Interested | 34 | 20. Embarrassed | 11 |
| 36. Accepted | 31 | 39. Energetic | 11 |
| 15. Discouraged | 30 | 42. Thirsty | 11 |
| 3. Worried | 29 | 24. Likeable | 9 |
| 14. Sad | 26 | 33. Rejected | 9 |
| 7. Inadequate | 25 | 23. Playful | 8 |
| 34. Trusting | 24 | 41. Hungry | 8 |
| 4. Calm | 23 | 26. Irritable | 7 |
| 9. Helpless | 23 | 19. Shy | 6 |
| 37. Tired | 23 | 31. Suspicious | 5 |
| 5. Relaxed | 22 | 38. Dull | 4 |
| 40. Alert | 22 | 12. Triumphant | 2 |
| 18. Optimistic | 21 | 29. Sympathetic | 2 |
| 21. Guilty | 18 | 43. Sexually aroused | 2 |
| 27. Angry | 18 | 44. Bladder pressure | 2 |
| 8. Inferior | 17 | 11. Superior | 1 |
| 35. Secure | 17 | 25. Bored | 1 |
| 6. Relieved | 16 | 30. Tender | 1 |
| 17. Cheerful | 14 | 45. Bowel pressure | 1 |
| 22. Confident | 14 | | |

therapist as feeling confident, whereas therapists exceeded patients in rating themselves as feeling preoccupied, frustrated, and tired.

## THERAPY AS RELATIONSHIP

Another facet of therapy dealt with in the TSRs pertains to the manner or style in which patients and therapists related to each other. The analysis of modes of relating, or interpersonal styles, applied in the questionnaires was developed by Orlinsky (1965). This analysis proposes four stylistic aspects of interaction in all interpersonal behavior, no matter what its substantive social content. These were: (1) the *structuring* or normative definition of interaction in terms of role and situational parameters; (2) the balance of *influence* or control over sanctions and rewards between the participants; (3) the *attitudinal valence* of

## TABLE 8

### Therapist TSR: Patient Feeling Process

| "How did your patient seem to feel during this session?" | Mean % Endorsement | "How did your patient seem to feel during this session?" | Mean % Endorsement |
|---|---|---|---|
| 2. Anxious | 51 | 34. Trusting | 16 |
| 1. Tense | 42 | 5. Relaxed | 15 |
| 13. Frustrated | 40 | 6. Relieved | 15 |
| 3. Worried | 29 | 22. Confident | 15 |
| 36. Accepted | 29 | 32. Hurt | 15 |
| 7. Inadequate | 27 | 4. Calm | 13 |
| 14. Sad | 26 | 8. Inferior | 13 |
| 28. Interested | 26 | 19. Shy | 13 |
| 15. Discouraged | 24 | 23. Playful | 13 |
| 9. Helpless | 22 | 37. Tired | 12 |
| 20. Embarrassed | 20 | 39. Energetic | 11 |
| 24. Likeable | 20 | 26. Irritable | 10 |
| 10. Effective | 19 | 35. Secure | 9 |
| 18. Optimistic | 19 | 38. Dull | 9 |
| 31. Suspicious | 19 | 33. Rejected | 7 |
| 40. Alert | 19 | 11. Superior | 4 |
| 21. Guilty | 18 | 12. Triumphant | 4 |
| 27. Angry | 18 | 29. Sympathetic | 3 |
| 16. Satisfied | 17 | 30. Tender | 3 |
| 17. Cheerful | 16 | 25. Bored | 1 |

the participants with respect to one another; and (4) the level of physical and emotional *responsiveness* of the participants. The configuration of an individual's orientation across these four aspects of interaction gives a systematic description of his manner or style of relating.

Each of the four aspects of interaction can be usefully construed as two-dimensional. Thus, an individual's orientation vis-à-vis the *structuring* of interaction can vary in regard to active assertion of situational and role definitions, and independently in regard to receptive accommodation to situational and role definitions. If each of these is dichotomized, the possibilities for orientation with respect to structuring the interaction are: to assert structure without being receptive (leading); to accommodate to structure without being assertive (following); to be both assertive and receptive in defining role and situational norms (reciprocating); to be neither assertive nor receptive (withdrawing).

An individual's orientation vis-à-vis *influence* can vary in regard to the degree of control exerted toward others, and in regard to the degree

## TABLE 9

### Patient TSR: Therapist Feeling Process

| "How did your therapist seem to feel during this session?" | Mean % Endorsement | "How did your therapist seem to feel during this session?" | Mean % Endorsement |
|---|---|---|---|
| 13. Interested | 80 | 9. Intimate | 5 |
| 1. Calm | 73 | 11. Detached | 5 |
| 2. Confident | 69 | 5. Apprehensive | 4 |
| 32. Alert | 56 | 16. Bored | 4 |
| 7. Involved | 53 | 26. Attracted | 4 |
| 3. Effective | 48 | 10. Preoccupied | 3 |
| 14. Sympathetic | 35 | 12. Withdrawn | 3 |
| 21. Optimistic | 29 | 22. Frustrated | 3 |
| 20. Cheerful | 28 | 17. Irritable | 2 |
| 25. Pleased | 22 | 18. Angry | 2 |
| 19. Satisfied | 19 | 24. Discouraged | 2 |
| 31. Energetic | 19 | 4. Tense | 1 |
| 8. Close | 16 | 6. Inadequate | 1 |
| 33. Tired | 9 | 23. Depressed | 1 |
| 27. Playful | 8 | 29. Repelled | 1 |
| 15. Tender | 7 | 30. Embarrassed | 1 |
| 28. Disappointed | 6 | 34. Dull | 1 |

of compliance with the sanctions of others. Dichotomized, these two dimensions give rise to four modes of orientation with respect to influence: controlling without compliance (dominance); compliance without controlling (dependence); both controlling and compliance (interdependence); neither controlling nor compliance (independence).

With respect to *attitudinal valence,* an individual's orientation can vary in the constituent dimensions of benevolence and malevolence. Thus, when these are dichotomized, four modes of orientation in regard to attitude are defined: benevolent but not malevolent (friendly); malevolent but not benevolent (hostile); both benevolent and malevolent (ambivalent); neither benevolent nor malevolent (neutral).

Finally, an individual's orientation vis-à-vis *responsiveness* can vary in the constituent dimensions of activity and affectivity. When activity and affectively are dichotomized, the four modes of orientation in level of responsiveness are: activity without affectivity (action); affectivity without activity (feeling); both activity and affectivity (animation); neither activity nor affectivity (impassiveness).

Styles of relating were assessed in the TSR by asking the participant to select, as descriptive of interaction in the session, one of the four

TABLE 10

Therapist TSR: Therapist Feeling Process

| "How did you feel during this session?" | Mean % Endorsement | "How did you feel during this session?" | Mean % Endorsement |
|---|---|---|---|
| 13. Interested | 87 | 5. Apprehensive | 6 |
| 1. Calm | 68 | 16. Bored | 6 |
| 7. Involved | 64 | 24. Discouraged | 6 |
| 32. Alert | 54 | 17. Irritable | 5 |
| 2. Confident | 47 | 34. Dull | 5 |
| 14. Sympathetic | 44 | 35. Hungry | 5 |
| 3. Effective | 38 | 38. Need to relieve bladder | 5 |
| 25. Pleased | 28 | 4. Tense | 4 |
| 8. Close | 25 | 6. Inadequate | 4 |
| 21. Optimistic | 24 | 27. Playful | 3 |
| 19. Satisfied | 23 | 37. Sexually aroused | 3 |
| 33. Tired | 20 | 12. Withdrawn | 2 |
| 26. Attracted | 18 | 18. Angry | 2 |
| 10. Preoccupied | 13 | 23. Depressed | 2 |
| 31. Energetic | 12 | 30. Embarrassed | 2 |
| 15. Tender | 11 | 29. Repelled | 1 |
| 20. Cheerful | 11 | 36. Thirsty | 1 |
| 11. Detached | 9 | 39. Need to relieve bowels | 1 |
| 22. Frustrated | 9 | | |
| 9. Intimate | 7 | | |
| 28. Disappointed | 7 | | |

possible modes of orientation for each of the four aspects—structuring, influence, attitudinal valence, and responsiveness. Each participant assessed his own style of relating, and the style of relating of the other.

The items that describe the patient's style of relating, and their endorsement percentages, are shown in Tables 11 and 12. The modes of orientation most frequently endorsed by patients indicated that they saw themselves as leading, independent, friendly, and animated. Patients and therapists were in close agreement about the dominant pattern of patient orientation. When their mean frequencies of endorsement for each item were compared, five of the sixteen differences were significant at or beyond the .05 level. Patients exceeded therapists in rating themselves as reciprocating in structuring, dependent in influence, and active in responsiveness. Therapists, on the other hand, exceeded patients in rating the patients as independent in influence, and feeling in responsiveness. Therapists tended to see their patients as more affectively

TABLE 11

## Patient TSR: Patient Style of Relating

| "How did you act toward your therapist during this session?" "During this session, I was mainly:" | Mean % Endorsement [a] |
|---|---|
| **[Structuring]** | |
| 1. Taking the lead: having my own ideas: bringing up things to talk about. | 53 |
| 3. Working together: joining in: cooperating. | 36 |
| 2. Following: receptive: waiting for direction from my therapist. | 15 |
| 4. Distant: reserved: holding back. | 7 |
| **[Influence]** | |
| 7. Able to compromise: sharing: "give and take." | 57 |
| 6. Agreeing: going along with: changing my mind. | 21 |
| 8. Independent: uninfluenced: making up my own mind. | 13 |
| 5. Determined: not giving in: firm. | 12 |
| **[Attitudinal Valence]** | |
| 9. Friendly: warm: respectful. | 50 |
| 11. Respectful but critical: both positive and negative: "mixed feelings." | |
| 12. Neutral: impartial: neither positive nor negative. | 12 |
| 10. Critical: negative: sarcastic. | 4 |
| **[Responsiveness]** | |
| 13. Excited: emotional: actively involved. | 35 |
| 14. Feeling deeply: moved but controlled: stirred up but quiet. | 33 |
| 15. Talkative: businesslike: active but not stirred up. | 27 |
| 16. Quiet: inactive: unemotional. | 7 |

[a] Total % may exceed 100%, since respondents might endorse more than one alternative in describing a therapy session.

involved, but less easily influenced, then the patients reported themselves to be.

The modes of therapist interpersonal style are shown in Tables 13 and 14. Therapists were most often viewed by patients as following, interdependent, friendly, and feeling. In other words, the therapists' style of relating was seen by patients as receptive to the structuring initiated by patients, mutually influencing, basically supportive in atti-

## TABLE 12

### Therapist TSR: Patient Style of Relating

| *"How did your patient act toward you during this session?"* <br> *"During this session,* my patient *was predominantly:"* | *Mean %* <br> *Endorsement* [a] |
|---|---|
| **[Structuring]** | |
| 1. Purposeful: taking the lead: initiating topics. | 53 |
| 3. Cooperating: joining in: working together. | 32 |
| 2. Responsive: waiting for direction: receptive. | 12 |
| 4. Distant: withdrawing from interaction: remote. | 9 |
| **[Influence]** | |
| 7. Mutually influencing: sharing: "give and take." | 55 |
| 8. Independent: making up own mind: uninfluenced. | 25 |
| 6. Agreeing: submissive: giving in. | 12 |
| 5. Insistent: controlling: unyielding. | 11 |
| **[Attitudinal Valence]** | |
| 9. Friendly: warm: engaging. | 51 |
| 11. Conflicted: ambivalent: "mixed feelings." | 38 |
| 12. Neutral: impersonal: impartial. | 9 |
| 10. Critical: negative: hostile. | 3 |
| **[Responsiveness]** | |
| 14. Deeply feeling: moved but expressively controlled: stirred. | 49 |
| 13. Animated: enthusiastic: excited. | 29 |
| 15. Businesslike: brisk: active but uninvolved emotionally. | 14 |
| 16. Impassive: unmoved: restrained. | 9 |

[a] See note to Table 11.

tudinal valence, and affectively responsive. Therapists were rarely seen by patients as neutral or impassive. Patients and therapists were also in close agreement regarding the dominant modes of therapist interpersonal style. Statistical comparison of the mean frequencies of patient and therapist endorsement for each of the sixteen items revealed that only two of the differences were significant at or beyond the .05 level. Patients exceeded therapists in rating therapists as leading in structuring, and as independent in influence.

In general, patients were viewed by therapists and by themselves as leading or reciprocating in structuring the session, whereas therapists were seen as following or reciprocating. Patients and therapists agreed

## TABLE 13

### Patient TSR: Therapist Style of Relating

| "How did your therapist act toward you during this session?" "During this session, my therapist was mainly:" | Mean % Endorsement [a] |
|---|---|
| **[Structuring]** | |
| 2. Attentive: waiting for me to lead: following. | 46 |
| 3. Joining in: working together: cooperating. | 42 |
| 1. Leading: directing: bringing up things to talk about. | 19 |
| 4. Distant: reserved: holding back. | 4 |
| **[Influence]** | |
| 7. Democratic: open minded: willing to compromise. | 48 |
| 8. Independent: uninfluenced: making up his own mind. | 28 |
| 5. Insistent: demanding: firm. | 14 |
| 6. Agreeing: going along with: doing what I wanted. | 14 |
| **[Attitudinal Valence]** | |
| 9. Friendly: helpful: on my side. | 51 |
| 11. Strict but fair: helpful but critical. | 39 |
| 12. Neutral: impartial: impersonal. | 10 |
| 10. Critical: negative: sarcastic. | 4 |
| **[Responsiveness]** | |
| 14. Moved but controlled: stirred: involved. | 62 |
| 15. Businesslike: active but uninvolved: brisk. | 24 |
| 13. Intense: enthusiastic: excited. | 8 |
| 16. Uninvolved: quiet: inactive. | 7 |

[a] See note to Table 11.

also in viewing both the patients and the therapists as predominantly interdependent in influencing each others' behavior. In attitudinal valence, patients were reported by both as primarily friendly, and secondarily ambivalent. The same modes of orientation predominated in reports of the therapists' attitudinal valence. In responsiveness, patients and therapists agreed that both participants were affectively involved, although the therapists' affective involvement was chiefly passive (i.e., feeling), whereas the patients were variously active (animated) and passive (feeling) in their emotional involvement. In sum, the stylistic or purely relational aspect of patient-therapist interaction was predominantly one of mutuality and warmth.

## TABLE 14

### Therapist TSR: Therapist Style of Relating

| *"How did you act toward your patient during this session?"* *"During this session, I was predominantly:"* | *Mean %* *Endorsement* [a] |
|---|---|
| **[Structuring]** | |
| 3.  Interacting: joining in: working together. | 57 |
| 2.  Receptive: attentive: responsive. | 32 |
| 1.  Structuring: intervening: initiating topics. | 12 |
| 4.  Reserved: distant: remote. | 4 |
| **[Influence]** | |
| 7.  Mutually influencing: sharing: "give and take." | 59 |
| 8.  Independent: uninfluenced: self-determining. | 18 |
| 5.  Determined: insistent: firm. | 12 |
| 6.  Agreeing: complying: going along with. | 12 |
| **[Attitudinal Valence]** | |
| 9.  Supportive: empathic: friendly. | 49 |
| 11. Supportive but critical: correcting but friendly. | 40 |
| 12. Neutral: impartial: impersonal. | 11 |
| 10. Reproving: correcting: critical. | 3 |
| **[Responsiveness]** | |
| 14. Moved but expressively controlled: emotionally responsive: stirred. | 49 |
| 15. Businesslike: brisk: active but uninvolved emotionally. | 35 |
| 16. Inactive: restrained: unmoved. | 9 |
| 13. Animated: enthusiastic: excited. | 7 |

[a] See note to Table 11.

## THERAPY AS EXCHANGE

The interactions of patient and therapist during a therapy session can be viewed as an "economic" transaction or exchange process (Homans, 1961; Blau, 1964). The inputs are the desires or intentions that patients and therapists seek to realize, and the outputs consist of the benefits or satisfactions that accrue to each. Accordingly, we wanted to know what the patient's hopes and wishes were, what the therapist's goals or intentions were, and what the patient felt she had gotten from the session.[2]

[2] Although therapists' satisfactions were not surveyed directly, an indication of those aspects of therapeutic experience that were most rewarding for the

## TABLE 15

### Patient TSR: Patient Aims

| *"What did you want or hope to get out of this session?"* *"This session, I hoped (or wanted) to:"* | *Mean %* *Endorsement* |
|---|---|
| 3. Get a better understanding of my feelings and behavior. | 67 |
| 15. Get help in talking about what is really troubling me. | 55 |
| 7. Work out a problem that I have. | 48 |
| 8. Get advice on how to deal with my life and with other people. | 47 |
| 14. Work together with my therapist on a person-to-person basis. | 47 |
| 17. Get better self control over my moods and over the things I do. | 39 |
| 1. Get relief from nervousness and bad feelings. | 36 |
| 2. Get a chance to let go and get things off my chest. | 32 |
| 19. Get straight on which things I feel and think are real and which are mostly in my mind. | 26 |
| 5. Get some reassurance about how I'm doing. | 22 |
| 20. Get my therapist to say what he (she) really thinks. | 18 |
| 6. Let my therapist see how I've improved. | 9 |
| 4. Show my therapist that I know what is going on, too. | 6 |
| 9. Get my therapist to like me better as a person. | 5 |
| 12. Find out more about my therapist as a person. | 5 |
| 16. Talk and just get the session over with. | 4 |
| 18. Get an emotional response from my therapist. | 3 |
| 10. Get my therapist to leave me alone for a while. | 1 |
| 11. Get my therapist to take my side. | 1 |
| 13. Get even with my therapist for the way I've been treated. | 1 |

Since the therapist's perception of what his patient wants is an essential condition of effective exchange, therapists as well as patients were questioned concerning these. It did not seem natural to ask patients what they thought their therapists' aims had been, however, nor did it seem directly relevant for therapists to report on patients' satisfactions. Thus, patients and therapists both reported on patients' wants, but only therapists reported on therapists' goals and only patients reported on patients' satisfactions.

The items representing the patients' aims and their endorsement percentages are shown in Table 15 for the patient TSR and in Table 16

therapists may be had by noting their preferences in dialogue, goals, feelings, and styles of relating (see Chapter 6).

## TABLE 16

### Therapist TSR: Patient Aims

| "What did your patient seem to want out of this session?" "During this session, my patient's behavior seemed aimed at:" | Mean % Endorsement |
|---|---|
| 3. Gaining insight and better self-understanding. | 52 |
| 5. Gaining attention, approval, sympathy, or affection. | 38 |
| 2. Getting relief by giving vent to suppressed or pent up feelings. | 35 |
| 6. Working through or resolving a recognized emotional conflict. | 35 |
| 1. Avoiding anxiety through defensive behavior and security operations. | 33 |
| 7. Getting "expert" advice, opinion, etc., on some problems. | 20 |
| 9. Withdrawal or evasion of contact with the therapist. | 16 |
| 14. Getting respite or relief from external involvements and pressure. | 15 |
| 13. Testing the limits of the therapist and the therapy relationship. | 14 |
| 15. Filling time to get through the therapy session. | 12 |
| 10. Winning the therapist as an ally in a dispute or conflict. | 10 |
| 17. Getting oriented to therapy and to being a patient. | 9 |
| 4. Competing with the therapist. | 8 |
| 8. Seductive provocation of the therapist. | 8 |
| 11. Gaining knowledge of the therapist's personal life. | 3 |
| 12. Revenge on or punishment of the therapist. | 3 |
| 16. Provocation of the therapist to criticism or anger. | 3 |

for the therapist TSR. Although the lists included aims both functional and dysfunctional for the conduct of therapy, patients only endorsed "good" or functional motives with a relatively high frequency. Patients and therapists agreed in rating insight and problem-resolution as the dominant goals of the patients, with relief as a prominent, although secondary, goal. Also clearly present was the patients' desire to maintain a good therapeutic relationship.

Of the items in the patient and the therapist TSRs, ten were sufficiently similar in substance and wording to permit a direct comparison. Four were found to differ significantly at or beyond the .05 level. Patients exceeded therapists in viewing patients as wanting to get better understanding of their feelings and behavior, and in seeking advice on how to deal with their lives and with other people. Therapists exceeded patients in seeing patients as wanting to get their therapists to

TABLE 17

**Therapist TSR: Therapist Goals**

| "In what direction were you working with your patient during this session?" "During this session, I was working toward:" | Mean Rating [a] |
|---|---|
| 2. Increasing my patient's insight and self-understanding. | 1.71 |
| 4. Moving my patient closer to experiencing her (his) real feeling, what she (he) really is. | 1.72 |
| 7. Engaging my patient in an honest person-to-person relationship, working together authentically. | 1.72 |
| 3. Supporting my patient's self-esteem. | 2.04 |
| 8. Helping my patient overcome her (his) resistance and defenses in order to get to what was of real concern to her (him). | 2.08 |
| 5. Helping my patient learn new or better ways of dealing with people and problems. | 2.17 |
| 1. Relieving my patient's tension and anxiety. | 2.43 |
| 10. Helping my patient gain better control over her (his) moods or impulses. | 2.55 |
| 6. Supporting my patient's defenses. | 2.62 |
| 9. Orienting my patient more effectively to interpersonal reality in order to discriminate and control autistic tendencies. | 2.62 |

[a] 1 = very much; 2 = moderately; 3 = little or not at all.

leave them alone for a while, and in seeking to get their therapists to side with them.

The items and mean ratings of therapists' goals are presented in Table 17. Referring to the most frequently endorsed patient aims (Tables 15 and 16), we note that patients' aims and therapists' intentions were in general highly congruent. The leading goals of both were deepened insight and problem-resolution for the patient. Trying to make the patient feel better was in general secondary for both patients and therapists.

Finally, the items and mean ratings by patients of their satisfactions are shown in Table 18. Reviewing the modal inputs and outputs of therapy as an exchange process, a rather direct connection between the two may be seen. What patients typically sought to get, what therapists typically sought to give, and what patients typically reported they got, were essentially the same: effective rapport, facilitation in focusing on important issues, and increased understanding.

TABLE 18

Patient TSR: Patient Satisfactions

| "What do you feel that you got out of this session?" "During this session, I feel that I got:" | Mean Rating [a] |
|---|---|
| 6. A sense of having an honest person-to-person relationship with my therapist, of working together. | 1.62 |
| 7. Help in being able to talk about what was troubling to me and really important. | 1.84 |
| 2. Better insight and self-understanding. | 2.01 |
| 3. Reassurance and encouragement about how I'm doing. | 2.16 |
| 4. Better ability to feel my feelings, to be what I really am. | 2.16 |
| 5. Ideas for new or better ways of dealing with people. | 2.25 |
| 8. A better ability to tell which of the things I felt and thought were real and which were mostly in my own mind. | 2.25 |
| 1. Relief from the tension I was under. | 2.29 |
| 9. Better self-control over my moods and actions. | 2.41 |

[a] 1 = very much; 2 = moderately; 3 = slightly, or not at all.

## THERAPY AS SESSION DEVELOPMENT

The model followed in designing items to survey session development was an adaptation of G. H. Mead's (1956) conception of the stages in the development of an act. Mead described the four stages as impulse, perception, manipulation, and consummation. Our adaptation of Mead's scheme to the dyadic situation of psychotherapy involved viewing the therapy session as an interpersonal act. The four stages in the development of this interpersonal act were construed as follows. Motivation to participate (impulse) was interpreted as the extent to which each participant looked forward to the session with positive anticipation. The patient's role-relevant perceptual task (perception) was interpreted as focusing on her inner feelings and associations, whereas the perceptual stage of the therapist's role implementation was defined as empathic understanding of the patient's behavior and subjective states. The patient's role performance (manipulation) was construed as free or unimpeded communication of her subjective states to the therapist, whereas that of the therapist was to respond in a helpful or facilitating way. Goal attainment (consummation) for both the patient and the therapist was indicated by a general sense of satisfaction with the session, and by a more specific sense that movement or progress in the direction of problem-resolution had been made.

Consequently, patients were asked how much they had been looking forward to their session, how clearly they had known what they wanted to talk about, how freely they had expressed themselves, how well their therapists had seemed to understand them, how helpful their therapists had been in responding to them, how they evaluated the session as a whole, and how much progress they felt they had made. They were also asked how much they were looking forward to their next session. Therapists were asked how much they had been looking forward to the session, how much they felt their patients had been looking forward to it, how freely their patients had expressed themselves and had focused on genuine concerns during the session, how much empathy and understanding they had experienced during the session, how helpful they felt they had been in responding, how they evaluated the session as a whole, and how much progress they felt the patient had made. To aid in the evaluation of patient progress, both patient and therapist were also asked to evaluate the patient's current state of psychological well-being. The specific items and their mean ratings are presented below.

### Motivation

The mean response of patients to the question, "To what extent were you looking forward to coming to this session?" was 2.11, indicating a response close to alternative 2: "I was somewhat looking forward to coming this session; was glad to get here." The mean response of therapists to the question, "How well motivated for coming to therapy was your patient this session?" was 1.81, indicating a response close to alternative 2: "My patient showed positive motivation for therapy once here, but didn't seem to have anticipated coming in particular." Patients and therapists seem to agree that patients typically felt some ambivalence about coming to therapy sessions, but that once there were positively motivated.

The therapist's motivation for participation in the session was assessed by the question, "To what extent were you looking forward to seeing your patient this session?" The mean response to this question was 1.89, indicating an answer close to alternative 2: "I was not anticipating this session in particular, but found myself pleased to see the patient when the time came." Like their patients, therapists apparently accepted the routine scheduling of therapy sessions, but found the immediate prospect of another session together a pleasing one.

We also asked the patients after each session to estimate their motivation for the following session. The mean rating given by patients to the question, "To what extent are you looking forward to your next session?" was 1.80, indicating a response close to alternative 2: "I am looking forward to my next session pretty much; will be ready for it when it comes."

## Perception

Patients responded to the question "How clearly did you know what you wanted to talk about during this session?" with a mean rating of 1.86, which is close to alternative 2: "I knew pretty much what I wanted to talk about this session, but sometimes I lost track." Therapists, by comparison, gave a mean rating of 2.93 in response to the question, "To what extent did your patient bring out the thoughts and feelings which really seemed to concern her during this session?" This rating is very close to alternative 3: "My patient had some difficulty in bringing out her real thoughts and feelings, but was able to deal with them to a considerable degree." Thus, from both points of view, the patient appeared to experience some interference in focusing upon her concerns.

The therapist's understanding of the patient was surveyed by asking the patient, "How well did your therapist seem to understand how you were feeling and what was really on your mind this session?" The mean rating given by patients was 1.37, which is close to alternative 1: "My therapist seemed to understand very well how I was feeling and what was on my mind during this session." Therapists were asked to rate their role-relevant perceptual functioning in terms of empathic and of conceptual understanding. They gave a mean rating of 1.77 in response to the question, "To what extent did you feel in rapport or empathically 'in touch' with what your patient was experiencing during this session?" Alternative 2 stated: "I felt mostly in touch with what my patient was experiencing during this session, but occasionally lost empathic contact with her." Therapists responded to the question, "How well do you feel you understood the meaning of what your patient said and did during this session (in whatever conceptual terms you find most useful for describing personality)?" with a mean rating of 1.72. This is close to alternative 2: "I understood a good deal of what my patient said and did, but remain uncertain about the meaning of important aspects of her behavior." Thus, therapists typically felt that they had an adequate if imperfect grasp of what their patients were up to, whereas patients typically felt that their therapists understood them very well.

## Performance

Understanding is mediated and made effective through communication. The patient must not only grasp what it is that concerns her, but also share this with her therapist. The therapist, for his part, must not only indicate that he knows what is troubling his patient, but must substantiate this claim with a response that is in some measure helpful. As a way of assessing their role performances, patients and therapists were asked to rate the patient's communicativeness and the therapist's helpfulness.

Patients were asked, "How freely were you able to talk with your therapist during this session?" The mean response of 3.22 was close to alternative 3: "I had occasional difficulty talking with my therapist, but for the most part I was able to express myself freely." Therapists were asked, "How freely did your patient express herself in this session?" Their mean rating of 3.25 was close to alternative 3: "My patient had occasional difficulty in communicating with me, but for the most part expressed herself adequately."

When asked, "Do you feel that what your therapist said and did this session was helpful to you?" patients gave a mean response of 2.04: "The things that my therapist said and did this session were pretty helpful to me" (alternative 2). In rating their own helpfulness, therapists were somewhat more conservative. Their mean response of 2.63 to the question, "How helpful do you feel that you were to your patient during this session?" fell between alternative 3 ("What I did this session seemed somewhat helpful to my patient") and alternative 2 ("What I did this session seemed pretty helpful to my patient").

Patients and therapists agreed concerning the patients' ability to communicate with considerable freedom. The therapists, in turn, were typically seen as moderately helpful. Here, as was also seen in assessing therapists' understanding, the patients gave a higher estimate of the therapists' helpfulness than the therapists did themselves.

## Goal Attainment

Consummation of the psychotherapy session for both patient and therapist was a sense of movement or progress toward the goal of problem-resolution. Patients were asked, "Do you feel that you made progress in this session in dealing with the problems for which you are in therapy?" They gave a mean rating of 2.11, indicating an answer close to alternative 2: "I made some progress in this session in dealing with my problems." A similar question for therapists was "To what extent did your patient seem to make progress during this session in dealing with the problems for which she is in therapy?" Their mean response of 1.95 was close to alternative 2: "My patient made some progress in this session dealing with her problems, but not very much." Thus, some progress was made in the typical therapy session. It is not clear, however, whether this average representation indicates that progress is made in every session or that little progress in some sessions is offset by a great deal of progress in others.

Consummation of the session was also assessed by the global evaluation, which was the first question presented in the TSRs. Patients gave a mean rating of 2.52 in response to the question, "How do you feel about the therapy session which you have just completed?" This value falls halfway between alternative 2 ("This was a really good session") and alternative 3 ("This was a pretty good session"). The conservatism of therapists relative to patients was again illustrated in their mean response of 2.91 to the same alternatives.

The therapy session also provides an opportunity to evaluate the psychological condition of the patient. On each such occasion, the therapist generally forms some impression of the patient's level of functioning. Therapists were asked, "At what level of effectiveness and integration (emotionally and psychologically) did your patient seem to be during this session?" Their mean rating of 1.82 was close to alternative 2: "My patient was functioning fairly well during this session, but still showed some distinct impairment in effectiveness and integration." Patients' estimates of their own functioning were at variance with those given by the therapists. In response to the question, "How well do you feel that you are getting along, emotionally and psychologically, at this time?" patients gave a mean response of 2.56. This is approximately halfway between alternative 3 ("I am getting along fairly well; manage to keep going with some effort") and alternative 2 ("I am getting along pretty well; have my ups and downs"). One reason for the patients' harsher estimates of their difficulties may be that they have direct knowledge of variations only in their own functioning, whereas therapists have a wider experience in judging psychopathology. The therapist is more likely to have seen severer forms of psychopathology, and in this context to judge the patient as relatively less disturbed. Patients, on the other hand, are more likely to judge themselves by the wishful ideal of problem-free functioning. In any event, therapists probably evaluate the functioning of their patients in relation to other patients, whereas patients evaluate themselves in relation to their "normal" friends and relatives.

## SUMMARY OF TYPICAL EXPERIENCES

The highlights of our findings concerning therapeutic experiences are given in Table 19. This table indicates what patients reported they wanted to get, talked about, felt, did in relation to their therapists, and actually got out of the typical therapy session. It also indicates what therapists reported they most frequently aimed toward, felt, and did in relation to their patients. To the extent that these findings are representative, Table 19 gives an idea of what most likely happens in the ordinary therapy session as it occurs in everyday practice.

What patients most frequently wanted from their therapy sessions were better self-understanding (67%), help in discussing difficult matters (55%), resolution of a particular problem (48%), collaboration on a person-to-person basis with the therapist (47%), and advice (47%). The predominant motivation of patients in coming to therapy thus

**TABLE 19**

**Typical Therapeutic Experiences**

| | |
|---|---|
| Patient wants to: | "Get a better understanding of my feelings and behavior." |
| | "Get help in talking about what is really troubling me." |
| | "Work out a problem that I have." |
| | "Work together with my therapist on a person-to-person basis." |
| | "Get advice on how to deal with my life and with other people." |
| Patient talks about: | "Feelings and attitudes toward myself." |
| | "Social activities and relationships, friends and acquaintances." |
| | "Relationship with spouse, boyfriend, or girlfriend." |
| Patient feels: | "Anxious." |
| | "Tense." |
| Patient relates by: | Leading. |
| | Being interdependent. |
| | Being friendly. |
| | Being animated or feeling. |
| Therapist tries to: | "Increase my patient's insight and self-understanding." |
| | "Move my patient closer to experiencing her real feelings, what she really is." |
| | "Engage my patient in an honest person-to-person relationship, work together authentically." |
| Therapist feels: | "Interested." |
| | "Calm." |
| | "Involved." |
| | "Alert." |
| | "Confident." |
| | "Sympathetic." |
| Therapist relates by: | Reciprocating. |
| | Being interdependent. |
| | Being friendly. |
| | Being feeling. |
| Patient gets: | "A sense of having an honest person-to-person relationship with my therapist, of working together." |
| | "Help in being able to talk about what was troubling to me and really important." |
| | "Better insight and self-understanding." |

appears to have been a desire to deepen their understanding of personal problems that were difficult for them to talk about. Presumably, this deepened understanding would alleviate the problems, or would at least make it possible for them to be dealt with more comfortably and effectively.

The areas of life that patients most frequently talked about in therapy were feelings and attitudes toward self (70%), social activities and relationships (52%), relationships with men friends (52%), inadequacies, fears, or successes in getting along (45%), work or school (43%), and feelings about being close to or needing someone (40%). From these reports it appears that the patients' problems were most frequently focused on themselves, in their current intimate relationships, and in their achievements and failures at work or school. In contrast to expectations based on clinical theory, relations with parents or siblings, memories of childhood experiences, and dreams or fantasies were reported discussed with considerably lesser frequency.

Although their sessions may have been helpful, patients typically reported feeling anxious and tense (both 41%) during interviews—not surprising in light of the fact that they were trying to discuss and understand their most difficult personal problems. Patients also reported feeling interested (34%), frustrated (34%), and accepted (31%), indicating a substantial degree of involvement despite the stress of the session.

Patients typically took the lead in bringing up things to talk about (53%), thereby exercising initiative in determining what happened during sessions. Although they saw themselves as having the initiative, however, patients typically felt that they did not dominate, but rather shared control of what happened with their therapists, engaging in an active give-and-take of influence (57%). Their typical attitude in relating to their therapists was reported by patients as friendly, warm, and respectful (50%), and their typical state as emotionally responsive (about 68%).

Patients, then, typically appeared to themselves as actively and positively involved in the therapeutic relationship, although experiencing considerable distress in dealing with problematic personal concerns. Although they came to be helped, they did not perceive themselves as helpless in relating to their therapists.

Viewing their own participation, therapists reported their typical goals in therapy as increasing the patient's insight and self-understanding, helping the patient to fully experience what she was feeling, and collaborating on a person-to-person basis with the patient. In the process, therapists typically reported feeling interested (87%), calm (68%), involved (64%), alert (54%), confident (47%), and sympathetic

(44%). As one would expect, therapists generally felt comfortable with, and positively responsive toward, their patients. The playful definition given to beginning therapists, which describes a therapist as the less anxious of the two persons in the office, seems borne out here by the facts.

How did the therapists typically act in relation to their patients? According to their reports, they were most often mutually influencing or interdependent (59%), reciprocating or sharing in structuring the session (57%), supportive and empathic toward the patient (49%), and moved but expressively controlled in feeling (49%). Therapists related to their patients in much the same manner in which patients related to them—collaboratively, positively, and feelingly.

Finally, patients typically reported finding the following satisfactions in their therapy sessions: a sense of having an honest person-to-person relationship with the therapist, of working together; help in talking about troubling but important matters; and better insight and self-understanding. To a large extent, patients seemed to get what they came to therapy for, and what their therapists hoped to be able to give them.

*Chapter 6*

# Ideal Psychotherapeutic Experiences

Psychotherapy appears to be a predominantly positive experience for its participants. Yet, as it typically occurs, it is undoubtedly a mixture of better and poorer elements. One way to focus on the essentials of the therapeutic process is to portray psychotherapy at its best, by isolating the better elements in this mixture.

Patients' and therapists' global evaluations of their sessions were used to distinguish better and poorer aspects of therapeutic experience. To take advantage of the evaluative judgments that patients and therapists spontaneously make, the first question in each form of the TSR was, "How do you feel about the therapy session which you have just completed?" Responses to this question reflected a sense of general satisfaction or dissatisfaction with the therapeutic encounter. By correlating these responses with responses to each of the other items in the TSRs, we obtained a composite portrait of "ideal" therapeutic experiences.

Patients' and therapists' immediate post-session evaluations of their experiences clearly constitute a subjective criterion. Although this criterion has obvious limitations, we should not lose sight of the fact that most patients enter therapy out of a genuine adult concern for their own well-being—expecting, or learning to expect, that they are letting themselves in for hard and often painful work. Nor should we forget the real degree to which therapists bring their training, experience, and maturity to bear in their practice of psychotherapy. It seems fair to say that the spontaneous and immediate post-session evaluations of therapy contain a great deal of informed critical judgment. The wearer of the shoe knows best if it pinches or if it fits him well.

The method of analysis utilized in this chapter provided control over differences in degree of enthusiasm between raters by characterizing the better session of each participant separately. These individual "ideals" were then combined to determine the modal values of patients and therapists (see Chapter 4 for details). By using the ratings of both patients and therapists on their common sessions, we gain the advantage of consensual judgment. As in the previous chapter, we present the correlates of session evaluation [1] for each facet of experience. We then describe and discuss patients' and therapists' ideal experiences. Finally, we compare these ideal experiences with the typical experiences presented in Chapter 5.

## DIALOGUE

Table 20 shows that eight of the eighteen topics of dialogue were significantly related to patients' and/or therapists' post-session evaluations. The one topic that both patients and therapists associated with "good" therapy sessions [2] was the patient's discussion of her childhood experiences with family members, suggesting the importance of a genetic or developmental focus in therapy. The apparent disagreement between patients and therapists concerning the other topics of dialogue they considered elements of the good therapy session is diminished if one reflects on the probable overlap between topics such as "relationship with spouse or boyfriend" (patient report) and "sexual feelings and experiences" (therapist report), or "social activities and friends" (patient report) and "feelings about being close to or needing someone" (therapist report). These clearly involve the erotic and the intimate relations of the patient. In general, the topics of dialogue associated with the patients' good therapy session appear to be phrased in terms of interpersonal aspects of the life-space, whereas the therapists' ideal seems more closely linked to topics phrased in terms of problem areas.

## FEELING PROCESS

The affective correlates of patients' and therapists' post-session evaluations are presented in Tables 21 and 22. There was general agreement

---

[1] The results presented in the accompanying tables were significant at or beyond the .01 level; those enclosed in brackets were significant at or beyond the .05 level, and are included as an aid to interpretation.

[2] Every statistically significant *positive* correlate of positive post-session evaluation is a significant *negative* correlate of negative post-session evaluation. That is, an experience whose presence defines the "good" therapy hour also defines, by its absence, the "poor" therapy hour; and vice versa.

TABLE 20

Topics of Dialogue: Correlates of Patients' and Therapists'
Session Evaluations

| Patients' Session Evaluations | | Therapists' Session Evaluations | |
|---|---|---|---|
| Patient Reports [a] | Therapist Reports [b] | Patient Reports [c] | Therapist Reports [d] |
| [Spouse or boyfriend] [e] | [Spouse or boyfriend] | Sexual feelings and experiences | Sexual feelings and experiences |
| [Dreams, fantasies] | | [Feelings and attitudes toward self] | Feelings and attitudes toward self |
| [Social activities, friends] | | Feelings about being close to or needing someone | [Feelings about being close to or needing someone] |
| [Childhood relations with parents, family] | | [Therapy, the therapist, being a patient] | Childhood relations with parents, family |

[a] $N = 60$
[b] $N = 28$
[c] $N = 28$
[d] $N = 31$
[e] In all tables, brackets indicate $p \leq .05$; absence of brackets indicates $p \leq .01$; N.S. indicates no significant relationships.

between patients and therapists that in good sessions *patients* (Table 21) tended to feel likeable, accepted, relieved, alert, interested, trusting, and optimistic. Patients' reports on their ideal sessions also included a number of other positive feelings. The major difference between patients' and therapists' views of patients' feelings lay in the area of negative affect. In their good sessions, patients characterized themselves as *not* feeling dull, tense, irritable, frustrated, discouraged, angry, inadequate, inferior, or tired. The only patient feeling incompatible with the therapists' view of the good session was "dull." Thus, as far as therapists were concerned, the good session was one in which the patient might (or might not) experience considerable negative affect, so long as key positive feelings were also present (e.g., relieved). Emotional liveliness seems to be what therapists were looking for in patients. Patients, somewhat understandably, excluded negative feelings from their own version of the ideal experience, since if they feel bad it hurt them, not their therapists.

Therapists' feelings in good sessions are shown in Table 22. Here

## TABLE 21

## The Patients' Feelings: Correlates of Patients' and Therapists' Session Evaluations

| Patients' Session Evaluations | | Therapists' Session Evaluations | |
|---|---|---|---|
| Patient Reports [a] | Therapist Reports [b] | Patient Reports [c] | Therapist Reports [d] |
| **A. Positive correlates** | | | |
| Relieved | Relieved | [Relieved] | Relieved |
| Trusting | [Trusting] | [Accepted] | [Trusting] |
| Accepted | | Optimistic | Accepted |
| Optimistic | | | [Optimistic] |
| Alert | | | [Alert] |
| Interested | | | [Interested] |
| [Likeable] [e] | | | [Likeable] |
| Calm | | | Embarrassed |
| Relaxed | | | |
| Secure | | | |
| Confident | | | |
| Satisfied | | | |
| [Effective] | | | |
| [Energetic] | | | |
| **B. Negative correlates** | | | |
| Dull | [Dull] | N.S. | Dull |
| Tense | Tense | | |
| [Tired] | Tired | | |
| Irritable | | | |
| Frustrated | | | |
| Discouraged | | | |
| Angry | | | |
| [Inadequate] | | | |
| [Inferior] | | | |

[a] $N=60$
[b] $N=28$
[c] $N=28$
[d] $N=31$
[e] See note e, Table 20.

one finds substantial agreement between patients and therapists on both positive and negative affects. In the ideal experiences of both participants, *therapists* tended to feel effective, interested, alert, confident, involved, optimistic, close, sympathetic, intimate, tender, and pleased. Also, therapists tended *not* to feel disappointed, dull, withdrawn, pre-

TABLE 22

## The Therapists' Feelings: Correlates of Patients' and Therapists' Session Evaluations

| Patients' Session Evaluations | | Therapists' Session Evaluations | |
|---|---|---|---|
| Patient Reports [a] | Therapist Reports [b] | Patient Reports [c] | Therapist Reports [d] |

**A. Positive correlates**

| | | | |
|---|---|---|---|
| Optimistic | [Optimistic] | [Optimistic] | Optimistic |
| Satisfied | [Satisfied] | [Satisfied] | Satisfied |
| [Close] [e] | Close | [Involved] | Close |
| Involved | [Effective] | [Alert] | Involved |
| Effective | | | Effective |
| Alert | | | Alert |
| Pleased | | | Pleased |
| Interested | | | [Interested] |
| Sympathetic | | | Sympathetic |
| [Cheerful] | | | Confident |
| | | | Intimate |
| | | | [Tender] |
| | | | [Attracted] |

**B. Negative correlates**

| | | | |
|---|---|---|---|
| Disappointed | [Disappointed] | [Withdrawn] | Disappointed |
| [Dull] | [Dull] | | [Dull] |
| [Withdrawn] | Frustrated | | [Withdrawn] |
| Preoccupied | | | Frustrated |
| Detached | | | Preoccupied |
| Bored | | | Detached |
| [Tired] | | | [Bored] |
| [Discouraged] | | | [Tired] |
| | | | Irritable |
| | | | [Inadequate] |

[a] $N=60$
[b] $N=28$
[c] $N=28$
[d] $N=31$
[e] See note e, Table 20.

occupied, detached, bored, or tired. These therapist feelings seem to cluster around the dimensions of adequacy and involvement. In good sessions, therapists felt both adequate (effective, confident) and involved (intimate, interested), whereas in poor sessions they felt inadequate (frustrated, dull) and uninvolved (preoccupied, detached).

## RELATIONSHIP

The qualities of relationship that patients and therapists associated with their ideal experiences are shown in Tables 23 and 24. These indicate which of the orientations to structuring, influence, attitudinal valence, and responsiveness were correlated with post-session evaluations. Table 23 shows that patients and therapists tended to value and disvalue the same qualities of patient behavior in their good sessions. Both agreed that the *patients'* ideal style of relating was reciprocating in structuring, interdependent in influence, friendly in attitudinal valence, and affective in responsiveness. They also agreed that the patients' ideal style of relating was *not* withdrawn, neutral or hostile, or impassive. Thus, the style of patient behavior found most desirable was warm, collaborative, equalitarian, and genuinely affective.

The qualities of therapist behavior found most desirable by patients and therapists are presented in Table 24. Both agreed that the *therapists'* ideal style of relating was reciprocating in structuring, interdependent in influence, and affective in responsiveness. They also agreed that the therapists' ideal style of relating was *not* withdrawn, neutral, or impassive. The fact that neutrality and impassiveness were found characteristic of therapists only in poor sessions stands in sharp contrast to the image of the therapist projected in classical psychoanalytic theory.

## EXCHANGE PROCESS

Psychotherapy involves an exchange of values between participants, in which patients and therapists both expect to get and to give something of value. What do patients expect and receive in ideal circumstances? What goals do therapists work toward in good sessions? What satisfactions, besides the receipt of his fee, accrue to the therapist? Tables 25 and 26 present data relevant to these questions.

Table 25 shows which patients' wants, therapists' goals, and patients' satisfactions were characteristic of the *patients'* ideal experience. Both participants concurred in seeing the patient as motivated for insight and involvement, and as wanting to please. The therapists' goals were to increase the patient's insight and to support the patient's self-esteem. As to benefits that patients said they received, the ideal session brought not only the sought for and intended satisfactions, but all nine possibilities listed. This seems less surprising when we consider that these associations represent the correlation of global satisfaction (post-session evaluation) with a number of specific satisfactions.

Basically the same pattern of exchange was found when the *therapists'* post-session evaluations were used as the criterion variable. Table 26

TABLE 23

**The Patients' Style of Relating: Correlates of Patients' and Therapists' Session Evaluations**

| Aspect of Interaction | Patients' Session Evaluations | | Therapists' Session Evaluations | |
|---|---|---|---|---|
| | Patient Reports[a] | Therapist Reports[b] | Patient Reports[c] | Therapist Reports[d] |
| **A. Positive correlates** | | | | |
| Structuring | Reciprocating [Leading] | N.S.[e] | N.S. | Reciprocating |
| Influence | Interdependent | Interdependent | Interdependent | Interdependent |
| Attitudinal valence | Friendly [Animated] | Friendly | N.S. | Friendly |
| Responsiveness | N.S. | Feeling | N.S. | Feeling |
| **B. Negative correlates** | | | | |
| Structuring | Withdrawn [Following] | Withdrawn | N.S. | Withdrawn |
| Influence | N.S. | Independent Dependent | [Dominant] | Independent |
| Attitudinal valence | Neutral Hostile | N.S. | N.S. | Ambivalent [Neutral] [Hostile] |
| Responsiveness | Impassive | N.S. | N.S. | Impassive Active |

a N=60
b N=28
c N=28
d N=31
e See note e, Table 20.

TABLE 24

**The Therapists' Style of Relating: Correlates of Patients' and Therapists' Session Evaluations**

| Aspect of Interaction | Patients' Session Evaluations | | Therapists' Session Evaluations | |
|---|---|---|---|---|
| | Patient Reports[a] | Therapist Reports[b] | Patient Reports[c] | Therapist Reports[d] |
| **A. Positive correlates** | | | | |
| Structuring | Reciprocating | N.S.[e] | [Reciprocating] | Reciprocating |
| Influence | Interdependent [Dependent] | N.S. | [Interdependent] | [Interdependent] |
| Attitudinal valence | Friendly Feeling | [Friendly] [Feeling] | [Ambivalent] | N.S. Feeling |
| Responsiveness | Animated | | N.S. | |
| **B. Negative correlates** | | | | |
| Structuring | Withdrawn | N.S. | N.S. | Following [Withdrawn] |
| Influence | [Independent] | N.S. | N.S. | N.S. |
| Attitudinal valence | Neutral Hostile | [Neutral] | Neutral | [Neutral] |
| Responsiveness | Impassive Active | N.S. | N.S. | Impassive [Active] |

[a] N = 60
[b] N = 28
[c] N = 28
[d] N = 31
[e] See note e, Table 20.

TABLE 25

**The Exchange Process: Correlates of Patients' Session Evaluations**

| Patient Wants (Viewed by Patients)[a] | Patient Wants (Viewed by Therapists)[b] | Therapist Goals (Viewed by Therapists)[c] | Patient Satisfactions (Viewed by Patients)[d] |
|---|---|---|---|
| [Better self-understanding] [e] | Gaining insight and better self-understanding | Increasing insight and self-understanding | Better self-understanding |
| Show how I've improved | [Gaining attention, approval, sympathy, or affection] | Supporting patient's self-esteem | Reassurance and encouragement |
| Working together with therapist on a person-to-person basis | (not) Withdrawal from contact with the therapist | | Working together with therapist |
| | (not) Filling time to get through the session | | Relief from tension |
| | | | Ideas for new ways of coping |
| | | | Help in talking about problems |
| | | | Better self-control |
| | | | Better sense of reality |
| | | | Better ability to feel real feelings |

[a] $N = 60$
[b] $N = 28$
[c] $N = 31$
[d] $N = 60$
[e] See note e, Table 20.

TABLE 26

**The Exchange Process: Correlates of Therapists' Session Evaluations**

| Patient Wants (Viewed by Patients)[a] | Patient Wants (Viewed by Therapists)[b] | Therapist Goals (Viewed by Therapists)[c] | Patient Satisfactions (Viewed by Patients)[d] |
|---|---|---|---|
| N.S.[e] | Gaining insight and better self-understanding | Increasing insight and self-understanding | Better self-understanding |
| | Work through an emotional conflict | Moving patient closer to experiencing real feelings | Help in talking about problems |
| | (*not*) Withdrawal from contact with therapist | [Supporting patient's self-esteem] | Reassurance and encouragement |
| | (*not*) Filling time to get through session | | Better sense of reality |
| | [(*not*) Avoiding anxiety] | | Relief from tension |
| | [(*not*) Relief from external pressure] | | [Ideas for new ways of coping] |
| | | | [Working together with therapist] |

[a] $N=28$
[b] $N=31$
[c] $N=31$
[d] $N=28$
[e] See note e, Table 20.

differs from the previous table only in showing no patient wants (as perceived by patients) associated with the therapists' ideal experience. In both versions, there was a convergent motivation for enhancing the patient's insight and for pleasing, or being supportive to, each other. These particular motivations seem conducive to all of the patient satisfactions that were surveyed.

An interesting question may be raised here concerning the personal satisfactions of therapists in the exchange process. These can be examined by reference to the topics, goals, feelings, and styles of relating that distinguished their ideal sessions. From these data, it appeared that the following elements of satisfaction accrued to the therapist: a feeling of efficacy or competence; an emotionally meaningful involvement in his work; a relationship of intimacy and trust, validating his own sense of worth as a helpful person; and an opportunity to examine and to influence the lives of his patients.

## SESSION DEVELOPMENT

The immediate post-session evaluations of patients and therapists, which have served as criterion variables for this chapter, constitute a part of the facet of experience we have called session development. Post-session evaluation was one of the ways by which the stage of consummation was assessed, the other being the patients' and therapists' sense of progress in problem resolution. Tables 27 and 28 show that the other stages of session development, and the other variable representing the stage of consummation, were positively associated with session evaluation. These results, of course, are predicted by the theoretical model in terms of which items for session development were framed. The ideal experience, reflecting the positive consummation of the interpersonal act, *should* follow from the exemplary implementation of their roles by patient and therapist. Thus, when patients are eager for their sessions, focus effectively on their real concerns, and communicate these freely to their therapists, a positive outcome should be obtained. Similarly, when therapists feel empathic rapport with their patients, understand their communications, and respond helpfully to them, a positive outcome should be obtained. The findings confirm these expectations, with only one deviant result: therapists' eagerness to see their patients was not significantly associated with their version of the good session, although it was with the patients' ideal.

## THE NATURE OF IDEAL EXPERIENCES

The portraits we have drawn of patients' and therapists' ideal experiences are empirical projections of trends found in patterns of correlations. As such, they may be considered as upper limits of quality. To the extent that any particular session approaches these ideals, it would be considered a good therapeutic experience. But this utopia does not *fully* exist in any therapist's office—it exists as a potentiality rather than as an actuality.

The ideal experiences we have described are also abstractions in the sense that they are averages or composites of positive tendencies within

## TABLE 27

### The Patients' Role Implementation: Correlates of Patients' and Therapists' Session Evaluations

| *Phase of Session Development* | *Patients' Session Evaluations* | | *Therapists' Session Evaluations* | |
|---|---|---|---|---|
| | *Patient Reports* [a] | *Therapist Reports* [b] | *Patient Reports* [c] | *Therapist Reports* [d] |
| *Motivation:* Looking forward to session. | $p < .01$ | $p < .001$ | N.S.[e] | $p < .001$ |
| *Perception:* Good focusing on own concerns. | $p < .001$ | $p < .001$ | $p < .02$ | $p < .001$ |
| *Performance:* Communicating freely with therapist. | $p < .001$ | N.S. | N.S. | $p < .001$ |
| *Consummation:* Sense of progress with problems. | $p < .001$ | $p < .001$ | $p < .001$ | $p < .001$ |

[a] $N = 60$
[b] $N = 28$
[c] $N = 28$
[d] $N = 31$
[e] See note e, Table 20.

## TABLE 28

### The Therapists' Role Implementation: Correlates of Patients' and Therapists' Session Evaluations

| Phase of Session Development | Patients' Session Evaluations | | Therapists' Session Evaluations | |
| --- | --- | --- | --- | --- |
| | Patient Reports[a] | Therapist Reports[b] | Patient Reports[c] | Therapist Reports[d] |
| *Motivation:* Looking forward to session. | —[e] | $p < .05$ | — | N.S.[f] |
| *Perception:* | | | | |
| (a) Empathy with patient | — | $p < .001$ | — | $p < .001$ |
| (b) Understanding of patient. | $p < .001$ | $p < .02$ | N.S. | $p < .001$ |
| *Performance:* Therapist's helpfulness. | $p < .001$ | $p < .001$ | $p = .001$ | $p < .001$ |
| *Consummation:* Patient's progress with problems. | $p < .001$ | $p < .001$ | $p < .001$ | $p < .001$ |

[a] $N=60$
[b] $N=28$
[c] $N=28$
[d] $N=31$
[e] Indicates absence of a parallel item.
[f] See note e, Table 20.

the many real experiences of different patients and therapists. Strictly speaking, the patterns of ideal therapeutic experience pertain directly to the group of patients and therapists as a whole, and cannot be attributed without caution to particular individuals within the group. There is demonstrable deviation in individual cases from tendencies found for particular items in the group as a whole. There were no individuals who were consistently deviant from the group across large numbers of items, however. When the correlations for each individual patient were intercorrelated and subjected to a cluster analysis (McQuitty, 1964) in search of different manifest types of ideal experience, no clearly distinguishable clusters were observed. The same procedure was followed for the sample of therapists, with the same result. Thus, individual patients and therapists approximate the patterns of ideal experience found for the group as a whole, but not in every detail.

Having made these cautions, what can we say with confidence about the nature of ideal experiences? First, it was strikingly clear that the ideal experiences projected from both the patient and the therapist groups were essentially similar. This indicates a commonality in their implicit conceptions of good psychotherapy. Several sources contribute to such commonality. The patients in our sample were not newcomers to psychotherapy; 62% had had some therapy prior to their current course of treatment. This suggests an extensive socialization to the normative culture of dynamic psychotherapy. Therapists, too, had a basis for sharing the criteria of session evaluation with their patients, in their own experiences as patients; 65% of the therapists had themselves undergone psychotherapy. Beyond these influences, it is likely—as Auerbach and Luborsky (1968) have suggested—that patients and therapists "all derive their standards (partly unwittingly) from a wider context: the notion of a good relationship, which is deeply rooted in our cultural values" (p. 166).

How, then, was the good therapy session defined? From the results we have obtained, the ideal experiences of these patients and therapists was "psychoanalytic" in content and "experiential" in manner. By content, we refer chiefly to the topics of dialogue, and to the patients' and therapists' aims or goals. By manner, we refer to the styles of relating and the affective character of the sessions.

The content of patients' and therapists' ideal experiences was psychoanalytic in the following respects. In dialogue, we found a focus on experiences of the most intimate personal relationships, past and present: early family relationships, erotic attachments, and explorations of fantasy and self-experience. We also found that patients and therapists approached these topics with the aims of achieving deeper insight and

TABLE 29

### Ideal Therapeutic Experiences

| Patient wants to: | "Get a better understanding of my feelings and behavior."<br>"Let my therapist see how I've improved."<br>"Work together with my therapist on a person-to-person basis." | | |
|---|---|---|---|
| Patient talks about: | "Relationship with spouse, boyfriend, or girlfriend."<br>"Dreams, fantasies."<br>"Social activities and relationships, friends and acquaintances."<br>"Childhood experiences with family members and feelings about them." | | |
| | | | *Not* |
| Patient feels: | "Relieved." | "Calm." | "Dull." |
| | "Trusting." | "Relaxed." | "Tense." |
| | "Accepted." | "Secure." | "Irritable." |
| | "Optimistic." | "Confident." | "Frustrated." |
| | "Alert." | "Satisfied." | "Discouraged." |
| | "Interested." | "Effective." | "Angry." |
| | "Likeable." | "Energetic." | "Tired." |
| | | | "Inadequate." |
| | | | "Inferior." |
| | | | *Not* |
| Patient relates by: | Reciprocating or leading. | | Withdrawing or following. |
| | Being interdependent. | | |
| | Being friendly. | | Being neutral or hostile. |
| | Being animated. | | Being impassive. |

resolution of emotional conflicts. These topics and goals are hallmarks of psychoanalytically-oriented psychotherapy.

The manner of therapeutic work in good sessions was remote from the image associated with the conduct of psychoanalytic therapy, however. The passive receptive attitude, the neutral stance, the impassiveness, and the detachment that are attributed to the classical psychoanalyst were for our patients and therapists correlates of *poor* therapy sessions. The manner of therapeutic work that patients and therapists both found most valuable was actively collaborative, genuinely warm, affectively expressive, and humanly involving. This experiential manner of participation was preferred *for* both the patient and the therapist, *by* both the patient

TABLE 29 (continued)

| Therapist tries to: | "Increase my patient's insight and self-understanding."<br>"Move my patient closer to experiencing her real feelings, what she really is."<br>"Supporting my patient's self-esteem." | | |
|---|---|---|---|

| | | | *Not* |
|---|---|---|---|
| Therapist feels: | "Optimistic." | "Interested." | "Disappointed." |
| | "Satisfied." | "Sympathetic." | "Frustrated." |
| | "Close." | "Confident." | "Preoccupied." |
| | "Involved." | "Intimate." | "Detached." |
| | "Effective." | "Tender." | "Irritable." |
| | "Alert." | "Attracted." | "Dull." |
| | "Pleased." | | "Withdrawn." |
| | | | "Bored." |
| | | | "Tired." |
| | | | "Inadequate." |

| | | *Not* |
|---|---|---|
| Therapist relates by: | Reciprocating. | Following or withdrawing. |
| | Being interdependent. | Being neutral. |
| | Feeling. | Being impassive or active. |

| Patient gets: | All listed satisfactions. |
|---|---|

and the therapist. Inspection of Tables 20 through 28 indicates that the most consistent, consensually valid signs of good therapeutic experience were: patients' feeling relieved and therapists' feeling satisfied and optimistic; patients' relating interdependently and therapists' not relating with neutrality; patients' focusing on their real concerns, therapists' responding helpfully, and each sensing that progress had been made.

## A COMPARISON OF IDEAL AND TYPICAL EXPERIENCES

The patterns of ideal experience define a potentiality of the therapy session. How close does the average or typical experience of psychotherapy come to fulfilling this potential? That is, to what extent is the typical session also a "good" session? The characteristics of typical experience were summarized in Table 19. Table 29 presents a parallel summary of ideal experience. This table gives highlights of patients' wants, dialogue, feelings, relational conduct, and satisfactions (from the patients' point of view), and therapists' goals, feelings, and relational conduct (from the therapists' perspective).

Three of the five typical patient aims were characteristic of the good therapy session: seeking better self-understanding, wishing to show improvement to the therapist, and wanting to work collaboratively on a person-to-person basis. The two typical aims *not* forming part of the ideal experience were seeking advice from the therapist, and hoping to resolve a particular problem. Thus, motivations for insight and for collaborative involvement made the average session a good one; the more intensely these were present, the closer therapeutic experience approximated the ideal pattern. Requests for advice and solutions to particular problems, on the other hand, were not part of this pattern—possibly because therapists would not or could not realistically fulfill them.

Similarities between typical and ideal patterns of experience also occurred in dialogue, although with suggestive differences in nuance. Two of the three most commonly discussed topics were characteristic of the good session: social activities and relationships with friends, and relationships with spouse or boyfriend. This consistent focus on adult interpersonal and heterosexual involvements appeared in a different context in the typical and the ideal patterns, however. In the average session, they were discussed against the pervasive background of conscious feelings and attitudes toward the self. In the ideal session, on the other hand, the patients' direct concern with self-image was replaced by a focus on dreams and fantasy, and on childhood experiences with family members. That is, in the ideal experience, the patient was more likely to be exploring the psychological roots of her heterosexual and interpersonal involvements. Thus, the ideal experience comes closer than does the typical experience to meeting the expectations of clinical theories about what it is most profitable to discuss in psychotherapy.

Patients' feelings in the typical session stand in marked contrast to those reported for the ideal experience. In the typical session, patients felt anxious and tense, and no positive feelings were reported commonly enough to be labeled "typical." In the ideal experience, patients felt relieved, trusting, accepted, optimistic, and ten other similar positive moods or emotions. Obviously, the good therapy session was something of a "peak" pleasurable experience for patients, whereas the typical experience was a rather more painful struggle.

Despite these differences in affective experience, patients tended to behave in much the same way in typical and ideal sessions. Patients' typical manner of relating was leading, interdependent, friendly, and animated or feeling. In their ideal session, the patients' manner of relating was leading or reciprocating (not following or withdrawing), interdependent, friendly (not neutral or hostile), and animated (not impassive).

Therapists' aims were also much the same in the two patterns: to increase their patients' insight and self-understanding, and to help their patients experience feelings more fully. These goals are what most theories of psychotherapy prescribe as appropriate. There was, however, an additional note in the therapists' motivation, which (like the patients') placed more emphasis on the positive or pleasing aspect of the relationship. In the ideal case, therapists' goals included support for the self-esteem of their patients. This reflects a clear intention to be rewarding or encouraging, and, like the patients' emphasis on showing how they had improved, may be more likely to happen once some real gains have been made.

The convergence of therapists' typical feelings on the ideal pattern is greater than was the case for patients' feelings. In the typical session, therapists reported feeling interested, involved, alert, confident, sympathetic, and calm. In the ideal pattern, therapists included these feelings (with the exception of calm!) along with optimistic, close, effective, satisfied, pleased, intimate, tender, and attracted. Thus, in the good session, therapists' feelings were warmer and distinctly more personal.

Therapists' manner of relating to their patients was essentially the same in the typical and the ideal pattern. Therapists' typical mode of relating was reciprocating, interdependent, friendly, and feeling. Similarly, in the ideal pattern, therapists were reciprocating (not following or withdrawn), interdependent, *not* neutral, and feeling (not active or impassive). The differences between typical and ideal modes of relating suggest that therapists value genuine affective involvement—nonneutrality rather than consistent friendliness, and feeling rather than mere activity or passivity.

If we conceive of a continuum from the best to the worst in psychotherapeutic experience, the typical or average session for both patients and therapists would be much closer to the best than to the worst. As the average experience approaches the ideal, dialogue becomes more dynamic in focus, and patients' wants become more congruent with what therapy can realistically provide. In the process, therapy becomes more pleasant and rewarding for the patient, and more interesting and personally involving for the therapist.

Part IV

# Differential Patterns of Psychotherapeutic Experience: Patients, Therapists, and Relationships

# Chapter 7

# Dimensions of Patient Experience

Therapy session experience exists for patients and therapists as a unified process. The separate facets of experience that were distinguished as a guide to constructing the TSR questionnaires represent different conceptual vantage points for observing that unified process. Talking, wanting, perceiving, feeling, and acting do not occur in isolation. They are woven together in patterns formed out of the differential association of particular topics, wishes, feelings, actions, etc. The *gestalt* or pattern of therapeutic experience comprises elements from the different facets that *tend to be present together*.[1]

Our questionnaires were designed to survey the range of potential experiences that patients and therapists might have during their sessions. From these potential experiences, we have reported those that proved to be most frequently encountered and most highly valued under actual conditions of psychotherapy. Another meaningful question to be asked about therapeutic experience is how it is patterned. A pattern of experience is more than, or at any rate significantly different from, the collection of individual elements (items) composing it. The empirical determination of patterns involved analysis of the TSR at a new level: the factorial dimensions extracted from the observed relationships among items.

---

[1] Two items can be highly correlated with a factor and not necessarily be highly correlated with each other. It is the pattern of relationships of each constituent item with the factorial dimension that serves to define that dimension.

As a transition from the preceding chapters, in which analyses were focused at the level of discrete items, it may be useful to recall the interconnection of the levels of analysis applied to the TSR. In Chapter 2, these levels were compared to the organization of musical sound: discrete *items* were likened to the notes of the scale; clusters of items representing *facet dimensions* were compared to chords; clusters of different facet factors representing *global experience dimensions* were identified with melodic themes. The analysis of typical experiences could be compared in this analogy to a study of the notes most frequently played in therapeutic sessions. The analysis of ideal experiences could then be described as a study of the most pleasing notes. Melodic themes (global dimensions) form the focus of analysis in this chapter. These describe the ways in which individual patients differed from each other in their experience of psychotherapy.

Eleven factorial dimensions of global patient experience were empirically determined. The variables that compose these dimensions are facet factors derived from the previous level of analysis. (These facet factors and the items that compose them are listed for reference in Appendix F.) In reading this chapter, it should be kept in mind that patient experience dimensions always represent the patients' perceptions of therapeutic process, even when the therapist is the target. To denote this fact, patient experience dimensions are prefixed with the letter P. The dimensions emerging from this factor analysis were identified as follows:

P-I:     Therapeutic satisfaction
P-II:    Painful self-exploration
P-III:   Toying with the therapist
P-IV:    Collaborative exploration of heterosexual involvements
P-V:     Courting a therapist who is seen as rejecting
P-VI:    Erotic transference resistance
P-VII:   Patient role ambivalence vs. Patient role acceptance
P-VIII:  Passive dependence vs. Independent introspection
P-IX:    Hostile provocation toward a seemingly noncommittal therapist
P-X:     Intrusiveness with a therapist felt to be tense and embarrassed
P-XI:    Therapist perceived as mean and attacking vs. Therapist perceived as involved and helpful.

## THE DIMENSIONS OF PATIENT EXPERIENCE

### P-I: Therapeutic Satisfaction

This factor represents a happy experience for both participants (in the patient's view). As shown in Table 30, the dominant patient feeling was euphoric, and the therapist was seen as feeling both effective and

## TABLE 30

**P-I: Therapeutic Satisfaction: Healing Progress and Good Relationship with a Therapist Seen as Pleased and Helpful**

| | | *Loading* | $h^2$ |
|---|---|---|---|
| Patient views herself as: | | | |
| P-6 | feeling *good* | .79[a] | .79 |
| P-41 | getting *relief and control* | .77 | .80 |
| P-40 | getting *insight and rapport* | .75 | .85 |
| P-44 | *doing well and making progress* | .73 | .79 |
| P-35 | wanting to *win the therapist's respect* | .67 | .71 |
| P-24 | relating with *enthusiastic acceptance* (vs. restrained emotion) | .60 | .55 |
| P-43 | *communicating effectively* | .52 | .63 |
| P-26 | relating with *warmth* (vs. ambivalence) | .45 | .71 |
| P-3 | talking about *social reality and "outer" concerns* | .43 | .45 |
| P-42 | *looking forward to sessions* | .43 | .64 |
| P-33 | wanting to *focus collaboratively and effectively on problematic issues* | .38 | .74 |
| P-22 | relating with *independent activity* (vs. emotional involvement) | .35 | .68 |
| Patient views therapist as: | | | |
| P-16 | feeling *pleased* | .80 | .80 |
| P-45 | *understanding and helpful* | .53 | .77 |
| P-12 | feeling *effective* | .48 | .69 |

[a] Italicized loadings indicate variables used in scoring each global experience factor.

accepting. The therapist was also seen as implementing his role effectively in the sense of being understanding and helpful toward the patient. The patient related to her therapist with enthusiastic warmth and acceptance, and was strongly motivated to gain the therapist's esteem and approval. The patient saw herself as communicating freely and effectively with her therapist, as looking forward to her sessions, and as realizing important satisfactions in the therapeutic exchange.

To the somewhat skeptical mind, the experience in P-I almost sounds too good to be true. On this factor, the patient's leading aim (win the therapist's respect) and focus of conversation (social reality and "outer" concerns) tend to reinforce this skeptical attitude. It is the social-emotional aspect of the therapeutic exchange that the patient finds so ameliorative to her spirits, rather than the task-instrumental aspect. The responsive presence of the therapist seems to be the focus of the patient's enthusiasm. Deeply personal probing into significant life experiences, in either an interpretive or an experiential-empathic manner, is notably absent.

### P-II: Painful Self-Exploration

The patient's characteristic affect in P-II was strongly dysphoric, contrasting sharply with P-I, although the therapist was viewed in similar terms. As shown in Table 31, the patient was clearly hurting, and strongly motivated to deal in a constructive manner with the psychological sources of her discomfort. She was involved in an emotional, collaborative manner in discussing such important areas of life experience as her childhood and current family relationships, her experience of herself as a person, problems relating to intimacy, dependency, and anger, and her dreams and fantasies. The patient's aims in approaching her sessions were appropriate to dynamic psychotherapy; she sought to unburden herself with candor to achieve a better understanding and mastery of herself. From many theoretical points of view, a patient having this kind of experience would be considered ideally motivated for therapy.

### P-III: Toying with the Therapist

The third global dimension was principally defined by patient and therapist feelings, as shown in Table 32. This dimension was distinguished by the salience of the therapist in the patient's experience

### TABLE 31

### P-II: Painful Self-Exploration: Seeking Help for Resolving Inner Conflicts Concerning Family Relations

|  |  | Loading | $h^2$ |
|---|---|---|---|
| Patient views herself as: |  |  |  |
| P-7 | feeling *bad* | .74[a] | .76 |
| P-39 | wanting to *get support for expressing feelings* | .71 | .71 |
| P-36 | wanting to *get help from the therapist* (vs. get the session over with) | .64 | .80 |
| P-1 | talking about *anger and family relations* | .60 | .59 |
| P-33 | wanting to *focus collaboratively and effectively on problematic issues* | .54 | .74 |
| P-4 | talking about *fantasy and "inner" concerns* | .50 | .59 |
| P-22 | relating with *emotional involvement* (vs. independent activity) | .46 | .68 |
| P-21 | relating *collaboratively* (vs. assertively) | .34 | .65 |
| Patient views therapist as: |  |  |  |
| P-12 | feeling *effective* | .39 | .69 |
| P-45 | *understanding and helpful* | .35 | .77 |

[a] See note to Table 30.

TABLE 32

**P-III: Toying with the Therapist: Seductiveness with a Therapist Perceived as Feeling Ineffective and Withdrawn**

|  | Loading | $h^2$ |
|---|---|---|
| Patient views herself as: | | |
| P-8    feeling *flirtatious* | .82[a] | .73 |
| P-25    relating with *aloofness* | .36 | .66 |
| Patient views therapist as: | | |
| P-13    feeling *ineffective* | .87 | .85 |
| P-17    feeling *"turned off"* | .57 | .70 |
| P-27    relating with *aloofness* | .51 | .67 |
| P-15    feeling *uneasy intimacy* | .46 | .67 |

[a] See note to Table 30.

and by her perception of him as being in trouble. The patient saw herself as having successfully manipulated the therapist into feelings that conflicted with his normal therapeutic functioning. The patient maintained a seductive posture—holding aloof in relating, but feeling playful, likeable, sympathetic, and superior. The pattern of seduction implied here does not involve a manifest erotization of the relationship. Rather, it focuses on the degree of interpersonal distance or intimacy that the therapist maintains. In this latter regard, the therapist was seen by the patient as having been thrown off balance—both in feeling an uneasy intimacy toward her (tender, intimate, close, apprehensive) and in withdrawing from her. The patient felt that she had successfully drawn the therapist to her, and then found him reacting defensively.

### P-IV: Collaborative Exploration of Heterosexual Involvements

The variables defining the fourth dimension of patient experience are presented in Table 33. The patient tended to talk about her spouse or boyfriend, her sexual feelings and experiences, her inadequacies, fears, and successes, and her feelings about being close to or needing others. She also examined her feelings and attitudes toward herself, and toward therapy and the therapist. These topics focus on her sense of identity and competence in heterosexual involvements, and were discussed with a real investment of feeling. The therapist was also seen as feeling involved, although not in the painful or distressing manner of P-III— the patient saw him as feeling intent (involved, alert, sympathetic, frustrated) and as feeling effective. There was an aura of close collaboration and mutual involvement in P-IV, both in terms of affective investment and in terms of the personal nature of the dialogue. There

TABLE 33

P-IV: Collaborative Exploration of Heterosexual Involvements

| | Loading | $h^2$ |
|---|---|---|
| Patient views herself as: | | |
| P-5    talking about *identity and competence in heterosexual relationships* | .68[a] | .70 |
| P-22   relating with *emotional involvement* (vs. independent activity) | .40 | .68 |
| Patient views therapist as: | | |
| P-18   feeling *invested* | .73 | .76 |
| P-12   feeling *effective* | .38 | .69 |

[a] See note to Table 30.

was a positive correlation of global session evaluation with this dimension ($r = .42$), indicating that the general tenor of the therapeutic exchange was rewarding for the patient.

### P-V: Courting a Therapist Who is Seen as Rejecting

The pattern of experience presented in Table 34 shows the patient as a supplicant for the indulgence and favor of a therapist who was seen as feeling rejecting toward her. She saw the therapist as feeling disappointed, angry, and repelled. The patient, in turn, felt trusting and tender toward the therapist. The sense of vulnerability suggested by the patient's feelings is reinforced by her wanting to "Get my therapist to like me better as a person," and to "Get my therapist to leave me alone for a while." These aims suggest the painfulness to the patient of the therapist's apparent displeasure, which she sought to reduce by trying to please him or at least get him to relent in his demands.

TABLE 34

P-V: Courting a Therapist Who is Seen as Rejecting

| | Loading | $h^2$ |
|---|---|---|
| Patient views herself as: | | |
| P-10   feeling *trusting warmth* (vs. "turned off") | .76[a] | .76 |
| P-37   wanting to *get lenient acceptance* | .71 | .62 |
| Patient views therapist as: | | |
| P-14   feeling *displeased* | .78 | .69 |

[a] See note to Table 30.

The situation depicted in this pattern is a dependency conflict, like that of a child who feels her parent is critical and rejecting toward her. The patient, like the child, is vulnerable to this felt rejection, yet still needs the parent too much to be able to leave the relationship or to tolerate open conflict. The child's only available options are to redouble her efforts to be a "good child," or to distract her parent's attention from her. The patient feels innocent of any particular wrongdoing in the relationship, yet feels she has somehow evoked the therapist's dislike. The conflictual aspect of this pattern stems from her dependent attachment to the therapist.

### P-VI: Erotic Transference Resistance

The salient characteristic of the sixth dimension was the sexual arousal felt by the patient. As shown in Table 35, this arousal was accompanied by feelings of embarrassment and shyness, a tendency to withdraw, and a serious blockage of communication. The patient was beset by feelings toward the therapist that she could neither deal with comfortably nor share with the therapist, even though she saw her therapist acting in a friendly, supportive manner. All of the turmoil the patient experienced was evidently kept locked within her. She could not relate her feelings to the therapist, and could not otherwise respond to his accepting and potentially helpful presence.

The pattern of experience depicted in P-VI seems to represent the sexual transference process described by Freud (1912a, 1915). More exactly, it reflects one phase of the sexual transference: the initial upsurge of the reaction that manifests itself defensively in the form of heightened resistance and blocking. One can well imagine that P-IV (*collaborative exploration of heterosexual involvements*) represents

**TABLE 35**

**P-VI: Erotic Transference Resistance: Blocking and Embarrassing Sexual Arousal with a Therapist Seen as Indulgent**

| | Loading | $h^2$ |
|---|---|---|
| Patient views herself as: | | |
| P-9  feeling *embarrassing sexual arousal* | .67[a] | .60 |
| P-25  relating with *aloofness* | .48 | .66 |
| P-43  not *communicating effectively* | .43 | .63 |
| Patient views therapist as: | | |
| P-29  relating with *indulgent acceptance* (vs. helpful strictness) | .70 | .66 |

[a] See note to Table 30.

the working through and resolution of erotic transference feelings. The difference between the two dimensions is that in P-IV there is an effective therapeutic alliance, whereas in P-VI the patient's feelings make any contact with the therapist too threatening.

### P-VII: Patient Role Ambivalence vs. Patient Role Acceptance

The seventh pattern of patient experience focused upon the patient's adaptation to the "patient role" in relating to the therapist. P-VII was a bipolar dimension, defined by the variables shown in Table 36. One pole of this dimension was characterized by the patient's preoccupation with domestic and household responsibilities and activities, and her ambivalent reaction to a therapist who seemed accomodating and willing to compromise. There was an implicit lack of genuine respect or acceptance toward the therapist on the patient's part. She seemed to define her problems as relating chiefly to the exigencies of her domestic situation and thus, presumably, not of an emotional or psychological nature.

At the opposite pole of P-VII, the patient talked about work or school, personal and social inadequacies or successes, childhood ex-

### TABLE 36

### P-VII+: Patient Role Ambivalence: Domestic Concerns and an Ambivalent Attitude with a Seemingly Persuasible Therapist

|  | Loading | $h^2$ |
|---|---|---|
| Patient views herself as: | | |
| P-2    talking about *domestic concerns* | .65[a] | .71 |
| P-26   relating with *ambivalence* | .59 | .71 |
| Patient views therapist as: | | |
| P-30   relating *persuasibly* | .64 | .70 |
| P-15   feeling *uneasy intimacy* | .36 | .67 |

### P-VII−: Patient Role Acceptance: Career Concerns and an Accepting Attitude with a Therapist Viewed as Independent

|  | Loading | $h^2$ |
|---|---|---|
| Patient views herself as: | | |
| P-2    talking about *career concerns* | .65 | .71 |
| P-26   relating with *warmth* | .59 | .71 |
| Patient views therapist as: | | |
| P-30   relating *independently* | .64 | .70 |
| P-15   not feeling *uneasy intimacy* | .36 | .67 |

[a] See note to Table 30.

periences in school and with friends, and current social activities and relationships. Her attitude in relating to the therapist was one of friendliness and respect, and she saw him as quite independent and inclined to be uninfluenced by her.

These two polar patterns define a continuum of adaptation to the "patient role" that clearly reflects different life styles and concerns. P-VII+[2] raises the image of a housewife immersed in domestic problems and interests, who has been referred for therapy but does not understand how talking to the therapist will help or have relevance to *her* complaints. She is not psychologically minded, and expects the therapist's behavior to be directive and prescriptive in conformity with the medical model. On the other hand, the patient depicted in P-VII— seems to live psychologically in a wider world of vocational and social concerns. She is more psychologically minded and her expectations of the therapist role seem to be more congruent with the therapist's, contributing to an effective rapport based on shared assumptions and values. The seventh dimension of patient experience thus reflects the relative ease with which the patient can comply with the demand characteristics of psychotherapy.

### P-VIII: Passive Dependence vs. Independent Introspection

Table 37 shows the variables that defined this bipolar dimension. In P-VIII+ the patient experienced herself as dependent on the therapist's direction. She saw the therapist as a forceful, intense, directive figure who was willing to lead her along lines he determined, and which she passively followed. Her inner experiences, whether in the form of dreams and fantasies or bodily need sensations, were not readily accessible. On the other hand, the patient in P-VIII— was quite sensitive to the promptings of her inner experience and relied on her introspective sense as a source of direction. She took initiative in focusing interaction upon the problems she experienced, and found the therapist more a collaborative partner than a directive leader.

The interpretation of this dimension as a continuum of interpersonal dependency suggests an important difference of emphasis in perceptual orientation among patients. Each person's phenomenal world is more or less firmly divided into an "outer world" of people, objects, and events, and an "inner world" of sensations, thoughts, feelings, and fantasy. Individuals differ in the extent to which one or the other of these spheres of experience is salient, however. The interpersonally independent person is more absorbed in her "inner world"; she scans this side of her experience with greater vigilance, and is more responsive to the demand

---

[2] The designation "+" or "−" in bipolar dimensions is purely arbitrary and does not reflect an evaluation of the quality of experience at each pole.

TABLE 37

**P-VIII+ : Passive Dependence with a Therapist Seen as Directive**

|  | Loading | $h^2$ |
|---|---|---|
| Patient views herself as: | | |
| P-23 relating with *passive compliance* | .68[a] | .63 |
| P-11 not feeling *bodily need sensations* | .42 | .45 |
| P-33 not wanting to *focus collaboratively and effectively on problematic issues* | .41 | .74 |
| P-4 not talking about *fantasy and "inner" concerns* | .37 | .59 |
| Patient views therapist as: | | |
| P-28 relating with *forceful direction* | .62 | .56 |

**P-VIII− : Independent Introspection with a Therapist Seen as Collaborative**

|  | | |
|---|---|---|
| Patient views herself as: | | |
| P-23 not relating with *passive compliance* | .68 | .63 |
| P-11 feeling *bodily need sensations* | .42 | .45 |
| P-33 wanting to *focus collaboratively and effectively on problematic issues* | .41 | .74 |
| P-4 talking about *fantasy and "inner" concerns* | .37 | .59 |
| Patient views therapist as: | | |
| P-28 relating with *collaboration* | .62 | .56 |

[a] See note to Table 30.

value of its stimuli. Her basic approach in therapy is to explore this side of her experience and to relate it to the therapist for whatever clarification and help he can offer. The interpersonally dependent person, in contrast, is more absorbed in the "outer world" of her experience; she is more immediately responsive to the people and events around her, and takes her lead from what she construes to be their cues for her behavior. She is very responsive to the actions and expressions of her therapist, and tends to fit her behavior to what she perceives as his expectations. This polarity may be similar to the psychological dimension of introversion-extraversion; it also resembles that of field dependence vs. field independence (Witkin, *et al.,* 1962).

### P-IX: Hostile Provocation Toward a Seemingly Noncommittal Therapist

The patient's desire to provoke the therapist was the most prominent variable defining the ninth dimension (see Table 38). The patient's aims in P-IX included wanting to "Get an emotional response from my thera-

TABLE 38

**P-IX: Hostile Provocation Toward a Seemingly Noncommittal Therapist**

|  | Loading | $h^2$ |
|---|---|---|
| Patient views herself as: |  |  |
| P-34 wanting to *get a rise out of the therapist* | .77[a] | .71 |
| Patient views therapist as: |  |  |
| P-32 relating with *attentive compliance* | .57 | .64 |
| P-12 not feeling *effective* | .35 | .69 |

[a] See note to Table 30.

pist," and wanting to "Get even with my therapist for the way I've been treated." The therapist's apparent receptiveness and openness of manner were evidently construed by the patient as a sign of weakness or ineffectuality. This view is suggested by the patient's tendency *not* to perceive the therapist as having feelings that *typically* are ascribed to therapists (see Chapter 5): effective, confident, calm, energetic, optimistic, alert, interested, sympathetic. Although feelings of anger toward the therapist were not reported for this pattern, the patient's aims with regard to him clearly had a vengeful or hostile overtone.

The aims that chiefly defined P-IX were infrequently endorsed in our sample, but the general pattern of experience is not an unfamiliar one in situations where therapist impassiveness is prescribed, e.g., classical psychoanalysis or orthodox client-centered therapy. Some patients find this impassive stance of the therapist very frustrating, and expend considerable ingenuity in attempting to "get a rise out of" the therapist. Perhaps for these patients a negative response from the therapist is better than no response at all.

### P-X: Intrusiveness with a Therapist Felt to be Tense and Embarrassed

The variables that defined the tenth dimension of patient experience are shown in Table 39. P-X centered in a cluster of patient aims and a cluster of perceived therapist feelings. The patient's predominant aims were to "Find out more about my therapist as a person," to "Get some reassurance about how I'm doing," and to "Get an emotional response from my therapist." The general theme of this cluster was the wish to establish a personal rather than a professional relationship with the therapist. In addition to her major aim of gaining personal acceptance from the therapist, the patient also sought a variety of other forms of active help from him. She did not hold aloof and did not want to "Talk

## TABLE 39

### P-X: Intrusiveness with a Therapist Felt to be Tense and Embarrassed

|  | Loading | $h^2$ |
|---|---|---|
| Patient views herself as: |  |  |
| P-38    wanting to *find out more about the therapist's personal life and feelings* | .73[a] | .71 |
| P-11    feeling *bodily need sensations* | .40 | .45 |
| P-36    wanting to *get help from the therapist* (vs. get the session over with) | .37 | .80 |
| P-25    not relating with *aloofness* | .36 | .66 |
| Patient views therapist as: |  |  |
| P-19    feeling *embarrassed and tense* | .54 | .72 |

[a] See note to Table 30.

and just get the session over with." Not at all shy or retiring, she rather sought to make herself the immediate object of the therapist's help and assistance. The image of the patient as a locus of highly clamorous needs was reinforced by her sensitivity to her own bodily need sensations. The therapist, on the other hand, was perceived as reacting to the patient's importunate pursuit of him with feelings of embarrassment and anxiety. The kind of response the patient sought from the therapist indicates a wish to be assured of a significant place in the therapist's personal life and feelings. To paraphrase Bruno Bettelheim, help is not enough. Although the patient is active and intrusive rather than passive and submissive, the very force of her needs places her paradoxically in a situation of felt dependency on the therapist. The perceived response of the therapist, however, seems to be one of confusion rather than nurturance.

### P-XI: Therapist Perceived as Mean and Attacking vs. Therapist Perceived as Involved and Helpful

The eleventh global experience dimension was a bipolar pattern that focused on the patient's perception of the therapist as either a helpful or a frightening person (see Table 40). P-XI+ marked the most negative pattern of patient experience. The therapist was perceived as an essentially attacking figure—as critical, negative, and unfeelingly active in relating to the patient—as feeling depressed and irritable, and as being neither understanding nor helpful. This harsh image of the therapist was complemented by an image of negative and deteriorative patient reaction. The therapist's perceived attack constituted a serious stress for the

## TABLE 40

### P-XI+ : Therapist Perceived as Mean and Attacking

|  | Loading | $h^2$ |
|---|---|---|
| Patient views herself as: |  |  |
| P-42   *looking forward to sessions* | .40 | .64 |
| P-41   not getting *relief and control* | .35 | .80 |
| P-44   not *doing well and making progress* | .35 | .79 |
| P-21   relating *assertively* | .34 | .65 |
| Patient views therapist as: |  |  |
| P-31   relating with *active criticism* | .77 [a] | .63 |
| P-20   not feeling *depressed and irritable* | .54 | .50 |
| P-45   not *understanding and helpful* | .54 | .77 |

### P-XI− : Therapist Perceived as Involved and Helpful

|  | Loading | $h^2$ |
|---|---|---|
| Patient views herself as: |  |  |
| P-42   *looking forward to sessions* | .40 | .64 |
| P-41   getting *relief and control* | .35 | .80 |
| P-44   *doing well and making progress* | .35 | .79 |
| P-21   relating *collaboratively* | .34 | .65 |
| Patient views therapist as: |  |  |
| P-31   relating with *affective involvement* | .77 | .63 |
| P-20   not feeling *depressed and irritable* | .54 | .50 |
| P-45   *understanding and helpful* | .54 | .77 |

[a] See note to Table 30.

patient, in response to which she showed tendencies to both fight and flight. The patient's manner of relating to the therapist was assertive and resistive, but she also dreaded coming to her sessions. The stressful nature of her contacts with the therapist also showed itself in the patient's report of obtaining little sense of relief or control in her sessions, and of making little if any improvement in her condition through therapy. Post-session evaluation was correlated significantly and negatively ($r = -.53$) with P-XI+, indicating that these sessions were generally considered poor in quality.

At the opposite pole, P-XI− depicted a pattern centering on the "good" therapist. The most salient characteristic of the good therapist in the patient's experience was his affective responsiveness, not excitedly or dramatically displayed but quietly, palpably present. He was also seen as clearly and fully understanding the patient's experience, and as helpful in what he said and did. No dysphoric affect of his own was felt by the patient to intrude on his rapport with her. In response to his presence, the patient was highly motivated to attend her sessions, felt that she got emotional relief and enhanced self-control, and believed that she was making good progress with the problems that brought her to treatment. She saw herself as relating collaboratively in her sessions, and as functioning well outside of them.

## THE STRUCTURE OF PATIENT EXPERIENCE

The eleven dimensions of individual differences reported above define the structure of patient experience as reported by the group of patients studied in the Psychotherapy Session Project. Clearly, these are not the only patterns of patient experience ever likely to be found. Patients with different personal characteristics, in different clinical settings, treated by therapists of distinctively different theoretical orientations and approaches, would probably develop somewhat different patterns of psychotherapeutic experience. Yet for this sample of not atypical patients, the eleven dimensions have been empirically established, and the clinical familiarity of the patterns suggests that many will be found to hold for other types of patients in different clinical situations. Taken all together, what do these patterns imply about the nature of patient experience?

Patient experience reflects both the nature of the patient's involvement with the therapist and the impact made on her by that involvement. The impact varies from positive (e.g., P-I) to neutral (e.g., P-VII—) to negative (e.g., P-XI+). The nature of the involvement seems to focus on one or more of four general areas of interpersonal relation: *task involvement, intimacy, dependency,* and *hostility.*

*Task involvement* was manifested in three of the eleven global dimensions. *Patient role ambivalence vs. patient role acceptance* (P-VII), reflecting the patient's adaptation to her role in therapy, is the most obvious case in point. *Painful self-exploration* (P-II) showed the patient effectively engaged in that mode of task involvement characteristically prescribed in insight-oriented psychotherapy. *Therapist perceived as involved and helpful* (P-XI—), on the other hand, showed the therapist functioning most successfully in the manner appropriate to his professional role.

*Intimacy* was reflected in two patterns of patient experience. *Collaborative exploration of heterosexual involvements* (P-IV) showed a mutually intimate involvement between patient and therapist successfully integrated into the therapeutic relationship. In contrast to this effectively sublimated intimacy, *erotic transference resistance* (P-VI) showed a strong erotic attraction or impulse for sexual intimacy that was disruptive to the therapeutic relationship.

*Dependency* appeared as a dominant theme in four of the eleven dimensions. *Passive dependence vs. independent introspection* (P-VIII) showed a continuum from extreme compliance in the face of therapist directiveness to extreme autonomy in which the therapist was accepted only in a collaborative role. *Intrusiveness with a therapist felt to be tense and embarrassed* (P-X), on the other hand, showed the patient overwhelming the therapist with demands for personal acceptance and response. Another permutation on the theme of dependency was seen in *toying with the therapist* (P-III), where the patient had reversed the normal direction of dependent attachment by manipulating the therapist into a weak, "one down" position. The fourth dimension in which dependency formed a dominant theme was *therapeutic satisfaction* (P-I). The clinical character of this dimension is especially interesting, in that it shows the potent beneficial impact of therapeutic dependency modeled upon the nurturance-succorance pattern of the successful parent-child relationship.

*Hostility* was a basic characteristic of three patterns of patient experience. In *hostile provocation toward a seemingly noncommittal therapist* (P-IX), the therapist was the object of the patient's vengeful prodding. In the other two, however, the patient experienced herself as the object of the therapist's hostility. *Courting a therapist who is seen as rejecting* (P-V) showed the patient seeking to reverse or neutralize what she perceived as the therapist's critical and rejecting feelings toward her. The hostility in *therapist perceived as mean and attacking* (P-XI+), however, was experienced as an aggressive onslaught by the therapist, from which she fearfully retreated.

The classification of patient experience into patterns of *task involvement, intimacy, dependency,* and *hostility* derives principally from a clinical interpretation of the dominant content themes. Different interpretive classifications of these patterns might be made on the basis of specific clinical theories. Rather than elaborate further *a priori* groupings, it seems more useful at this point to offer an empirical analysis of the configurations of experience dimension profiles. Chapter 8 presents this analysis, together with an investigation of the determinants of patient experience types.

*Chapter 8*

# Patient Experience-Types and their Correlates

The patterns of experience described in Chapter 7 were discovered through the systematic comparison of differences between patients. As such, they consist of dimensions defining the structure of experience within the entire patient sample. Each of these group dimensions represents a single unitary aspect of therapeutic experience, and the experiences of an individual patient could be characterized by her score on that dimension.

In the present chapter, we focus on the total pattern of experience, rather than on single components. The relevant analyses involved characterizing the total pattern of experience for patients as individuals, and then determining groups or clusters of patients on the basis of similarities of these patterns. This approach allowed us to isolate and to describe *types* of patients, to determine the personal and social characteristics of those persons who shared a common type of experience, and to predict for future samples what type of experience an individual of given characteristics is likely to have in psychotherapy.

The total pattern of experience for an individual patient was represented by the *profile* of her scores on the eleven dimensions derived from the patient form of the TSR. A profile shows the level of scores relative to each other,[1] and thereby suggests which dimensions were more

---

[1] The score of a patient on each dimension was in standard score terms, and thus represented her position relative to the other patients on that dimension. A profile of these scores represents a configuration of these relative positions, and should not be interpreted in absolute terms.

or less prominent in each patient's experience. The difference between comparing the separate scores of two patients and the profiles of those two patients may be readily illustrated. Each patient might have approximately the same score on *therapeutic satisfaction* (P-I), but for one patient that score might be the highest of her eleven scores, whereas for the other that score might be only the fourth or fifth highest. By inspecting their profiles, we would be likely to conclude that P-I was quite prominent in the experience of the former but not of the latter—a conclusion we could not have drawn simply by comparing the two scores alone.

Since our interest here is in the experiences that patients have, rather than in the individual patients themselves, the analysis was designed to isolate groups of patients on the basis of the similarity of their profiles. The procedures used are outlined in detail in Chapter 4. Four major clusters of profiles emerged, permitting the classification of fifty of the sixty patients in our sample. Each cluster was characterized by a composite profile that defined a distinctive pattern of experience. Score profiles of patients were inspected to determine the dimensions of therapeutic experience that seemed to organize each cluster, i.e., dimensions that were consistently high or low for the patients in that cluster. These organizing dimensions were used as the basis for interpreting each type. The four patient experience-types were identified as:

P-A:  Helpful experience
P-B:  Stressful experience
P-C:  Dependent experience
P-D:  Counter-dependent experience.

## PATIENT EXPERIENCE-TYPES

### P-A: Helpful Experience

The pattern of experience that distinguished one group of patients seemed to realize the most positive or helpful potentials of the therapeutic encounter. The composite profile for this group was organized around the following dimensions: *therapist perceived as involved and helpful* (P-XI−), *therapeutic satisfaction* (P-I), and *collaborative exploration of heterosexual involvements* (P-IV). That is, scores on these three dimensions were distinctly higher than scores on the other profile dimensions for patients of type P-A.

This experience-type embodies the textbook expectation of what psychotherapy should be like. Both the character of the patient's involvement with the therapist and the apparent impact of that involvement on her condition are seen in a positive light. These patients experienced a sense of progress, satisfaction, and mutual involvement in working with their therapists. They tended to perceive their therapists as effective, emotionally responsive, and accepting. The predominant feeling was that their therapists were helpful, and that their therapeutic experiences were helping them to solve their problems.

21 of the sixty patients in the sample were included in type P-A (one third of all the patients, and two fifths of those classifiable in one of the four types). Thus, for a substantial minority, experiences that conformed to the most optimistic or ideal expectations of psychotherapy were salient. The fact that this pattern of experience emerged lends empirical support to clinical formulations concerning the essential characteristics of the helpful relationship. It is worth noting, however, that a majority of patients did *not* have this type of experience.

### P-B: Stressful Experience

A second group of patients was distinguished by a pattern of experience that emphasized the negative or stressful potentials of the therapeutic encounter. The composite profile of this type was organized by the elevation of *therapist perceived as mean and attacking* (P-XI+) and *erotic transference resistance* (P-VI), and by the depression of *therapeutic satisfaction* (P-I) and *collaborative exploration of heterosexual involvements* (P-IV). This pattern is essentially the mirror image of *helpful experience*.

In type P-B, patients seemed to feel threatened both by their own feelings toward their therapists and by their perceptions of their therapists' responses to them. Embarrassing sexual arousal and defensive blocking of communication tended to characterize the patient's subjective position. At the same time, these patients tended to respond with anxiety to their sense of being trapped in an encounter with an actively critical therapist. Other evidence (cf. Chapter 11) suggests that the patient's perception of the therapist may represent a defensive projection of her own aggressive impulse. The patient may, in effect, be viewing the therapist as her own harsh conscience. The experience of distressing sexual and aggressive impulses appears to preclude the simultaneous experience of therapy as a positive and collaborative involvement.

Seven of the sixty patients in our sample were included in this experience-type. For these patients, therapy seems to have produced a heightening rather than a reduction in the level of experienced conflict. The extent to which this pattern represents a breakdown, or merely a difficult phase, or even a necessary stage in the development of the therapeutic process, clearly requires further study.

### P-C: Dependent Experience

Another group of patients was distinguished by a pattern of experience in which passive dependence was the distinctive feature. The composite profile of this group was organized by the elevation of *passive dependence* (P-VIII+), and by the depression of *painful self-exploration* (P-II), *collaborative exploration of heterosexual involvements* (P-IV), and *intrusiveness with a therapist felt to be tense and embarrassed* (P-X). Patients of this type tended to experience themselves predominantly as the passive and submissive objects of their therapist's initiative and activity. This compliant attitude, in addition to limiting the development of a collaborative relationship, precluded extensive self-exploration or independent introspective openness on the patient's part.

Eighteen of the sixty patients in the sample (nearly one-third of the total) were included in this experience-type. A substantial minority of patients thus seem to adopt a dependent stance vis-à-vis the therapist. The absence of the patient's active participation also seems to result in a lack of the kind of positive therapeutic impact noted in type P-A.

### P-D: Counter-Dependent Experience

A final group of patients shared a pattern of experience in which resistance to the influence of the therapist was a central feature. The composite profile of this type was organized by the elevation of *intrusiveness with a therapist felt to be tense and embarrassed* (P-X), *independent introspection* (P-VIII−), and *patient role ambivalence* (P-VII+), and by the depression of *erotic transference resistance* (P-VI). This pattern is, in effect, the mirror image of *dependent experience*.

In type P-D, patients seem to have sought various devices to forestall the development of a passive dependent attachment to the therapist. These included the vigorous and importunate pursuit of help from the therapist, the exaggeration of autonomous therapeutic behavior to keep initiative from the therapist, and a reluctance to comply with the norms of the patient role. The common result of these different tactics was a maintenance of distance from the therapist and his potential influence.

Only four patients were included in this type. Thus, although dependency on the therapist or submission to his influence was a salient feature of experience in both types P-C and P-D, most of the patients who were affected by it were those who also yielded to it.

## COMPARISON OF PATIENT EXPERIENCE-TYPES

Only one of the four types of patient experience showed a markedly positive therapeutic impact upon the patient. In terms of the components of intimacy, task-involvement, dependency, and hostility that were discussed in Chapter 7, *helpful experience* may be viewed a sa successful blend of intimacy, task involvement, and dependency. It was the only experience-type that included positive task involvement as a major component. In contrast, the other three types showed either an absence of positive therapeutic impact or an apparently negative therapeutic impact upon the patient.

From another perspective, the four experience-types may be viewed as constituting two distinct pairs. Types P-A and P-B focused on the issue of helpful vs. stressful experience in therapy, whereas types P-C and P-D focused on the issue of dependent vs. resistive response to the therapist's influence. The differentiation between *helpful experience* and *stressful experience* appears to lie along an axis of *reduction or mobilization of anxiety* for the patient. The differentiation between *dependent experience* and *counter-dependent experience* seems to lie along a second axis of *acceptance or rejection of influence* from the therapist. These two axes might be hypothesized as the higher order components of structure in shaping the patients' global psychotherapeutic experience.

## CORRELATES OF PATIENT EXPERIENCE-TYPES

How do the four types of experience relate to the personal and social characteristics of patients and of their therapists? Are certain types of experience more likely to occur for specific kinds of patients or for the patients of particular kinds of therapists? The data pertinent to this issue are presented in Tables 41 and 42. Each of the characteristics surveyed is shown with its internal classifications (e.g., Age: 20-26, 27-36, 37-60), and the number of patients in each experience-type for each classification is shown in the adjacent columns.

None of the personal and social characteristics significantly differentiated patients who had a *helpful experience* from those in the other experience-types. Certain characteristics of these patients' therapists were differentially associated with type P-A, however. These were sex and profession.[2] Patients whose therapists were women, and/or psychiatric social workers, had a *helpful experience* more frequently than did others. The distinguishing qualities of such therapists (at least by common cultural attribution) are a readiness to be helpful, to care for others, and to respond to feelings. Women in our culture have been expected to possess these qualities more than do men, and have been more rewarded for manifesting them. Furthermore, among the three principal mental

---

[2] Many of the characteristics of patients and of therapists were confounded. The relationships reported do not imply that *all* the characteristics associated with a particular experience-type need be present together.

health professions, social work has been more committed by its professional ideology to value "helping" relationships. On the other hand, it may also be that patients find it easier to identify with, and accept help from, therapists of the same sex. Our data give no clear indication as to whether therapists' attributes, or some interaction between attributes of patients and therapists, determine this sex effect.

Patients for whom therapy was a *stressful experience* tended to be disproportionately 26 or younger, and/or single. In addition, patients who found therapy to be a *stressful experience* tended to have *therapists* who were disproportionately from upper-middle-class backgrounds, and/or only children. Thus, the predisposition toward a *stressful experience* seems to be a function of both patient and therapist characteristics. The life situation of the unattached, psychologically disturbed young woman probably offers few reliable opportunities for emotional gratification. Because of this, the therapeutic relationship may become a major arena for the expression of her personal needs. On the other hand, the therapist from a small family of relatively elite status probably is accustomed to being the object of intense emotional investment. The combination of unfulfilled need in the patient and readiness to absorb emotional investment on the part of the therapist offers a plausible hypothesis concerning the disposition to *stressful experience*. Contrary to expectation, the sex of the therapist was not disproportionately associated with this type.

Patients for whom therapy was a *dependent experience* were disproportionately 37 to 60 years of age, and/or from three- or four-child families (but *not* from two-child families). Patients who had a *dependent experience* also tended to have *therapists* who had children, and/or were from families of three or more children (but *not* from one- or two-child families). Older patients, reared in the family values of an earlier generation, probably tend to assimilate perceptions of the therapist to the image of an authoritarian parent. This tendency is probably reinforced by the fact that their therapists actually have children, and may transfer to dependent patients attitudes similar to those they have toward their own children. In addition, for this experience-type, both patients and therapists tended to come from large multi-sib families—families in which there is considerable status differentiation among sibs. Socialization in such a family might predispose one to conceive of a helping relationship in terms of dominant and dependent roles. In any event, *dependent experience* clearly has sources in the family experiences of both participants.

Patients for whom therapy was a *counter-dependent experience* were disproportionately Jewish and/or from two-child families. Such patients experienced themselves as assertive and demanding in relation to

## TABLE 41

## Number of Profiles of Each Patient Type in Each of the Patient Background Groups

| Patient Background Groups | Patient Experience-Types | | | | |
|---|---|---|---|---|---|
| | A | B | C | D | % [a] |
| **Age** | | | | | |
| 20-26 | 8 | 6 * | 6 * | 2 | 44 |
| 27-36 | 9 | 1 | 5 | 1 | 32 |
| 37-60 | 4 | 0 | 7 | 1 | 24 |
| **Marital status** | | | | | |
| Single | 8 | 6 * | 7 | 1 | 44 |
| Married | 5 | 0 | 7 | 1 | 26 |
| Formerly married | 8 | 1 | 4 | 2 | 30 |
| **Parental status** | | | | | |
| No children | 11 | 6 | 10 | 2 | 58 |
| Children | 10 | 1 | 8 | 2 | 42 |
| **Employment** | | | | | |
| Employed | 18 | 7 | 14 | 4 | 86 |
| Not employed | 3 | 0 | 4 | 0 | 14 |
| **Social class of origin** | | | | | |
| Upper middle and middle | 5 | 2 | 3 | 1 | 22 |
| Lower middle | 7 | 1 | 5 | 1 | 28 |
| Upper lower | 9 | 3 | 9 | 1 | 44 |
| Lower and lower lower | 0 | 1 | 1 | 1 | 6 |
| **Education** | | | | | |
| High school graduate or less | 7 | 1 | 7 | 2 | 34 |
| Some college | 10 | 3 | 4 | 1 | 36 |
| College graduate or more | 4 | 3 | 7 | 1 | 30 |
| **Religion** | | | | | |
| Protestant | 9 | 4 | 9 | 1 * | 46 |
| Catholic | 8 | 3 | 6 | 1 | 36 |
| Jewish | 3 | 0 | 1 | 2 | 12 |
| Other or none | 1 | 0 | 2 | 0 | 6 |
| **Family size** | | | | | |
| Only child | 3 | 1 | 3 * | 0 * | 14 |
| One sib | 5 | 2 | 0 | 3 | 20 |
| 2-3 sibs | 7 | 3 | 10 | 0 | 40 |
| 4 or more sibs | 6 | 1 | 5 | 1 | 26 |
| **Birth order** | | | | | |
| Oldest | 8 | 3 | 9 | 3 | 46 |
| Middle | 7 | 2 | 4 | 1 | 28 |
| Youngest | 6 | 2 | 5 | 0 | 26 |

## TABLE 41 (continued)

| Patient Background Groups | Patient Experience-Types | | | | |
|---|---|---|---|---|---|
| | A | B | C | D | % [a] |
| **Age at family disruption** | | | | | |
| Under 5 | 2 | 2 | 2 | 1 | 14 |
| 6-10 | 2 | 1 | 1 | 0 | 8 |
| 11-15 | 2 | 0 | 1 | 0 | 6 |
| 16 plus, or never | 15 | 4 | 14 | 3 | 72 |
| **Diagnosis** | | | | | |
| Depressive reaction | 7 | 5 | 6 | 2 | 40 |
| Anxiety reaction | 4 | 1 | 3 | 1 | 18 |
| Personality disorder | 6 | 0 | 6 | 1 | 26 |
| Schizophrenia | 4 | 1 | 3 | 0 | 16 |
| **Previous psychotherapy** | | | | | |
| Yes | 11 | 5 | 11 | 2 | 58 |
| No | 10 | 2 | 7 | 2 | 42 |
| **Weeks of current therapy** | | | | | |
| 1-26 weeks | 9 | 3 | 8 | 2 | 44 |
| 27-52 weeks | 5 | 2 | 6 | 0 | 26 |
| 53 or more weeks | 7 | 2 | 4 | 2 | 30 |
| **Number of patients** | 21 | 7 | 18 | 4 | |

[a] % based on 50 classified patients.

* $\chi^2$ statistically significant ($p < .05$) for comparison of column distribution with pooled distribution of other types. The italicized entries indicate major contributors to obtained significant $\chi^2$.

their therapists. In addition, patients who had this type of experience tended to have *therapists* who were only children, and/or had more than six years of professional experience. The patients' socialization in dyadic sibships probably prepared them for more peer-like and direct emotional exchanges. Their therapists, on the other hand, were probably inclined to maintain a greater emotional distance, as a function of being only children and/or as a result of being more highly professionalized. It is noteworthy that when patients had a *counter-dependent experience,* both they and their therapists tended to come from small families, whereas in cases of *dependent experience* both tended to come from large families.

## PREDICTORS OF PATIENT EXPERIENCE-TYPES

The personal and social characteristics that contributed to each type of patient experience were presented in the preceding section. These same data may be utilized to answer a related question: What types of

## TABLE 42

### Number of Profiles of Each Patient Type in Each of the Therapist Background Groups

| Therapist Background Groups | Patient Experience-Types | | | | % [a] |
| | A | B | C | D | |
| --- | --- | --- | --- | --- | --- |
| **Age** | | | | | |
| 29-35 | 9 | 4 | 6 | 1 | 40 |
| 36 or over | 12 | 3 | 12 | 3 | 60 |
| **Marital status** | | | | | |
| Single | 7 | 3 | 5 | 2 | 34 |
| Married | 8 | 3 | 9 | 2 | 44 |
| Formerly married | 6 | 1 | 4 | 0 | 22 |
| **Parental status** | | | | | |
| No children | 17 | 6 | 10 * | 2 | 70 |
| Children | 4 | 1 | 8 | 2 | 30 |
| **Social class of origin** | | | | | |
| Upper middle and middle | 9 | 6 * | 9 | 2 | 52 |
| Lower middle and upper lower | 12 | 1 | 9 | 2 | 48 |
| **Religion** | | | | | |
| Protestant | 6 | 1 | 2 | 2 | 22 |
| Catholic | 3 | 1 | 3 | 0 | 14 |
| Jewish | 8 | 3 | 7 | 1 | 38 |
| Other or none | 4 | 2 | 6 | 1 | 26 |
| **Sex** | | | | | |
| Male | 10 * | 5 | 13 | 3 | 62 |
| Female | 11 | 2 | 5 | 1 | 38 |
| **Family size** | | | | | |
| Only child | 1 | 2 * | 0 * | 2 * | 10 |
| One sib | 5 | 2 | 1 | 1 | 18 |
| Two or more sibs | 15 | 3 | 17 | 1 | 72 |
| **Birth order** | | | | | |
| Oldest | 7 | 4 | 5 | 2 | 36 |
| Middle | 9 | 2 | 6 | 1 | 36 |
| Youngest | 5 | 1 | 7 | 1 | 28 |
| **Profession** | | | | | |
| Psychiatry | 10 * | 4 | 12 | 3 | 58 |
| Psychology | 4 | 2 | 5 | 0 | 22 |
| Social work | 7 | 1 | 1 | 1 | 20 |
| **Years of experience** | | | | | |
| 0-5 years | 11 | 2 | 10 | 0 * | 46 |
| 6 or more years | 10 | 5 | 8 | 4 * | 54 |

TABLE 42 (continued)

| Therapist Background Groups | Patient Experience-Types | | | | |
|---|---|---|---|---|---|
| | A | B | C | D | % [a] |
| **Personal psychotherapy** | | | | | |
| Yes | 16 | 7 | 12 | 2 | 74 |
| No | 5 | 0 | 6 | 2 | 26 |
| **Number of patients** | 21 | 7 | 18 | 4 | |

[a] % based on classified patients.

* $\chi^2$ statistically significant ($p < .05$) for comparison of column distribution with pooled distribution of other types. The italicized entries indicate major contributors to obtained significant $\chi^2$.

experience are specific kinds of patients, or patients assigned to specific kinds of therapists, likely to have in therapy? If patient experience can be predicted on the basis of readily available information about patients and therapists, case assignment and treatment planning can be practiced with less reliance on purely intuitive judgments.

The answer to this question involved determination of the most probable experience-type membership for each subgroup of each patient or therapist characteristic. The data for this analysis are reported in Tables 41 and 42. The analysis consisted in the computation of the percentage of cases in each experience-type for each subgroup of a background characteristic. Where more than 50% of the persons with a particular characteristic were in one of the experience-types, the characteristic was considered differentially predictive of patient experience. In general, it should be noted that the most likely experience-type for a patient was *helpful experience* (35%), followed by *dependent experience* (30%), *stressful experience* (12%), and *counter-dependent experience* (7%).[3]

Patients for whom psychotherapy was a predominantly *helpful experience* shared the following characteristics: they were between 27 and 36 years of age, were formerly married, had some college education, and came from families that were disrupted when they were between 6 and 15 years old. These women are young adults, old enough to have had some experience of life, who have had personal misfortunes in childhood and/or adult family relations. Such persons seem best prepared to appreciate the positive qualities of the therapeutic relationship. The prob-

[3] Ten of the sixty patients were not classifiable into the four experience-types. In what follows, we shall report distributions based only on the 50 classifiable patients. The assumption here is that all patients are ultimately classifiable into one of the four types and that the expected distribution over these types would be 42%, 36%, 14%, and 8%, respectively.

ability of a patient's having a *helpful experience* was also enhanced if her therapist was a woman, was formerly married, came from a dyadic sibship, was Protestant, and was a psychiatric social worker. Since all but one of the psychiatric social workers were female, and all of the formerly married therapists in our sample were female, it is probable that the sex of the therapist is the primary influence in these cases. The potential for mutual identification between patient and therapist may provide a basis for the empathy, collaboration, and positive transference that defined a *helpful experience.*

Since only seven patients had a *stressful experience,* no background characteristic was distributed such that over 50% of the patients in any subgroup had this experience. No matter what a patient's or her therapist's characteristics were, it was unlikely that she would find therapy a *stressful experience.* Several characteristics did seem to *preclude* a *stressful experience,* however. Patients who were over 27 years of age, were currently or formerly married, had children, had no college education, and were diagnosed as personality disorders were unlikely to have distressing sexual or aggressive impulses conflictually mobilized in the therapeutic relationship. These older, less-well-educated housewives seem to be people whose emotional impulses are stably bound in relationships outside of psychotherapy. The probability that a patient would have a *stressful experience* was also reduced if her therapist came from a working-class background, and had not had personal psychotherapy.

The patients who were most likely to have a *dependent experience* in psychotherapy were over 36 years of age, married, and not currently employed. These patients were highly similar to those least likely to have a *stressful experience.* Patients whose therapists had children were also more likely to be included in type P-C. On the other hand, patients whose therapists came from small (one- or two-child) families were *less* likely to find therapy a *dependent experience.* In a similar vein, patients who had one sibling were also less likely to be in type P-C.

Only four patients in our sample had a predominantly *counter-dependent experience.* It was never the case that more than 50% of the patients in a subgroup were in this type. There were, however, some patient and therapist characteristics that decreased the likelihood of a *counter-dependent experience.* Patients who were youngest children and from large (three or more child) families were *unlikely* to have a *counter-dependent experience.* Patients whose therapists came from large (three or more child) families, and had less than six years of experience in the practice of psychotherapy, were also unlikely to have this experience. These findings suggest that the size of the sibship in which a person has been socialized is an important determinant of the expression of dependency in psychotherapy.

## SUMMARY

We have focused attention in this chapter on total patterns of experience in psychotherapy. Analysis of the profiles of patients resulted in the definition of four experience-types: *helpful experience, stressful experience, dependent experience,* and *counter-dependent experience.* The internal composition of these experience-types suggested that they might be viewed more generally as two pairs. One pair (*helpful/stressful*) seemed to reflect the reduction or mobilization of anxiety in the patient's experience during therapy sessions. The other pair (*dependent/counter-dependent*) appeared to reflect the patient's acquiescence to, or resistance against, the therapist's influence. A second line of evidence, derived from analyses of the personal and social characteristics of patients and therapists in relation to the four experience-types, tended to reinforce this conception of two dichotomous pairs. Patients and therapists who were associated with patients' *dependent experience* usually had characteristics opposite to those of patients and therapists associated with *counter-dependent experience;* e.g., patients and therapists from larger families were associated with the former type, whereas those from smaller families were associated with the latter type.

Certain personal and social characteristics also differentially predicted the type of experience a patient would tend to have during therapy sessions. For example, if a woman were married and/or over 36 years of age, she was most likely to have a *dependent experience* and not a *stressful experience;* if formerly married and/or between 27 and 36 years old, she was most likely to have a *helpful experience* and not a *stressful experience.* The *stressful experience* type, although not frequent, tended to be associated with women who were unmarried and under 27 years of age. Although the evidence is as yet rather fragmentary, it seems clear that the personal and social characteristics of patients and therapists are important determinants of the patients' experience of psychotherapy. Further data and discussion about the impact of these characteristics are presented in Chapters 10 and 12.

# Chapter 9

# Dimensions of Therapist Experience

From a traditional viewpoint, the significance of the therapist's experience of therapy is secondary to that of the patient. The patient is the "official" focus of interest in the therapeutic enterprise; it is her private experiences that are expressed, probed, and analyzed. Furthermore, the patient's experience is the target at which therapy is aimed. But for all that the therapist's experiences are kept to the sidelines, masked in the reserve of the therapist role, they are part of the therapeutic process and an important object of study. Therapists' experiences form the source of most theoretical formulations about psychotherapy and personality. Learning how therapists cognitively structure their subjective participation in the therapeutic process therefore becomes a major step in refining our present theories.

Another reason for studying the therapist's experience relates more directly to clinical practice. For the most part, knowledge about the patient's experience in therapy is based on the *therapist's* experience of the patient. Knowledge of the patient's experience is thus filtered through the therapist's perceptions, and the therapist who seeks to act on his understanding of what his patient is experiencing is faced with the difficult task of judging the extent to which his perception is a projected or a veridical image. We have recorded and analyzed the patient's experiences independently of the therapist's. We can therefore determine the salient dimensions of therapists' experiences and correlate them with the concurrent experiences of their patients. The resulting estimate of congruence or discrepancy between the therapist's perception of his patient and her own perception of herself can serve as a useful guide and corrective to his clinical intuition (see Chapter 13).

This chapter and the next present our findings on the dimensions, the types, and the correlates of therapists' experiences. The global dimensions of individual differences among therapists, presented in this chapter, were derived by the factor analytic procedures described in Chapter 4.

Eleven factorial dimensions of global therapist experience were empirically determined. The variables that compose these dimensions are facet factors derived from the previous level of analysis. (These facet factors and the items that compose them are listed in Appendix G.) Therapist experience dimensions always represent the therapists' perceptions of therapeutic process, even when the patient is the target. To denote this fact, therapist experience dimensions are prefixed with the letter T. The eleven dimensions were identified as follows:

T-I: Depressive stasis vs. Effective movement
T-II: Sympathetic involvement vs. Uncaring detachment
T-III: Strengthening defenses vs. Stimulating insight
T-IV: Calm frank facilitation vs. Intent supportiveness
T-V: Uneasy intimacy
T-VI: Engagement with a patient perceived as enthusiastic and open vs. Reserve with a patient perceived as feeling uncomfortably involved and mistrustful
T-VII: Cheerful warmth
T-VIII: Collaborative relationship vs. Abiding a patient perceived as passively dependent
T-IX: Unresponsive activity with a patient seen as passively dependent
T-X: Felt mutual failure
T-XI: Erotic countertransference.

## THE DIMENSIONS OF THERAPIST EXPERIENCE

### *T-I: Depressive Stasis vs. Effective Movement*

This dimension of therapist experience reflects the mood and momentum of the therapeutic relationship as alternatively bogged down in mutual depression or progressing in effective collaboration. The variables that defined T-I are shown in Table 43. At one pole (T-I+[1]), the

---

[1] The designation "+" or "−" for bipolar dimensions is purely arbitrary (as is the numbering of the factors) and does not reflect an evaluation of the quality of experience at each pole.

## TABLE 43

### T-I+: Depressive Stasis: Resignation Over Impasse with a Patient Perceived as Depressed and Narcissistic

|  | Loading | $h^2$ |
|---|---|---|
| Therapist views patient as: | | |
| T-13  feeling *depressed* | .81[a] | .78 |
| T-41  not making *therapeutic progress* | .76 | .88 |
| T-5   talking about *somatic and domestic concerns* | .72 | .76 |
| T-9   feeling *anxious* | .62 | .82 |
| T-34  wanting to *gain sympathy* | .52 | .81 |
| T-24  relating with *unresponsive activity* | .41 | .94 |
| T-42  not *communicating effectively* | .37 | .77 |
| T-37  wanting to *obstruct therapy* | .35 | .79 |
| Therapist views himself as: | | |
| T-22  feeling *resigned* | .77 | .76 |
| T-43  not *motivated and understanding* | .53 | .78 |
| T-31  relating *frankly* | .39 | .77 |

### T-I−: Effective Movement: Sense of Progress with a Patient Seen as Responsive and Motivated

|  | Loading | $h^2$ |
|---|---|---|
| Therapist views patient as: | | |
| T-13  not feeling *depressed* | .81 | .78 |
| T-41  *making therapeutic progress* | .76 | .88 |
| T-5   not talking about *somatic and domestic concerns* | .72 | .76 |
| T-9   not feeling *anxious* | .62 | .82 |
| T-34  wanting to *work at problems* | .52 | .81 |
| T-24  relating with *mutuality* | .41 | .94 |
| T-42  *communicating effectively* | .37 | .77 |
| T-37  wanting to *gain insight* | .35 | .79 |
| Therapist views himself as: | | |
| T-22  not feeling *resigned* | .77 | .76 |
| T-43  *motivated and understanding* | .53 | .78 |
| T-31  relating *supportively* | .39 | .77 |

[a] Italicized loadings indicate variables used in scoring each global experience factor.

patient's mood was perceived as primarily one of depression and anxiety. The patient was seen as feeling sad, bored, dull, and discouraged; anxious, tired, and worried. Her conversation focused heavily upon somatic concerns, such as body functions and physical symptoms, and upon household activities and responsibilities. She was seen as seeking sympathy, attention, affection, and advice from the therapist, in contrast to working toward resolution of her emotional problems. With all of this apparent distress, she seemed essentially unable to express or deal with her real concerns. Her emotions, although evident to the therapist, were felt to be narcissistically unavailable to his influence. Although verbally active in the sessions, she was not seen as affectively responsive or involved. The therapist viewed the patient as poorly motivated for attending sessions, and as not making much noticeable progress in them.

The therapist's own mood of resignation appeared largely responsive to his perception of the type of patient with whom he was working. His salient feelings were boredom and discouragement. He did not look forward with much anticipation to sessions with the patient, nor did he feel himself able to develop much useful rapport or understanding with her. His post-session evaluations were generally low, and his manner of relating during their sessions tended to be openly evaluative rather than supportive. There was a symmetrical quality to the therapist's perception of his own and his patient's mood and motivation, a sense that they were going through the motions of therapy without really being involved or getting anywhere.

At the opposite pole $(T-I-)$, the therapist saw the patient as strongly motivated to work toward a resolution of her emotional problems, and as progressing readily toward that goal. He felt she was eager to come to their sessions, and that she was able to focus on and express her concerns effectively. The patient was viewed as relating in an affectively responsive manner, and as sustaining a good rapport in the relationship. In response to this perception of the patient, the therapist tended to look forward more positively to their sessions and to make more positive post-session evaluations. His own style of relating was more empathic, supportive, and emotionally responsive. The total impression conveyed by the therapist's perception was one of an effective therapeutic alliance between the patient and himself.

Our interpretation of this dimension is that it reflects the therapist's reaction to the patient's approach to therapy. The patient who attributes her depressive and anxious feelings to external influences, and who seems to view therapy as an opportunity to get sympathy, elicits from the therapist a sense of disinterest and resignation. On the other hand, a patient who appears committed to working on her problems, responds affectively, and seems to make progress engages the therapist's interest and encouragement. The sense of the whole dimension develops around the therapist's perception of the patient's ability or inability to form a meaningful object-relationship with him and his concomitant of movement or impasse.

### T-II: *Sympathetic Involvement vs. Uncaring Detachment*

A second dimension of therapist experience reflects the felt quality of the therapist's involvement with his patient. The variables that define T-II are shown in Table 44. In T-II+, the therapist felt involved, pleased, and interested. His manner of relating was affectively responsive, frankly evaluative, and mutually influencing. He looked forward

### TABLE 44

### T-II+: Sympathetic Involvement: Active Supportive Involvement with a Patient Seen as Anxious and Communicative

|  |  | Loading | $h^2$ |
|---|---|---|---|
| Therapist views patient as: |  |  |  |
| T-42 | communicating *effectively* | .60[a] | .77 |
| T-9 | feeling *anxious* | .53 | .82 |
| T-4 | not talking about *social and vocational concerns* | .52 | .91 |
| T-3 | not talking about *familial and therapeutic concerns* | .46 | .75 |
| T-35 | wanting to *gain support and relief* | .40 | .74 |
| Therapist views himself as: |  |  |  |
| T-18 | feeling *involved* | .85 | .85 |
| T-39 | aiming to provide an *active supportive relationship* | .82 | .82 |
| T-29 | not relating with *impassive control* | .77 | .88 |
| T-43 | *motivated and understanding* | .60 | .78 |
| T-32 | relating with *affective involvement* | .49 | .83 |

### T-II−: Uncaring Detachment: Passive-Aggressive Response to a Patient Felt to be Intellectualizing

|  |  | Loading | $h^2$ |
|---|---|---|---|
| Therapist views patient as: |  |  |  |
| T-42 | not *communicating effectively* | .60 | .77 |
| T-9 | not feeling *anxious* | .53 | .82 |
| T-4 | talking about *social and vocational concerns* | .52 | .91 |
| T-3 | talking about *familial and therapeutic concerns* | .46 | .75 |
| T-35 | not wanting to *gain support and relief* | .40 | .74 |
| Therapist views himself as: |  |  |  |
| T-18 | feeling *withdrawn* | .85 | .85 |
| T-39 | not aiming to provide an *active supportive relationship* | .82 | .82 |
| T-29 | relating with *impassive control* | .77 | .88 |
| T-43 | not *motivated and understanding* | .60 | .78 |
| T-32 | relating with *unresponsive activity* | .49 | .83 |

[a] See note to Table 43.

with pleasant anticipation to his meetings with the patient, felt that he understood her well, and had a good rapport with her. His aims in the session were educative and supportive, viewed as operating through the medium of the immediate personal relationship between the patient and himself. He sought to help his patient learn new or better ways of dealing with people and problems, to support his patient's self-esteem, to engage her in an honest person-to-person relationship, and to relieve her tension and anxiety. The patient was seen as able to communicate her concerns to the therapist freely and effectively, but as experiencing a considerable amount of anxiety. The therapist saw her as chiefly motivated to win him as an ally and to get respite or relief from distressing external involvements and pressures. She was also seen as seeking an opportunity to give vent to suppressed feelings, and to get advice from the therapist. The therapist saw the patient's relationship with him as a safe haven for her, and saw himself as a supportive mentor. He did not hesitate to criticize when necessary, but did so in a way that aimed at helping the patient improve her ability to cope with her life.

At the opposite pole of this factor (T-II−), the therapist felt detached, dull, repelled, and withdrawn, and related to the patient in an impassively controlling or passive-aggressive manner. The therapist also looked forward with reluctance to his sessions with the patient, and felt little rapport with her. The patient was seen as talking intellectually about her life. She was seen as exhibiting little or no anxiety or motivation to gain support and relief, and as having a difficult time talking freely about her felt concerns.

In this dimension of experience, the therapist's own behavior and feelings were most salient. The total dimension shows the therapist as approaching or retreating from the patient. This contrasts with T-I (*depressive stasis vs. effective movement*), in which the therapist's perception of the patient's approach to therapy was more focal. T-II defines one particular manner of fulfilling, or failing to fulfill, the therapist role. In fulfilling his role, the therapist experienced himself as the patient's backstop, the man in her corner who salves her wounds, cheers her up, and offers advice and encouragement. This therapeutic stance most naturally fits the struggling, manifestly anxious patient who is beleaguered by difficulties in her life situation. The pronounced failure of the therapist to take this stance occurs in an unpleasant emotional context, amid efforts at withdrawal and control on his part.

### T-III: Strengthening Defenses vs. Stimulating Insight

Whereas T-II stressed the therapist's sense of helpfulness or inability to help, T-III emphasizes the kind of help the therapist aims to offer (see Table 45). His intentions appear to range along a continuum of confrontation from passive non-directive support to active experiential

## TABLE 45

### T-III+ : Strengthening Defenses: Soothing Attitude Toward Perceived Patient Distress

| | | Loading | $h^2$ |
|---|---|---|---|
| Therapist views patient as: | | | |
| T-1 | talking about *anger, intimacy, and competence in personal relationships* | .84 [a] | .89 |
| T-4 | talking about *social and vocational concerns* | .47 | .91 |
| T-2 | talking about *heterosexual concerns* | .46 | .78 |
| T-35 | wanting to *gain support and relief* | .36 | .74 |
| Therapist views himself as: | | | |
| T-38 | aiming to provide *emotional stability* | .81 | .90 |
| T-30 | relating with *attentive compliance* | .44 | .80 |
| T-19 | feeling *calm* | .36 | .76 |

### T-III− : Stimulating Insight

| | | Loading | $h^2$ |
|---|---|---|---|
| Therapist views patient as: | | | |
| T-1 | not talking about *anger, intimacy, and competence in personal relationships* | .84 | .89 |
| T-4 | not talking about *social and vocational concerns* | .47 | .91 |
| T-2 | not talking about *heterosexual concerns* | .46 | .78 |
| T-35 | not wanting to *gain support and relief* | .36 | .74 |
| Therapist views himself as: | | | |
| T-38 | aiming to provide *experiential insight* | .81 | .90 |
| T-30 | relating with *collaborative intervention* | .44 | .80 |
| T-19 | feeling *intent* | .36 | .76 |

[a] See note to Table 43.

probing. His choice in this regard seemed to be a function of the amount of distress perceived in the patient. At T-III+, the patient was seen as expressing a large variety of concerns. Chief among these were angry and aggressive feelings; inadequacies, fears, and successes; feelings about being close to or needing someone; feelings and attitudes toward self; and strange or unusual experiences. The therapist viewed the patient as seeking support and relief and felt that she was coping poorly with her problems.

The most salient feature of the therapist's experience in T-III+ was his aim of affording relief to the patient. The therapist's goals involved supporting the patient's defenses, relieving her tension and anxiety, helping her gain better self-control, and orienting her to reality more effectively. These aims all involve an attempt to stabilize the patient's emotional equilibrium and to forestall deteriorative trends. The therapist's manner in implementing this contrasts strikingly with the active supportive style noted in T-II+. In T-III+, the therapist described himself as attentive and compliant in relating to the patient, rather than as actively collaborative. The calm mood he reported was congruent with his aim and manner.

T-III— gives no positive indication of the patient's participation. Indirectly, we gather that the patient was *not* preoccupied by the variety of concerns manifested at T-III+, nor viewed by the therapist as in need of emotional support and relief. He therefore seemed to feel free to probe the patient's feelings to stimulate the development of further insight. In doing so, he felt intent rather than calm, and related in an actively collaborative manner.

Factor III focuses on the degree of *provocativeness* in the therapist's participation. T-III+ represents a dampening of provocativeness in an attempt to avoid further upsetting the patient's emotional balance; T-III— depicts a heightening of provocativeness in an attempt to push the patient into new depths of feeling and awareness. In this latter orientation, the therapist tended to evaluate the patient's emotional balance positively, that is, to see her as someone who was "able to take it."

### T-IV: Calm Frank Facilitation vs. Intent Supportiveness

This dimension of therapist experience reflects the therapist's approach to the patient as a function of the patient's resistance or accessibility in the therapeutic relationship. The defining variables are shown in Table 46. At T-IV+, the goals of the therapist were to help the patient overcome her resistance and defensiveness to get to what was of real concern to her and to give her a more realistic orientation to social situations. The therapist reported feeling calm in working toward these goals. His manner of relating to the patient was supportive but critical, correcting but friendly, yet reserved and distant. This reserve does not reflect a lack of activity or affect on his part, but indicates instead a disinclination either to provide structure for the patient or to accept her attempts to structure the situation. The patient was seen by the therapist as withdrawing from interaction, as negative and hostile, and as controlling. Their conversation was focused on the therapeutic relationship and on familial relationships past and present. She also was viewed as feeling relaxed, calm, and confident. Although the topics discussed might be construed as therapeutically appropriate, the therapist's view of his patient's affective tone and manner of relating suggests that there was not an effective therapeutic alliance.

### TABLE 46

### T-IV+ : Calm Frank Facilitation

|  |  | Loading | $h^2$ |
|---|---|---|---|
| Therapist views patient as: |  |  |  |
| T-27 | relating with *hostile withdrawal* | .49[a] | .64 |
| T-4 | not talking about *social and vocational concerns* | .44 | .91 |
| T-3 | talking about *familial and therapeutic concerns* | .41 | .75 |
| T-11 | feeling *relaxed* | .35 | .80 |
| Therapist views himself as: |  |  |  |
| T-40 | aiming to provide *facilitation and clarification* | *.84* | .89 |
| T-19 | feeling *calm* | *.70* | .76 |
| T-31 | relating *frankly* | *.64* | .77 |
| T-33 | relating with *animated responsiveness* | .40 | .78 |

### T-IV− : Intent Supportiveness

|  |  | Loading | $h^2$ |
|---|---|---|---|
| Therapist views patient as: |  |  |  |
| T-27 | not relating with *hostile withdrawal* | .49 | .64 |
| T-4 | talking about *social and vocational concerns* | .44 | .91 |
| T-3 | not talking about *familial and therapeutic concerns* | .41 | .75 |
| T-11 | feeling *embarrassed* | .35 | .80 |
| Therapist views himself as: |  |  |  |
| T-40 | not aiming to provide *facilitation and clarification* | *.84* | .89 |
| T-19 | feeling *intent* | *.70* | .76 |
| T-31 | relating *supportively* | *.64* | .77 |
| T-33 | relating with *independence* | .40 | .78 |

[a] See note to Table 43.

At the opposite pole (T-IV−), the therapist reported feeling intent rather than calm, and relating in a supportive, empathic, and friendly, although independent, manner. There was little overt attempt to facilitate the patient's involvement, and little perception of the patient as being negativistic or tending to withdraw from interaction. The patient, instead, was viewed as occupied with social activities and relationships, and experiences with others at work or at school. She also was seen as feeling embarrassed, shy, and tense.

Taken together, the poles of T-IV reflect the therapist's response to the patient's perceived withdrawal or lack of withdrawal in the therapeutic relationship. When the therapist saw the patient as accessible (not hostile and withdrawn), he responded with empathic attention to her concerns. When, on the other hand, he saw the patient as resistive, he responded interpretively in an attempt to facilitate a more productive involvement.

### T-V: Uneasy Intimacy

In T-V, the therapist appeared to experience an uncomfortably personal response to the seductive provocations of his patient (see Table 47). The patient was viewed by the therapist as tending to feel playful, sympathetic, likeable, interested, secure, trusting, accepted, tender, and alert. This pattern of feeling gains in clarity when seen in conjunction with the provocative aims also discerned in the patient's behavior. These goals included gaining knowledge of the therapist's personal life; punishment of the therapist; provocation of the therapist to criticism or anger; seductive provocation of the therapist; testing the limits of the therapist and the therapy relationship; and withdrawal or evasion of contact with the therapist. The resulting image suggests an attempt to manipulate the therapist into a personal involvement that is usually felt to be incompatible with the therapist role.

The therapist's response to this seemingly innocent although provocative behavior was primarily affective. The therapist reported feeling embarrassed, playful, intimate, attracted, satisfied, and tense. He also tended to report feeling tender, energetic, alert, close, sympathetic, and involved. These feelings indicate that the therapist was far from immune to the patient's provocative conduct. He found himself drawn into the patient's playful spiderweb, although clearly not without misgivings manifested in his feeling embarrassed and tense. This factor bears a

### TABLE 47

**T-V: Uneasy Intimacy: Uneasy Nurturant Warmth with a Patient Perceived as Warm and Seductive**

|  | Loading | $h^2$ |
|---|---|---|
| Therapist views patient as: | | |
| T-14    feeling *flirtatious* | .82[a] | .81 |
| T-7    feeling *trusting warmth* | .66 | .75 |
| T-36    wanting to *provoke the therapist* | .63 | .85 |
| Therapist views himself as: | | |
| T-16    feeling *uneasy intimacy* | .82 | .82 |
| T-23    feeling *nurturant warmth* | .44 | .90 |

[a] See note to Table 43.

strong resemblance to the patient experience defined in factor P-III, *toying with the therapist* (see Chapter 7).

### T-VI: Engagement with a Patient Perceived as Enthusiastically Accepting and Open vs. Reserve with a Patient Perceived as Feeling Uncomfortably Involved and Mistrustful

A sixth dimension reflects the therapist's perception of the patient as either enthused and personally open or ambivalently involved and mistrustful (see Table 48). At one pole (T-VI+), the patient was perceived as relating with enthusiastic acceptance, i.e., as being animated, enthusiastic, excited, friendly, warm, and engaging. The patient was described as feeling relaxed, relieved, optimistic, effective, cheerful, etc., and as distinctly *not* feeling suspicious, frustrated, irritable, or inferior.

### TABLE 48

#### T-VI+: Engagement with a Patient Perceived as Enthusiastically Accepting and Open

|  | Loading | $h^2$ |
|---|---|---|
| Therapist views patient as: |  |  |
| T-25   *relating with enthusiastic acceptance* | .86[a] | .83 |
| T-10   not feeling *mistrustful* | .72 | .79 |
| T-2   talking about *heterosexual concerns* | .51 | .78 |
| T-11   feeling *relaxed* | .41 | .80 |
| T-6   feeling *good* | .39 | .86 |
| T-36   not wanting to *provoke the therapist* | .37 | .85 |
| Therapist views himself as: |  |  |
| T-33   relating with *animated responsiveness* | .56 | .78 |

#### T-VI−: Reserve with a Patient Perceived as Feeling Uncomfortably Involved and Mistrustful

|  | Loading | $h^2$ |
|---|---|---|
| Therapist views patient as: |  |  |
| T-25   relating with *ambivalent involvement* | .86 | .83 |
| T-10   feeling *mistrustful* | .72 | .79 |
| T-2   not talking about *heterosexual concerns* | .51 | .78 |
| T-11   feeling *embarrassed* | .41 | .80 |
| T-6   not feeling *good* | .39 | .86 |
| T-36   wanting to *personally provoke the therapist* | .37 | .85 |
| Therapist views himself as: |  |  |
| T-33   relating with *independence* | .56 | .78 |

[a] See note to Table 43.

The patient's conversation tended to focus on her relationship with spouse or boyfriend, sexual feelings and experiences, expectations of the future, and dreams and fantasies. From the therapist's viewpoint, the patient appeared to find therapy a happy experience, with a wholly positive impact upon her.

In contrast to this differentiated view of the patient, the therapist reported only that his style of participation was both actively and affectively responsive. No specific modes or directions of therapeutic activity were reported in association with this enthusiastically positive patient response. The therapist evidently saw the source of the patient's response as residing more within herself than in what he was doing for her. The only qualification to this latter notion is that the therapist was a fully responsive participant. This line of interpretation suggests a strong resemblance between T-VI+ and patient factor P-I, *therapeutic satisfaction,* described and discussed in Chapter 7. Both of these appear to reflect a process of positive transference in the patient.

In T-VI−, the patient was viewed as relating in a conflicted and ambivalent manner, but deeply feeling, stirred, and moved although expressively controlled. In addition, the therapist saw the patient's feelings as markedly suspicious, frustrated, irritable, inferior, and helpless, as well as embarrassed, shy, tense, and guilty. The apparent lack of openness and trust in the patient's relationship with the therapist was emphasized by a tendency to avoid discussion of heterosexual concerns, and to behave in a way that was felt to be personally provocative. That this mode of being with the therapist was far from pleasant for the patient (as the therapist reported it) was underscored by the tendency toward *not* "feeling good" (optimistic, effective, cheerful, confident, etc.). The therapist viewed himself as independent, uninfluenced, and self-determined. The quality of the patient's reaction, which has a paranoid flavor, seems again to have been largely conditioned by inner determinants rather than by the actions of the therapist. If, at T-VI+, the patient reacted as though she were once more in the healing presence of the "good parent," at T-VI− she reacted as if she were in the potentially harmful presence of the "bad parent."

Our interpretation of T-VI is cast in terms of the transference potential that the relationship to the therapist, in and of itself, holds for the patient. This is not the familiar erotic or competitive pattern that has its roots in the oedipal period of development. It seems, rather, to involve a pre-oedipal response to the therapist as a parent on whom one is dependent and to whom one comes for help. The mere presence of this earlier-experienced and more omnipotent parent conveys either a benign or a baleful influence. The benign influence is one that allows the parent to assuage a small child's hurt by "kissing it better." The baleful influence is one that permits the parent to frighten a child by looking at her hatefully or with malice. Re-experiencing such past encounters of early childhood, perhaps with partial or subtle support in the therapist's behavior, may be the source of this experiential dimension.

### T-VII: Cheerful Warmth

This dimension of therapist experience was primarily concerned with the therapist's mood in the relationship (see Table 49). The therapist feelings that most notably defined this dimension were cheerful, effective, optimistic, confident, pleased, and sympathetic. With somewhat lesser emphasis, the therapist reported feeling tender, energetic, alert, close, and involved. These positive indications of the therapist's mood were supplemented by the tendency *not* to report feeling physical discomforts, such as bowel or bladder tension, or feeling depressed, angry, and tense. Although the therapist was experiencing pleasant, kindly, and outgoing feelings, the patient was viewed as feeling rejected, inadequate, inferior, hurt, helpless, and guilty. That is, the patient was seen as feeling herself to be a poor ineffectual soul whom no one could want or respect. From his superior state, the therapist experienced a flow of good-natured caring toward his patient.

### T-VIII: Collaborative Relationship vs. Abiding a Patient Perceived as Assertively Narcissistic

T-VIII reflects the basic aim or thrust of the patient's motivation, as this was perceived by the therapist. This thrust was seen as moving in one of two opposed directions: toward a collaborative resolution of her problems, or toward an aggressive evasion of her problems (see Table 50). At T-VIII+, the therapist viewed the patient's behavior as actu-

### TABLE 49

**T-VII: Cheerful Warmth: Self-Confident Nurturant Warmth
with a Patient Seen as Feeling Inferior**

|  | Loading | $h^2$ |
|---|---|---|
| Therapist views patient as: |  |  |
| T-8 feeling *inferior* | .39 | .83 |
| Therapist views himself as: |  |  |
| T-15 feeling *good* | .82[a] | .85 |
| T-23 feeling *nurturant warmth* | .59 | .90 |
| T-21 not feeling *distress* | .46 | .63 |

[a] See note to Table 43.

TABLE 50

**T-VIII+: Collaborative Relationship: Responsive Intervention with a Patient Perceived as Wanting Insight and Relating Collaboratively**

| | Loading | $h^2$ |
|---|---|---|
| Therapist views patient as: | | |
| T-37   wanting to *gain insight* | .78[a] | .79 |
| T-24   relating with *mutuality* | .74 | .94 |
| T-28   relating with *collaboration* | .71 | .85 |
| T-6   not feeling *good* | .71 | .86 |
| Therapist views himself as: | | |
| T-30   relating with *collaborative intervention* | .56 | .80 |
| T-32   relating with *affective involvement* | .43 | .83 |
| T-33   relating with *animated responsiveness* | .37 | .78 |

**T-VIII—: Abiding a Patient Perceived as Assertively Narcissistic**

| | Loading | $h^2$ |
|---|---|---|
| Therapist views patient as: | | |
| T-37   wanting to *obstruct therapy* | .78 | .79 |
| T-24   relating with *unresponsive activity* | .74 | .94 |
| T-28   relating with *assertion* | .71 | .85 |
| T-6   feeling *good* | .71 | .86 |
| Therapist views himself as: | | |
| T-30   relating with *attentive compliance* | .56 | .80 |
| T-32   relating with *unresponsive activity* | .43 | .83 |
| T-33   relating with *independence* | .37 | .78 |

[a] See note to Table 43.

ated by a search for insight and better self-understanding. The concurrent perception of the patient as *not* feeling good (i.e., not feeling optimistic, effective, cheerful, confident, satisfied, etc.) lends an edge of authenticity or seriousness of motivation to the patient's insight-seeking orientation. The manner of the patient's behavior in relating to the therapist, in his view, also reinforces this impression of serious involvement and commitment. Her participation was seen as mutually influencing or sharing, as deeply feeling but expressively controlled, and as receptive. She was also seen as cooperative, although as somewhat restrained. This combination of motivation for insight, discomfort with self, availability of affect, and collaborative involvement in the therapeutic alliance defines by most of the usual criteria the patient for whom therapy is ideally suited. The therapist's style of participation was actively collaborative, feelingly involved, and fully responsive. The therapist tended to rate sessions at T-VIII+ as good therapy hours (see Chapter 6).

The other pole of this dimension (T-VIII−) showed the patient's behavior to be actuated (from the therapist's point of view) by such aims as simply filling time to get through the therapy session, and competitiveness with the therapist. The patient's aim seemed to be that of obstructing fruitful collaborative work. The patient's manner of behavior in relating to the therapist reflected this same orientation. The therapist described the patient as active but emotionally uninvolved, independent and uninfluenced, leading, and controlling. This active pattern of assertive resistance contrasts with the withdrawing resistance noted in T-IV+. The kind of affect the therapist perceived in the patient was the euphoric potency and narcissism associated with feeling "Good": optimistic, effective, cheerful, confident, satisfied, superior, energetic, likeable, triumphant, playful, alert. Apparently the resistance described here was not perceived by the therapist as having the hostile quality associated with the patient's withdrawal from interaction in T-IV+. The patient did not seem to withdraw so much as to narcissistically insulate herself from being affected by therapy, by being active and yet refusing to collaborate in an emotionally real or meaningful way. The pattern of therapist response reflected in T-VIII− was essentially one of detachment. The therapist reported himself to be receptive and compliant, but independent and businesslike. This combination of nondirective acceptance and "professionalism" suggests that the therapist tended to assume a strategy of waiting out the patient.

### T-IX: Unresponsive Activity with a Patient Seen as Passively Dependent

This dimension reflects the therapist's perception of the patient's dependency in the therapeutic relationship (see Table 51). The therapist described the patient as submissive, waiting for direction, and neutral in attitude. This compliant manner was motivated, in the therapist's view, by her desires to win the therapist as an ally, to get relief and respite from external pressures, and to get expert advice. There was some tendency to avoid discussion of heterosexual concerns. The therapist's evaluation of the patient's psychological functioning tended also to be low ($r = -.36$). The therapist's manner of relating was active but emotionally uninvolved, and independent. The therapist also tended *not* to report experiencing a need to relieve bowels or bladder, depression, anger, or tenseness. Thus, although the therapist responded actively to his passive dependent patient, he did not experience any personal involvement in the process.

## TABLE 51

### T-IX: Unresponsive Activity with a Patient Seen as Passively Dependent

|  |  | *Loading* | $h^2$ |
|---|---|---|---|
| Therapist views patient as: |  |  |  |
| T-26 | relating with *passive dependence* | *.73* [a] | .65 |
| T-35 | wanting to *gain support and relief* | *.49* | .74 |
| T-2 | not talking about *heterosexual concerns* | *.39* | .78 |
| Therapist views himself as: |  |  |  |
| T-32 | relating with *unresponsive activity* | *.41* | .83 |
| T-21 | not feeling *distress* | *.41* | .63 |

[a] See note to Table 43.

### T-X: Felt Mutual Failure

The tenth dimension reflects the therapist's sense of inefficacy in the treatment process (see Table 52). At the extreme, he felt that he was failing to respond effectively to a rather ineffectual-feeling patient. The therapist reported feeling disappointed, inadequate, frustrated, and apprehensive. This sharply dysphoric cluster centered on the apparent failure of the therapist's efforts and expectations concerning the therapy, and carried a note of anxiety with it. The therapist's sense of failure was supplemented by a view of himself as relating in an impassively controlling manner, rather than with genuine responsiveness. This manner included behavior that was impersonal, critical, inactive, restrained, and insistent. Thus, along with his feeling of failure, the therapist also felt himself caught in a somewhat passive-aggressive style of relating.

## TABLE 52

### T-X: Felt Mutual Failure: Sense of Failure with a Patient Perceived as Feeling Inferior

|  |  | *Loading* | $h^2$ |
|---|---|---|---|
| Therapist views patient as: |  |  |  |
| T-8 | feeling *inferior* | *.61* [a] | .83 |
| T-34 | wanting to *gain sympathy* | *.45* | .81 |
| T-25 | relating with *ambivalent involvement* | *.36* | .79 |
| Therapist views himself as: |  |  |  |
| T-20 | feeling a *sense of failure* | *.88* | .85 |
| T-29 | relating with *impassive control* | *.38* | .88 |

[a] See note to Table 43.

The patient was viewed as feeling rejected, inadequate, inferior, hurt, helpless, and guilty. This cluster of patient feelings might also be referred to as a sense of failure, reinforcing the impression of a symmetrical state of mutual failure. Curiously, patient and therapist were not seen as angry with each other, but each as angry with or blaming himself. The patient's affective experience was accompanied, in the therapist's judgment, by behavior activated by a wish to elicit sympathy, attention, and approval, and to avoid anxiety. The patient's manner of relating was seen as ambivalent, and moved but expressively controlled.

The presence of several bipolar variables in this factor suggests that an interpretation of the opposite end of the continuum might also be instructive. Such an interpretation is secondary, as none of these bipolar variables was salient. Nevertheless, a low score on T-X would indicate a marked absence of guilt or ambivalence in both patient and therapist, and a frankness or openly evaluative personal responsiveness in the therapist complementing a well-motivated and warmly accepting pattern of behavior in the patient. The total dimension thus defined seems to reflect the presence (or absence), in the therapist's experience, of a mutually guilty or intrapunitive orientation in both participants.

### T-XI: Erotic Countertransference

The final dimension concerned the therapist's feelings of disturbance over his sexual arousal in the relationship. The variables that defined T-XI are shown in Table 53. The principal feelings reported by the therapist were sexually aroused, irritable, thirsty, and, to a lesser extent, frustrated, hungry, and tired. The therapist also tended to report feeling depressed, angry, tense, and a need to relieve bowels and bladder. The patient, too, was seen as beset by her feelings while the therapist

### TABLE 53

### T-XI: Erotic Countertransference: Distressing Bodily Arousal with a Patient Perceived as Feeling Angry and Guilty

|  | Loading | $h^2$ |
|---|---|---|
| Therapist views patient as: | | |
| T-12 feeling *angry and guilty* | *.85* [a] | .89 |
| T-3 talking about *familial and therapeutic concerns* | .39 | .75 |
| T-11 feeling *embarrassed* | .36 | .80 |
| Therapist views himself as: | | |
| T-17 feeling *disturbing sexual arousal* | *.79* | .69 |
| T-21 feeling *distress* | .39 | .63 |

[a] See note to Table 43.

struggled with his. The therapist perceived the patient as feeling angry, guilty, triumphant, embarrassed, shy, and tense.[2] Thus, in addition to his awareness of his own bodily needs and feelings (including sexual arousal), the therapist felt that both he and his patient were unhappy with him. The source of this distress seemed to be the intrusion of his personal needs in a forceful way during the therapy sessions. Interestingly, these feelings occurred in the context of discussing familial and therapeutic relationships.

This pattern of perceptions suggests an erotic countertransference, probably accompanied by an erotic transference process in the patient. Although this transference-countertransference experience seemed to the therapist to be painful for both participants, there was a concurrent effort to focus on these feelings in the therapeutic dialogue, and to analyze them with reference to familial antecedents and the wishful impulses revealed in dream and fantasy material.

## THE STRUCTURE OF THERAPIST EXPERIENCE

Six of the eleven dimensions of therapist experience have been interpreted as bipolar factors. For purposes of discussion, the resulting seventeen patterns may be classified into four categories: *helping, dealing with difficult patients, nontherapeutic responses,* and *personal distress.* These four are not the only ways of grouping the patterns of therapist experience, but they encompass all the patterns and are clinically meaningful and relevant.

### Helping

Eight of the seventeen patterns of therapist experience showed ways in which psychotherapy seemed to be helpful to patients. These may be further divided according to whether the source of help, as viewed by the therapist, came principally from the therapist's participation, from the patient's participation, or from the interaction of the two participants.

Five patterns suggest that the primary source of help lay in the therapist's participation. These were:

T-II+ Sympathetic involvement: active supportive involvement with a patient seen as anxious and communicative.

---

[2] We know, too, from the correlation of patient and therapist facet factors that patients included sexual arousal in this cluster of feelings. This suggests that the sexual arousal indicated by the therapist in his report of this dimension may also have been present in the patient. There was no way for the therapist to report sexual arousal *per se* in the patient using the questionnaire provided him.

T-III+ Strengthening defenses: soothing attitude toward perceived patient distress.
T-III— Stimulating insight.
T-IV— Intent supportiveness.
T-VII Cheerful warmth: self-confident nurturant warmth with a patient seen as feeling inferior.

T-II+ and T-III— show the therapist taking an active approach toward the patient, the former to convey encouragement and advice, and the latter to deepen the patient's felt self-awareness. On the other hand, T-III+ shows the therapist as cautiously restricting his own activity and interventions. The patterns depicted in T-IV— and T-VII differ from these and from each other. In T-IV—, the therapist is seen as cultivating the friendly and supportive aspects of the relationship, i.e., as offering a positive and empathic response to the patient's concerns. In T-VII, the therapist seems to feel that his presence as a caring person is itself a benign influence upon the patient.

In contrast to these, two other patterns suggest that the therapist felt the help that the patient got was principally a function of the qualities she herself brought to therapy. These were:

T-I— Effective movement: sense of progress with a patient seen as responsive and motivated.
T-VI+ Engagement with a patient perceived as enthusiastically accepting and open.

In T-I—, the key quality perceived in the patient's participation was her ability to make a genuine emotional investment in the therapeutic relationship. The patient's emotional commitment seemed to be object-related rather than narcissistic, giving the patient an evident leverage in pursuing the understanding and resolution of her problems. In T-VI+, the patient apparently did not pursue and resolve her problems but found them magically gone. Here it seems that being in contact with the therapist was sufficient to confirm the patient's expectation of help from a powerful, benign, and trusted figure.

Finally, one pattern appeared to locate the primary source of help in the therapeutic relationship:

T-VIII+ Collaborative relationship: responsive intervention with a patient perceived as wanting insight and relating collaboratively.

This pattern focuses on the mutual involvement and collaborative effort of patient and therapist in the task of broadening the patient's effective self-understanding.

The fact that therapy is viewed as a helping experience in these eight patterns does not, of course, necessarily imply that the patient in any or all of these situations is actually being helped. The data in hand refer only to the therapist's perceptions of the psychotherapeutic process.

### Dealing with Difficult Patients

Three patterns represented the therapist's (more or less deliberately strategic) dealings with a difficult patient. These were:

T-VI+ Calm frank facilitation.
T-VI− Reserve with a patient perceived as feeling uncomfortably involved and mistrustful.
T-VIII− Abiding a patient perceived as assertively narcissistic.

In each, the therapist seemed to be attempting to cope with, or mitigate, a type of patient behavior that was sufficiently deviant from the norms of the patient role to make efforts at social control necessary. In T-IV+, the approach of the therapist to the wary, hostile, withdrawing patient seems to be "Come, let us reason together." In T-VI−, on the other hand, the therapist's reserve with the suspicious, uncomfortable patient seemed intended to allow the patient to test the situation to her satisfaction and gradually to overcome her discomfort and reservations. A more precipitous pursuit of the suspicious patient might conceivably frighten her off altogether. The attitude of the therapist toward the aggressively obstructive, narcissistic patient (T-VIII−) seemed to be one of waiting for the force of the patient's resistance to spend itself. When the resistive behavior has run its course, the patient might be amenable to influence; during its height, the narcissistic quality it has makes it impervious to intervention.

### Nontherapeutic Responses

Four patterns represented situations in which the therapist found himself responding in a nontherapeutic manner toward his patient. This sort of response suggests a difficult but not necessarily personally distressing impasse, due primarily to the therapist's having allowed himself to be maneuvered into a disadvantageous position. The four patterns were:

T-I+ Depressive stasis: resignation over impasse with a patient perceived as depressed and narcissistic.

T-II— Uncaring detachment: passive-aggressive response to a patient felt to be intellectualizing.

T-V Uneasy intimacy: uneasy nurturant warmth with a patient perceived as warm and seductive.

T-IX Unresponsive activity with a patient seen as passively dependent.

In T-I+, the therapist has become discouraged over the possibility of making effective progress with his patient, and seems to have caught her depressed mood. In T-II —, the therapist appeared to respond in an extremely nonsupportive, or even hostile, fashion to a patient with whom he felt little empathic rapport. In T-V, the therapist seemed to succumb with a mixture of pleasure and misgiving to the manipulative, seductive blandishments of his patient. Finally, in T-IX the therapist reacted with increased activity to the patient's passive dependent solicitation to be told what to do. This activity may have gratified the patient's wish for direction, but at the same time it seemed to be a defense on the therapist's part against the evocation of his own dependent needs. In each of these patterns, the therapist appears to have responded to a difficult patient, not with a technically correct intervention, but with a defensive personal response that failed to facilitate movement in the relationship.

### Personal Distress

Two patterns reflected situations in which the therapist became involved in ways that caused him to experience personal distress. In addition to offering a manifestly nontherapeutic response to the patient, the therapist appeared to have introduced aspects of his own patient vectors into the relationship. The two patterns were:

T-X Felt mutual failure: sense of failure with a patient perceived as feeling inferior.

T-XI Erotic countertransference: distressing bodily arousal with a patient perceived as feeling angry and guilty.

In T-X, the therapist appeared to fall into a pattern of self-rejection that suggests the irrational intrusion of superego impulses. In T-XI, inappropriate erotic and dependent needs of the therapist seemed to intrude. These countertransference reactions, although distressing to the therapist and an inevitable burden upon the therapeutic relationship, may not in themselves preclude an eventually effective therapeutic resolution.

In interpreting these dimensions, it is important to note once more that these do not represent all the possible patterns of therapist experience in the psychotherapeutic process. The inclusion of different therapists, or different patients, in the sample might well have produced a different set of factors. Moreover, we must have correspondingly greater sensitivity to this limitation with the therapist factors, as there was a small number of therapists surveyed. The factors described above represent the dimensions along which the therapists in this sample varied from one another in their experiences of a block of therapy sessions. The generalizability of these findings will be tested intuitively by other therapists who find these patterns of experience similar to their own, and will be tested empirically by the extension of the method we have described to different therapists in different clinical settings. We do feel, however, that most of the patterns described in this chapter will have appeared familiar to experienced therapists.

# Chapter 10

# Therapist Experience-Types and their Correlates

In this chapter, we focus on the total pattern of therapist experience, rather than on single dimensions. The total pattern of experience for each therapist can be represented by the profile of his scores on the set of eleven dimensions described in Chapter 9. Our principal interest here is the definition of therapist experience-types, and the study of these types in relation to the personal and social characteristics of the participants in psychotherapy.

The method for determining therapist experience-types was the same as that used to define patient experience-types in Chapter 8 (see Chapter 4 for details of method). A profile of scores on the global experience dimensions was constructed for each therapist, and groups or clusters of therapists were determined on the basis of similarity of profiles. A composite profile defining a distinctive type or pattern of total therapist experience was obtained from each cluster. Score profiles of therapists within each of these clusters were inspected to determine the dimensions that organized the cluster, i.e., which seemed to be consistently high or low. Two therapist experience-types were thus identified as:

T-A:  Helping experience
T-B:  Stressful experience.

## THERAPIST EXPERIENCE-TYPES

### T-A: Helping Experience

One group of therapists shared a pattern of experience distinguished by a warm and effective therapeutic engagement. T-A was defined by the *presence* of *effective movement* (T-I−), *sympathetic involvement* (T-II+), *engagement with a patient perceived as enthusiastic and open* (T-VI+), and by the *absence* of *felt mutual failure* (T-X), *erotic countertransference* (T-XI), and *uneasy intimacy* (T-VI). Scores on these six dimensions were distinctly higher or lower than scores on the other profile dimensions for therapists of type T-A. Ten of the fifteen [1] therapists who could be classified into a type found therapy to be a predominantly *helping experience*.

The core of the *helping experience* was the therapist's perception of himself and his patient as positively and comfortably involved with one another in a productive relationship. Therapy was seen as going well. The therapist was emotionally responsive in a way that was consistent with his therapeutic role; he felt sympathetic, supportive, and confident. He particularly did not experience feelings that put to question the professional basis of his involvement, such as excessive intimacy and nurturance, sexual or other physical arousal, and guilt toward the patient. Neither did he find himself in emotional retreat from the patient. From his own point of view, he seemed to have found an optimal balance of genuine involvement and professional objectivity. In addition, the patient was perceived as emotionally involved in a fashion consistent with the patient role, bringing feelings of anxiety and depression, and a desire to work them out, into a relationship where she felt relaxed and accepting. She, too, was not perceived as having feelings that made her involvement with the therapist difficult or problematic for him. She was neither seductively provocative nor overtly angry, nor did she narcissistically shield her feelings from the therapist's influence.

### T-B: Stressful Experience

The pattern of experience that distinguished the second group of therapists focused on their sense of difficulty in dealing with nontherapeutic personal reactions, and with uncooperative, discomforting patients. The profiles in T-B were organized by the following dimensions: *calm frank facilitation* (T-IV+), *reserve with a patient perceived as*

---

[1] One representative case was selected for each of the therapists who reported on more than one patient. Thus, the sample size for the typal analysis of therapist experience was seventeen, of whom fifteen proved classifiable.

*feeling uncomfortably involved and mistrustful* (T-VI—), *abiding a patient perceived as assertively narcissistic* (T-VIII—), *erotic countertransference* (T-XI), *uncaring detachment* (T-II—), and *felt mutual failure* (T-X). Five of the fifteen classifiable therapists found therapy to be a predominantly *stressful experience.*

The experiences that defined T-B were to a great extent the opposite of those that defined T-A. Thus, the core of the *stressful experience* appears to be an imbalance in the emotional relationship between patient and therapist. From the therapist's point of view, either he or his patient has become excessively or insufficiently involved. Although this state of affairs may bring considerable discomfort, it is worth noting that this pattern does not seem to preclude effective therapeutic movement. Therapists in this cluster did not feel themselves to be in control of the relationship, however, and tended to respond with defensive withdrawal.

Although 59% of the therapists in our sample found therapy to be an expectably *helping experience,* for a significant minority (29%) therapy became a *stressful experience.* This seems like a high proportion for a sample of experienced therapists. It is not yet clear whether this indicates a poor outcome or merely a difficult phase in the therapeutic process.

## CORRELATES OF THERAPIST EXPERIENCE-TYPES

How do the types of therapist experience relate to the individual characteristics of therapists and patients? Are certain types of experience more likely to occur for specific kinds of therapists or for therapists of specific kinds of patients? The data pertinent to this question are presented in Tables 54 and 55, the former showing the patient characteristics and the latter the therapist characteristics associated with therapist experience-types. Each of the characteristics surveyed is shown with its internal classification (as in Tables 41 and 42), with the number of therapists in each experience-type for each classification shown in the adjacent columns.

Patients of therapists who had a *helping experience* were most frequently diagnosed as anxiety reactions or as schizophrenics. Such patients probably exhibit high levels of manifest anxiety, to which therapists can relate their helping interventions. Therapists who had a *helping experience* were also more likely to be past the first year of treatment with the patient. This finding might be explained in two ways. It may be that only those cases where help is effectively given survive into the second year of treatment. Alternatively (although not incompatibly), it may be that the patient and therapist have learned to work together more effectively by the second year. The correlates of type T-A suggest that the therapist's *helping experience* is to some significant degree a function of the availability of the patient's anxiety in the context of a securely established therapeutic relationship.

Patients of therapists who had a *stressful experience* were disproportionately: between 20 and 26 years old; not mothers; Protestants; college graduates; and diagnosed as depressive reactions or personality disorders. Therapists who had a *stressful experience* were more often male, and from upper-middle or middle class backgrounds. Finally, therapists of type T-B were more likely to be in the first year of treatment with their patients. These factors point to several possible sources of stress for the therapist. The youthfulness, absence of strong emotional life commitments, and highly educated and presumably intelligent character of these women patients might well make them tempting targets of personal involvement for their male therapists. This suggestion finds support in the prominence of *erotic countertransference* (T-XI) in the profile of type T-B. Another possible source of stress for the therapist might be frustration encountered in working with patients diagnosed as depressive reactions or personality disorders, as these patients tend to be relatively unavailable for emotional involvement. An interesting point is that both types of therapist experience seem to be primarily functions of patient characteristics, rather than of therapist characteristics.

## PREDICTORS OF THERAPIST EXPERIENCE-TYPES

Which type of experience are therapists of certain characteristics likely to have? The previous section focused on a basically descriptive problem. In this section, the same data (Tables 54 and 55) are used to discover the personal and social characteristics that best predict each experience-type. As in Chapter 8, the analysis involved computation of the percentage of cases in each experience-type for each subclass of a background characteristic. It should be noted that, for this sample in general, the most likely therapist experience-type was *helping experience*. Only those personal and social characteristics that substantially improve the base-rate prediction [2] will be noted below.

### Helping Experience

Therapists who were most likely to find psychotherapy a *helping experience* were: female (86%); over 35 years of age (78%); parents (80%); and psychiatric social workers (100%). They tended to be

---

[2] Based on the fifteen classifiable therapists, 67% had a *helping experience* and 33% had a *stressful experience*.

## TABLE 54

### Number of Profiles of Each Therapist Type in Each of the Patient Background Groups

| Patient Background Groups | Therapist Experience-Types | | |
| | A | B | % [a] |
| --- | --- | --- | --- |
| **Age** | | | |
| 20-26 | 4 | 5 | 60 |
| 27-36 | 2 | 0 | 13 |
| 37-60 | 4 | 0 | 27 |
| **Marital status** | | | |
| Single | 4 | 3 | 47 |
| Married | 3 | 1 | 27 |
| Formerly married | 3 | 1 | 27 |
| **Parental status** | | | |
| No children | 4 | 5 | 60 |
| Children | 6 | 0 | 40 |
| **Employment** | | | |
| Employed | 9 | 5 | 93 |
| Not employed | 1 | 0 | 7 |
| **Social class of origin** | | | |
| Upper middle and middle | 2 | 2 | 27 |
| Lower middle | 3 | 1 | 27 |
| Upper lower | 3 | 2 | 33 |
| Lower and lower lower | 2 | 0 | 13 |
| **Education** | | | |
| High school graduate or less | 4 | 1 | 33 |
| Some college | 4 | 1 | 33 |
| College graduate or more | 2 | 3 | 33 |
| **Religion** | | | |
| Protestant | 2 | 3 | 33 |
| Catholic | 5 | 1 | 40 |
| Jewish | 2 | 1 | 20 |
| Other or none | 1 | 0 | 7 |
| **Family size** | | | |
| Only child | 1 | 0 | 7 |
| One sib | 3 | 2 | 33 |
| 2-3 sibs | 2 | 2 | 27 |
| 4 or more sibs | 4 | 1 | 33 |
| **Birth order** | | | |
| Oldest | 3 | 3 | 40 |
| Middle | 4 | 1 | 33 |
| Youngest | 3 | 1 | 27 |

TABLE 54 (continued)

| Patient Background Groups | Therapist Experience-Types | | |
|---|---|---|---|
| | A | B | %[a] |
| **Age at family disruption** | | | |
| Under 5 | 2 | 0 | 13 |
| 6-10 | 2 | 0 | 13 |
| 11-15 | 0 | 0 | 0 |
| 16+, or never | 6 | 5 | 73 |
| **Diagnosis** | | | |
| Depressive reaction | 1 | 2 | 20 |
| Anxiety reaction | 3 | 1 | 27 |
| Personality disorder | 1 | 2 | 20 |
| Schizophrenia | 5 | 0 | 33 |
| **Previous psychotherapy** | | | |
| Yes | 3 | 1 | 27 |
| No | 7 | 4 | 73 |
| **Weeks of current therapy** | | | |
| 1-26 weeks | 4 | 2 | 40 |
| 27-52 weeks | 0 | 2 | 13 |
| 53 or more weeks | 6 | 1 | 47 |
| **Number of cases** | 10 | 5 | |

[a] % based on 15 classified therapists.

later born children (78%), with two or more siblings (78%), from families of lower-middle or upper-lower socioeconomic status (83%). These therapists appear to be mature women in whom the maternal component of feminine character has been maximized, and the narcissistic component minimized (Deutsch, 1945). We presume that being a later born child in a large family of lower socioeconomic status would tend to inhibit rather than encourage the expression of narcissistic traits. It seems likely that the basic emotional orientation of such people *is* toward helping others.

The probability of a therapist's having a *helping experience* was also enhanced if the patient was (in addition to being a woman) over 26 years old (100%), a mother (100%), and diagnosed as an anxiety reaction or schizophrenic (89%). Other patient characteristics included: being later born (78%); having four or more siblings (80%); having experienced familial disruption as a child (100%); being Catholic (83%); and not being a college graduate (80%). The implication is that patients with these characteristics are more readily helped. They are older and more settled in their lives; they come from more overtly disturbed family

TABLE 55

## Number of Profiles of Each Therapist Type in Each of the Therapist Background Groups

| Therapist Background Groups | Therapist Experience-Types | | |
| --- | --- | --- | --- |
| | A | B | % [a] |
| **Age** | | | |
| 29-35 | 3 | 3 | 40 |
| 36 or over | 7 | 2 | 60 |
| **Marital status** | | | |
| Single | 4 | 2 | 40 |
| Married | 3 | 2 | 33 |
| Formerly married | 3 | 1 | 27 |
| **Parental status** | | | |
| No children | 6 | 4 | 67 |
| Children | 4 | 1 | 33 |
| **Social class of origin** | | | |
| Upper middle and middle | 5 | 4 | 60 |
| Lower middle and upper lower | 5 | 1 | 40 |
| **Religion** | | | |
| Protestant | 3 | 1 | 27 |
| Catholic | 0 | 1 | 7 |
| Jewish | 4 | 1 | 33 |
| Other or none | 3 | 2 | 33 |
| **Sex** | | | |
| Male | 4 | 4 | 53 |
| Female | 6 | 1 | 47 |
| **Family size** | | | |
| Only child | 1 | 2 | 20 |
| One sib | 2 | 1 | 20 |
| Two or more sibs | 7 | 2 | 60 |
| **Birth order** | | | |
| Oldest | 3 | 3 | 40 |
| Middle | 4 | 1 | 33 |
| Youngest | 3 | 1 | 27 |
| **Profession** | | | |
| Psychiatry | 5 | 4 | 60 |
| Psychology | 1 | 1 | 13 |
| Social work | 4 | 0 | 27 |
| **Years of experience** | | | |
| 0-5 years | 5 | 2 | 43 |
| 6 or more years | 5 | 3 | 57 |
| **Personal psychotherapy** | | | |
| Yes | 8 | 3 | 73 |
| No | 2 | 2 | 27 |
| **Number of cases** | 10 | 5 | |

[a] % based on 15 classified therapists.

backgrounds, and are more manifestly anxious; their later born position in large families (as with the therapists) probably discouraged the development of narcissistic traits.

A final factor was time in treatment. Having gone beyond the first year of therapy with a patient made it likely (86%) that the therapist would have a *helping experience*.

### Stressful Experience

Therapist type T-B was predicted by having patients who were: in the second six months of their current treatment (100%); diagnosed as depressive reactions or personality disorders (67%); between 20 and 26 years of age (56%); not mothers (56%); Protestants (60%); and college graduates (60%). These figures are substantially higher than the base rate prediction of 33% for type T-B. Strikingly, there were no therapist characteristics that predicted a *stressful experience* for the therapist. It was the patient, and the period of treatment, that appeared to determine this type of therapist experience. (Our finding may offer some solace to the therapist who finds himself personally distressed in dealing with a patient.) This troubling situation is likely to occur after the initial phase of therapy, but before a long-standing working alliance has been achieved. It is also more likely to occur with a highly educated, emotionally unsettled but interpersonally unavailable, young woman. Such patients were also more likely themselves to find therapy a *stressful experience* (see Chapter 8, type P-B).

### SUMMARY

An analysis of profiles of therapist global dimensions resulted in the discrimination of two clusters defined by relatively polar types of experience. *Helping experience* for therapists centered on the perception of a gratifying, productive, and mutually comfortable involvement, achieved by the successful balancing of emotional responsiveness and professional objectivity. *Stressful experience* for therapists centered on a perceived failure to attain such a balance, resulting either in painful overinvolvement or in wearisome negotiation from defensively withdrawn emotional positions. Ten of the fifteen therapists in our sample formed the first cluster, and five composed the second. It was noted, however, that patient characteristics more frequently determined the type of experience a therapist had than did the personal or social characteristics of the therapist. Patients whose attributes generally pointed toward an anaclitic or interpersonally responsive emotional orientation were those with whom therapists tended to have a *helping experience*. By contrast, patients who seemed disposed toward a narcissistic or interpersonally unresponsive emotional orientation were those with whom therapists more frequently had a *stressful experience*. These same orientations among therapists had a noticeable, although slighter, effect on therapist experience-type. In general, the most difficult period of treatment was the second six months of the relationship. *Helping experience* was commoner in same-sex therapeutic dyads, whereas *stressful experience* was more common in cross-sex dyads.

Sample limitations (such as the absence of male patients and the relatively small number of therapists) require that these findings and the interpretations based on them be taken as tentative indications of how the questions posed in this chapter may be answered. In Chapter 12 we shall consider these questions further, bringing these data into relation with those reported in Chapter 8 as well as with those that emerge from the conjoint analysis of experience in patient-therapist dyads, to which we now turn.

*Chapter 11*

# Dimensions of Conjoint Experience: The Relationship as a Unit

The experiences of the psychotherapist form one part of the inner world of the therapeutic relationship; those of the patient form yet another part. Separate empirical analyses of the experiences of patients and of therapists have yielded a number of coherent and clinically meaningful patterns. These analyses have broadened and refined the understanding of patients' and therapists' experiences, and have placed that understanding on a more rigorous empirical foundation. Patients' and therapists' experiences, however, when considered in isolation from each other, do not provide a view of the psychotherapeutic relationship as a whole. To gain an understanding of the relationship *per se,* analysis must focus on the experiences of both participants simultaneously. In such an analysis, one looks for coherent patterns that meaningfully integrate the experiences of both participants. To our knowledge, a view of psychotherapy from this dyadic perspective has never been attempted.

The question we ask in this chapter is: How do the experiences of individuals participating in therapeutic dyads fit together? An answer to this question was sought through the correlation of patterns of patient experience with patterns of therapist experience in those cases where both participants completed Therapy Session Reports for the same sessions. 28 such cases were available in the present sample. Each of the patient-therapist pairs was scored on the eleven patient factors and the eleven therapist factors, and the intercorrelations between these 22 scores across the set of 28 matched pairs were computed.[1] The inter-correlation matrix was factor analyzed, and the resultant factors were rotated using the criterion of maximum common factors employed throughout this study.[2]

By the procedures described above, seven dimensions of conjoint experience were isolated and identified, as follows:

J-I:   Therapist agency vs. Therapist catalysis
J-II:  Patient agency vs. Patient passivity
J-III: Productive rapport vs. Unproductive contact
J-IV:  Ambivalent nurturance-dependence
J-V:   Healing magic vs. Uncomfortable involvement
J-VI:  Sympathetic warmth vs. Conflictual erotization
J-VII: Therapeutic Alliance vs. Defensive impasse.

The variables that compose these factors are the patient and therapist global experience dimensions presented in Chapters 7 and 9, respectively. The salient variables for each conjoint factor are shown in Tables 56 through 62. These tables are arranged so that all positive loadings, including positively loaded poles of the bipolar global experience factors, are grouped together; negative loadings, including negatively loaded poles of the bipolar global experience factors, are separately grouped. Conjoint factors are prefixed by the letter J to distinguish them from the patient (P) and therapist (T) factors that define them.

## THE DIMENSIONS OF CONJOINT EXPERIENCE

The first two dimensions of conjoint experience stand apart from the others in being defined primarily either by patient or by therapist experiences. These dimensions reflect the individual participant's approach to the enactment of his role in the therapeutic encounter. The remaining five dimensions are each defined by patient *and* therapist experiences. These represent five statistically independent aspects of the phenomenological interior of the therapeutic relationship.

### J-I: Therapist Agency vs. Therapist Catalysis

The first dimension of conjoint experience reflects the therapist's implicit conception of himself as a change agent (see Table 56). At J-I+, the therapist conceived his function as that of stimulating change

---

[1] Due to the relatively small subsample of matched-pair cases (in relation to the number of variables), the results of this analysis must be regarded as suggestive hypotheses that require replication.

[2] See Chapter 4 for a more detailed discussion of this analysis.

**TABLE 56**

**J-I+ : Therapist Agency**

|  |  | Loading | $h^2$ |
|---|---|---|---|
| Therapist experiences: |  |  |  |
| T-IV — | *intent supportiveness* | .82[a] | .79 |
| T-III — | *stimulating insight* | .70 | .78 |
| T-I + | *depressive stasis:* resignation over impasse with a patient perceived as depressed and narcissistic | .44 | .81 |

**J-I— : Therapist Catalysis**

|  |  | Loading | $h^2$ |
|---|---|---|---|
| Therapist experiences: |  |  |  |
| T-IV + | *calm frank facilitation* | .82 | .79 |
| T-III + | *strengthening defenses:* soothing attitude toward perceived patient distress | .70 | .78 |
| T-I — | *effective movement:* sense of progress with a patient seen as responsive and motivated | .44 | .81 |

[a] Italicized loadings indicate variables used in scoring each conjoint experience factor.

in the patient. A sense of concentration and of effort on the therapist's part was noticeable, as though he were attempting to produce some positive transformation through his own input. The analogy to a chemical agent, combining directly with another agent as an active ingredient in the process, suggests itself as a way of describing this mode of approach to the therapist role. The load of T-I+ (*depressive stasis*) at this pole of J-I seems to reflect the therapist's frustration with this approach in a situation where the patient's emotional unresponsiveness renders it ineffective.

At J-I—, by contrast, the therapist viewed himself primarily as the facilitator rather than the producer of change within the patient. He functioned as a kind of Socratic midwife, assisting in the patient's effort to give birth to a new self—clarifying, soothing, or appreciative, as needed. Reverting to our chemical analogy, this mode of approach to the therapist role may be described as essentially catalytic. A catalyst may accelerate or retard change, but does not produce it.

This bipolar dimension was significantly loaded exclusively by therapist global experience factors, despite the fact that both patient and therapist factors were incorporated in the basic matrix of intercorrelations. Thus, it appears that this stylistic difference in enacting the therapist role, however significant an issue it may be for professionals of differing temperament or ideology, makes little if any impact on the patient's experience of psychotherapy.

### J-II: Patient Agency vs. Patient Passivity

A second dimension reflects the patient's approach to her role as a help-taker in the therapeutic encounter (see Table 57). At J-II+, the patient is seen in active pursuit of the therapist as a source of help. The initiative clearly rested with her, whether she was pressing the therapist for more open and personal involvement (as in P-X and P-III) or was focusing on her inner experience (as in P-VIII−). In both cases, the therapist was seen as responding to the patient's input. When her attention was introspectively focused, the therapist was viewed as respond-

TABLE 57

**J-II+ : Patient Agency**

| | | Loading | $h^2$ |
|---|---|---|---|
| Patient experiences: | | | |
| P-X | *intrusiveness with a therapist felt to be tense and embarrassed* | .87 [a] | .90 |
| P-VIII − | *independent introspection with a therapist seen as collaborative* | .78 | .85 |
| P-III | *toying with the therapist:* seductiveness with a therapist perceived as feeling ineffective and withdrawn | .57 | .63 |
| Therapist experiences: | | | |
| T-V | *uneasy intimacy:* uneasy nurturant warmth with a patient perceived as warm and seductive | .61 | .61 |

**J-II− : Patient Passivity**

| | | Loading | $h^2$ |
|---|---|---|---|
| Patient experiences: | | | |
| P-X | little *intrusiveness with a therapist felt to be tense and embarrassed* | .87 | .90 |
| P-VIII + | *passive dependence with a therapist seen as directive* | .78 | .85 |
| P-III | little *toying with the therapist* | .57 | .63 |
| Therapist experiences: | | | |
| T-V | little *uneasy intimacy* | .61 | .61 |

[a] See note to Table 56.

ing collaboratively. When the patient's importunate demands or seductive energy were focused on him, however, the therapist appeared to react with some discomfort. The strength of this reaction is attested by the appearance of T-V (*uneasy intimacy*) on a dimension otherwise loaded exclusively by patient factors. The patient was intent upon, and evidently successful in, eliciting a degree of personal intimacy from the therapist that he found difficult to reconcile comfortably with the customary limitations of his professional role.

In the contrasting pattern defined by J-II−, the patient viewed herself as the passive target of the therapist's initiative and direction. Her approach to the help-taking role was receptive and submissive, with control over the process ceded entirely to the doctor. Thus, she was not only in need of help, but needed to have that help delivered to her by the therapist's intervention.

The dimension of *patient agency vs. patient passivity* both resembles and complements the previous dimension of *therapist agency vs. therapist catalysis*. Both involve the manner in which the persons fit themselves into their respective roles in therapy. The process is analogous to the professional actor's establishing a "character" by feeling his way into the part he is to play in a drama. For both patient and therapist, the stylistic options in their role enactment seem to hinge on the degree of self-assertiveness with which the part is engaged.

### J-III: Productive Rapport vs. Unproductive Contact

A third dimension includes both the patient's and the therapist's experience of the quality of personal communication in the therapeutic relationship (see Table 58). There is either a static or a flowing quality, a sense of alienation or of rapport, a feeling of missing or of resonating to each other's "vibrations." The resonant, flowing quality appears to result from a meshing of *expectations about* each other with *experiences of* each other; the static, alienated quality results from a failure of experience to fit expectation.

At J-III+, the patient and therapist seemed well pleased with the role qualifications of the other. The patient focused her concerns on work activities and relationships, and responded with acceptance to the professional, independent manner she perceived in the therapist. The therapist, on his part, felt that progress was being made and looked forward to contact with a patient whom he found adept at functioning in the patient role—i.e., able to work collaboratively, able to communicate freely and responsively, and interested in gaining insight into her problems.

At J-III−, neither the patient nor the therapist seemed to fit each

TABLE 58

### J-III+ : Productive Rapport

|  | Loading | $h^2$ |
|---|---|---|
| Patient experiences: |  |  |
| P-VII — *patient role acceptance:* career concerns and an accepting attitude with a therapist viewed as independent | .83[a] | .80 |
| Therapist experiences: |  |  |
| T-I — *effective movement:* sense of progress with a patient seen as responsive and motivated | .63 | .81 |

### J-III— : Unproductive Contact

|  | Loading | $h^2$ |
|---|---|---|
| Patient experiences: |  |  |
| P-VII + *patient role ambivalance:* domestic concerns and an ambivalent attitude with a seemingly persuasible therapist | .83 | .80 |
| Therapist experiences: |  |  |
| T-I + *depressive stasis:* resignation over impasse with a patient perceived as depressed and narcissistic | .63 | .81 |

[a] See note to Table 56.

other's ideal. To put the matter more bluntly, each fell far short of the other's ideal or even reasonable expectation. The patient, for her part, was absorbed in complaints of a domestic and somatic nature, and found the therapist all too agreeable to suit her taste. "He seems a nice enough person, to be sure, and after all he is the doctor, but frankly I don't see what talking to him can do to change things"—thus we imagine the patient's train of thought. From the therapist's point of view, on the other hand, the patient was hardly an ideal candidate for psychotherapy. "She is miserable and worried and beset with ills beyond her share, but she is emotionally inaccessible and unresponsive to all of my efforts to help her; we are getting nowhere at all"—so we imagine the therapist's train of thought. He saw the patient as locked in her depression, and had similarly resigned himself to being locked in a "weary, flat, stale, and unprofitable" relationship with her. What emerges in terms of conjoint experiential process is a rather severe mismatching of role expectations with the reality presented by the other. The patient did not qualify for the kind of help the therapist felt capable of giving, and the therapist did not qualify to give the kind of help the patient felt she needed.

Neither one seemed really relevant to the enterprise the other had in mind.

The total dimension defined by *productive rapport vs. unproductive contact* revolves around the issue of congruence vs. incongruence between the expectations held by patient and therapist concerning the behavior of the other person, and that person's actual (perceived) behavior. To the extent that congruence exists, the relationship is an effective vehicle for therapeutic interaction. To the extent that incongruence exists, no real communication takes place in the relationship. Each participant sends messages that are irrelevant or contrary to the expectations of the other. The failure to make meaningful contact in the relationship looks, from the therapist's perspective, like emotional narcissism or a lack of object-relatedness in the patient. In other words, the patient does not allow that the therapist is a real, present person with some potentially significant emotional connection to her. This does not prevent the patient from proclaiming her distress, but it makes the therapist irrelevant to her distress, and therefore makes her problems inaccessible to influence.

Congruence between role expectation and role performance is a significant issue in all interpersonal relationships. It seems to be the key to rapport based upon the mutual understanding that the other person will behave in ways that can be reliably anticipated and normatively approved.

### J-IV: Ambivalent Nurturance-Dependence

A fourth dimension of conjoint experience reflects the sense of acceptance, and the distribution of influence, in the therapeutic relationship (see Table 59). These interwoven themes define a monopolar continuum whose null point consisted of a relation of personal equality and mutual acceptance between patient and therapist, and whose extreme accentuated the dominant-nurturant and submissive-dependent qualities latent in their respective roles. At one end of the continuum, influence and openness to influence was mutual; at the other end, influence flowed only in one direction, but encountered a substantial undertow of inner resistance from both participants.

J-IV was characterized by a markedly passive-dependent patient, who strongly needed the therapist's initiative and tended to react submissively toward his actual or construed directions. There was a tendency in the patient to feel inferior and to expect rejection, and apparently to behave in a way that was self-rejecting and found rejection from others. Despite this set, the patient continued to search (without real hope of success) for approval and acceptance. The therapist reacted to the patient's ambivalent, dependent demands with attempted nurturance and then,

## TABLE 59

### J-IV: Ambivalent Nurturance-Dependence

| | | Loading | $h^2$ |
|---|---|---|---|
| Patient experiences: | | | |
| P-V | courting a therapist who is seen as rejecting | .65[a] | .72 |
| P-VIII + | passive dependence with a therapist seen as directive | .39 | .85 |
| Therapist experiences: | | | |
| T-IX | unresponsive activity with a patient seen as passively dependent | .81 | .75 |
| T-X | felt mutual failure: sense of failure with a patient perceived as feeling inferior | .70 | .66 |
| T-III + | strengthening defenses: soothing attitude toward perceived patient distress | .39 | .78 |

[a] See note to Table 56.

since the patient was unable to accept his nurturance, reacted to her frustration of his efforts with a self-rejecting sense of personal failure. Even when most active, the therapist did not seem to have his heart in it, and was not warm or affectively responsive. This suggests a forced attitude of nurturance that was perhaps as ambivalent and self-doubting as the patient's dependence. The patient seemed caught in a form of guilty taking and the therapist in a form of guilty giving that by its nature could not be truly satisfying to either. The therapist tended to view the patient as a fragile, threatened, needy individual who required careful and solicitous handling. This view matched the patient's own self-fulfilling attitude toward herself as a helpless and worthless person.

The antithesis to the process described as *ambivalent nurturance-dependence* emphasizes genuine give-and-take in a relationship between equals. There was an evident honesty of expression and personal openness that occurred between two persons who were accepting of each other and self-accepting. This mutual openness included, on the therapist's part, an inclination to be frankly evaluative and interpretively confronting, to "level" with the patient and let her know what was on his mind. The therapist's openness with the patient was matched by the patient's openness in making her inner feelings and sensations available to the therapist. Part of the therapist's confidence in the patient rested on his esteem for her as a person who could "take it," and who could therefore be treated with the genuine respect accorded to a peer. The patient's confidence in the therapist seemed, in a similar way, to rest upon his acceptance of her as an equal partner in the relationship, and his respect for her ability to participate as an adult.

*Ambivalent nurturance-dependence* appears to evolve from a basic distinction in the mode of exchange and influence possible in any intensive dyadic relationship. Two strands that are woven together in this dimension may be distinguished. The first is that of equality, or the acceptance of coordinate status, vs. inequality, or the acceptance of a subordinate/superordinate status arrangement. The second strand is that of personality vs. impersonality. This entails an engagement of self and other as two subjective and self-regarding participants in a mutual endeavor, in contrast to an approach to the other as a more or less powerful object that must be handled or manipulated appropriately. Equality and personality are joined at the null point of this dimension in a relationship of peerhood; inequality and impersonality are joined at the positive pole in a relationship of estrangement. In the context of the therapeutic relationship, peerhood manifested itself in the collaboration of adults in a person-to-person encounter, whereas estrangement manifested itself in the co-manipulation of a "pretend" parent and a "pretend" child.

### J-V: Healing Magic vs. Uncomfortable Involvement

A fifth dimension of conjoint experience reflected the degree of charismatic faith, of trusting enthusiasm or suspicious wariness, mobilized in the therapeutic encounter (see Table 60). J-V+ may be easily interpreted as a state of positive transference in the patient. An aura of beneficent healing power surrounds her experience of the therapist, and she feels happy, trusting, and well in his presence. Patients' and therapists' views of the situation showed considerable agreement. The patient felt eager to be with her therapist, euphoric in his presence, and thoroughly satisfied after their contact. The therapist seemed to embody the essential qualities a small child seeks in the "good parent": effective power and benevolent acceptance. This attitude in the distressed child creates the magical "kiss better" potential of the parent, i.e., the parent's ability to give effective balm simply by a symbolic act or gesture that indicates the balm is given. The therapist did not appear to hold such a view of himself, nor to attribute the patient's reaction primarily to his behavior. From the therapist's point of view, what stood out most about his part in the interaction was the responsiveness of his participation, his active and affective involvement. Assuming the therapist's benevolent intentions, this responsive involvement may provide sufficient support for the crystallization of a positive transference in the patient. The enthused satisfaction and happy response the patient evinced leads us to view the experiential process in operation here as a variety of the "kiss better" phenomenon.

## TABLE 60

### J-V+ : Healing Magic

|  |  | Loading | $h^2$ |
|---|---|---|---|
| Patient experiences: |  |  |  |
| P-I | *therapeutic satisfaction:* healing progress and good relationship with a therapist seen as pleased and helpful | *.85*[a] | .84 |
| Therapist experiences: |  |  |  |
| T-VI + | *engagement with a patient perceived as enthusiastically accepting and open* | .72 | .60 |
| T-V | little *uneasy intimacy* | .40 | .61 |

### J-V — : Uncomfortable Involvement

|  |  | Loading | $h^2$ |
|---|---|---|---|
| Patient experiences: |  |  |  |
| P-I | little *therapeutic satisfaction* | .85 | .84 |
| Therapist experiences: |  |  |  |
| T-VI — | *reserve with a patient perceived as feeling uncomfortably involved and mistrustful* | .72 | .60 |
| T-V | *uneasy intimacy:* uneasy nurturant warmth with a patient perceived as warm and seductive | .40 | .61 |

[a] See note to Table 56.

At J-V— the patient found little *therapeutic satisfaction* (P-I). She felt emotionally involved, but with considerable ambivalence. She felt reluctant to come to sessions, took little pleasure in them, and got little from them. The therapist's perceptions suggest that the patient's lack of trust or faith in him lay behind this general dissatisfaction. The therapist sensed the ambivalence and discomfort in her involvement with him, and experienced a similar uneasy involvement with the patient. Neither seemed to feel safe in the relationship. This extreme polarity emphasizes the extent to which a sense of personal safety is involved in the development of positive transference.

The total dimension reflects the degree to which the therapist comes to have a charismatic influence on the patient. Charismatic authority consists of the direct popular appeal or "personal magnetism" of a leader for his followers (Weber, 1964). It is the leader's ability to sway his audience by virtue of the values he dramatically embodies. The leader's personal qualities are the focus of his followers' attention, and the legitimation of their enthusiastic compliance. Charismatic influence, however, is a function of the relation between the leader and follower. The power does not inhere solely in the personality of the one to whom it is attributed. That person is endowed with the power by those who need to have it work. The person who is thus endowed must respond in a way that attracts and supports the attribution; his charismatic "gift" must be tested and proven. Although charismatic influence has been seen as operative mainly in the context of religion and political leadership, the relevance of the concept for psychotherapy is evident. The convergence of this application of charisma with Freud's concept of transference suggests that this "magical" potential in interpersonal relations is a legacy that the child's experience of parental power has bequeathed to the adult personality.

### *J-VI: Sympathetic Warmth vs. Conflictual Erotization*

The sixth dimension of conjoint experience reflects the development of a libidinal bond between the participants, taking either the sublimated form of affectionate good will or the unsublimated (and emotionally threatening) form of sexual desire (see Table 61). This polarization of the erotic potential in therapy into nurturant and sexual modes corresponds to the parental and conjugal modes of intimacy that anthropologists find basic to the American kinship system (Schneider, 1968). The conjugal mode engendered considerable anxiety and defensiveness in both participants, whereas the parental mode was experienced with greater comfort (particularly by the therapist).

The interpretation of J-VI — (*conflictual erotization*) seems relatively unambiguous. There was a private awareness of sexual arousal in each of the participants, and a considerable amount of defensiveness attendant upon it. Although each participant was uncomfortably aware of his own sexual arousal, this state of feelings was not explicitly communicated between them. Communication was, in fact, considerably impaired by the mutual defensive reactions that were engendered. The patient tended to "block" and found it difficult to express herself to the therapist. Her behavior, as she saw it, was hostile and provocative. This hostility seemed to serve both as a defense against her sexual responsiveness to the therapist and as a provocative attempt to engage the therapist from his own defensive withdrawal. The therapist saw the patient as being angry and guilty, and as communicating without appropriate affect (intellectualizing). Thus, in the course of struggling to contain her sense of attraction, the patient managed to convey a rather misleading impression of her feelings.

The therapist, on the other hand, was viewed by the patient as being accepting but also noncommittal, unwilling to take initiative with re-

## TABLE 61

### J-VI+ : Sympathetic Warmth

| | | Loading | $h^2$ |
|---|---|---|---|
| Patient experiences: | | | |
| P-VI | little *erotic transference resistance* | .77[a] | .73 |
| P-IX | little *hostile provocation toward a seemingly noncommital therapist* | .61 | .58 |
| P-II | little *painful self-exploration* | .40 | .83 |
| P-III | little *toying with the therapist* | .38 | .63 |
| Therapist experiences: | | | |
| T-II + | *sympathetic involvement:* active supportive involvement with a patient seen as anxious and communicative | .71 | .63 |
| T-XI | little *erotic countertransference* | .57 | .65 |
| T-VII | *cheerful warmth:* self-confident nurturant warmth with a patient seen as feeling inferior | .56 | .46 |

### J-VI− : Conflictual Erotization

| | | Loading | $h^2$ |
|---|---|---|---|
| Patient experiences: | | | |
| P-VI | *erotic transference resistance:* blocking and embarrassing sexual arousal with a therapist seen as indulgent | .77 | .73 |
| P-IX | *hostile provocation toward a seemingly noncommital therapist* | .61 | .58 |
| P-II | *painful self-exploration:* seeking help for resolving inner conflicts concerning family relations | .40 | .83 |
| P-III | *toying with the therapist:* seductiveness with a therapist perceived as feeling ineffective and withdrawn | .38 | .63 |
| Therapist experiences: | | | |
| T-II − | *uncaring detachment:* passive aggressive response to a patient felt to be intellectualizing | .71 | .63 |
| T-XI | *erotic countertransference:* distressing bodily arousal with a patient perceived as feeling angry and guilty | .57 | .65 |
| T-VII | little *cheerful warmth:* self-confident nurturant warmth with a patient seen as feeling inferior | .56 | .46 |

[a] See note to Table 56.

spect to her. From the therapist's point of view, this was with good reason: he was disturbed by his sexual responsiveness to the patient, and did not trust himself to take initiative. He experienced himself as passively and somewhat hostilely detached from the patient. He saw her suffering with whatever uncommunicated feelings she had, but could not move to ease her impasse because of his own distressingly nontherapeutic reaction. Again, we see a manner of hostility as part of the defense mobilized against the emerging sexual impulses, although the therapist's passive-aggressive expression of this contrasts with the patient's sometimes attacking, provocative manner.

The inability to communicate, the superficial irritation, and the inner excitement and distress noted in J-VI— suggest that patient and therapist are (against their wills) strongly attracted to each other, each doing his best to deny and counter these unwelcome feelings. The state of affairs is reminiscent of Freud's (1912a, 1915) description of "transference love." This implies that the sexual desire patient and therapist experience is an inappropriate intrusion from past relationships. Although sexual transference is not in itself therapeutic, and presents certain dangers of acting out, its development may indicate the formation of a transference neurosis, which, in theory, is an essential phase of psychoanalytic treatment. The development of an erotic countertransference in the therapist may be viewed either as a misfortune for treatment or as a transient "countertransference neurosis," which complements and in a sense validates the transference neurosis. Whatever its causes and consequences, the fact that this phenomenon was recognized quite early in the history of psychotherapy suggests that it is a common and powerful process. As Lucia Tower (1956) has noted, "Virtually every writer on the subject of countertransference states unequivocally that no form of erotic reaction to a patient is to be tolerated. This would indicate that temptations in this area are great, and perhaps ubiquitous." If so, then a transference interpretation of these feelings has at least the moral utility, for the participants, of making the improper spurious.

The opposite pole, J-VI+, was defined for the patient only by the decided absence of the experience of *conflictual erotization*. Sexual and hostile feelings were equally lacking, as were other indications of the patient's state. The therapist, however, saw the patient as feeling anxious and inferior, as someone needing his help. His sympathetic, nurturant manner of response to the patient suggests a basically parental attitude. Feeling a great deal of self-confidence and affection, the therapist tried to provide an actively supportive relationship for the patient. There was neither the sense of equality implied in considering the patient as a potential sexual intimate, nor the sense of attraction toward the patient that figured so prominently in J-VI—. The affectionate involvement felt by the therapist was comfortably compatible with his professional role, but evidently made little impact on the patient's experience.

The process revealed in J-VI constitutes what would seem to be a possibility inherent in any intensive dyadic relationship, a broad capacity for erotization. Libidinous feeling, especially when partially inhibited or sublimated, forms an important source of cohesion in social relationships and groups. When it emerges directly and strongly in a relationship that prohibits overt sexual feeling, however, it tends to have a disruptive influence. This seems to have been the situation in J-VI, where at one pole the patient and therapist tried to mask their feelings with silence or a show of hostility, and at the other extreme retreated into a generous if possibly vacuous display of supportive affection.

### J-VII: Therapeutic Alliance vs. Defensive Impasse

The degree of effective collaboration between patient and therapist in the task of therapy—their progress or impasse as a work team—defines the seventh dimension of conjoint experience (see Table 62).

At J-VII+, three elements stand out strongly: an effective working relationship, an emotionally meaningful exploration of the patient's self-experience and personal involvements, and a sense of progress in resolving the patient's problems. These were reported by both patient and therapist. Each participant was experienced by the other as functioning effectively and had confidence in the other's ability to carry their partnership forward. The nonsalient loading of factor P-V may reflect the nature of the patient's experience on those occasions when "the going got too rough." J-VII+ in these ways approximated the ideal patient-therapist relationship described in the clinical literature.

J-VII— reflected the experience of an open aggression in the therapeutic relationship. The remarkable thing about this experience, however, is that each participant attributed the aggression to the other. The therapist was seen by the patient as actively critical and attacking. The patient, on the other hand, was viewed by the therapist as actively and assertively attempting to defeat his therapeutic influence. Neither of them experienced any aggression originating with himself, but rather felt himself in a basically defensive position. The patient's major sense of her participation was one of flight from the threat posed by the therapist. She perceived him as feeling depressed and irritable, and as destructively venting his spleen on her. She dreaded coming to their sessions, withdrew from any collaboration in them, and simply did her best to protect herself from his malign impact. From the therapist's point of view, the patient appeared to make herself narcissistically inaccessible in the relationship—seemingly feeling good, but pursuing an obstructive and unresponsive line of action. The therapist attempted to wait out the

TABLE 62

J-VII+ : Therapeutic Alliance

| | | Loading | $h^2$ |
|---|---|---|---|
| Patient experiences: | | | |
| P-XI — | *therapist perceived as involved and helpful* | .82[a] | 76 |
| P-IV | *collaborative exploration of heterosexual involvements* | .67 | .63 |
| P-II | *painful self-exploration:* seeking help for re-solving inner conflicts concerning family relations | .65 | .83 |
| P-V | *courting a therapist who is seen as rejecting* | .44 | .72 |
| Therapist experiences: | | | |
| T-VIII + | *collaborative relationship:* responsive inter-vention with a patient perceived as want-ing insight and relating collaboratively | .64 | .64 |
| T-I — | *effective movement:* sense of progress with a patient seen as responsive and motivated | .38 | .81 |

J-VII— : Defensive Impasse

| | | Loading | $h^2$ |
|---|---|---|---|
| Patient experiences: | | | |
| P-XI + | *therapist perceived as mean and attacking* | .82 | .76 |
| P-IV | little *collaborative exploration of hetero-sexual involvements* | .67 | .63 |
| P-II | little *painful self-exploration* | .65 | .83 |
| P-V | little *courting a therapist who is seen as re-jecting* | .44 | .72 |
| Therapist experiences: | | | |
| T-VIII — | *abiding a patient perceived as assertively nar-cissistic* | .64 | .64 |
| T-I + | *depressive stasis:* resignation over impasse with a patient perceived as depressed and narcissistic | .38 | .81 |

[a] See note to Table 56.

patient's defensiveness by taking a somewhat detached and non-challeng-ing attitude toward her.

Two interpretations of this apparently paradoxical situation suggest themselves. On the one hand, the patient might be viewed as projecting on to her perception of the therapist threatening aggressive or libidinal impulses that contact with him evokes in her. Such a view would be consistent with the therapist's experience, and places the burden of the impasse on the patient. But, on the other hand, the therapist might be seen as insensitive to the degree to which he is threatening the patient's defenses by stimulating her impulses to a greater extent than he realizes or intends. The two interpretations are not logically incompatible, and might both find some support in the view of an external observer. What is clear at any rate is that this pattern represents a probably unstable impasse in the therapeutic relationship. Either the patient will flee from therapy altogether, completing her defensive withdrawal, or the therapist will find a way to provide enough security to enable her to be a more collaborative participant in the relationship.

The total dimension defined by J-VII reflects a process common to intensive dyadic relationships having some significant task orientation. The parties to such a relationship either may work well together, combining their efforts effectively, or they may interfere with each other and distract each other from their task. This aspect of collaboration hinges not so much on the relative presence or absence of skills in each participant, as upon the cooperative meshing of their assertive and adaptive energies.

## THE STRUCTURE OF EXPERIENCE IN THERAPEUTIC DYADS

The dimensions of conjoint experience presented in this chapter reflect differences between therapeutic dyads. Each factor represents one aspect of the complex unity constituted by the experiences of patient-and-therapist. Thus, interpretive comment is properly focused on the relationship, rather than on either of the participants in it.

From a descriptive viewpoint, the seven dimensions fit readily into two broad categories: *presentational style,* comprising each participant's manner of approach to therapy, and *relational process,* reflecting emergent interactive properties of the dyad.

The therapeutic relationship is in one sense, like other relationships, a system of roles. Presentational style derives from the fact that, like actors, the participants in therapy are confronted with the problem of interpreting their roles. The task around which the therapist's role is constructed is that of giving help. The complementary task in the patient's role is that of getting and using help. The manner in which each participant approaches his task is a major determinant of his "presentation of self" in the relationship.

The therapist's interpretation of his role was reflected in J-I, *therapist agency vs. therapist catalysis.* The former emphasizes a style of helping by stimulating or provoking a constructive experience and awareness in the patient. Although the therapist is not necessarily overtly active, he injects a good deal of personal energy into encouraging the patient to move more deeply into the sense of her experience. *Therapist catalysis,* on the other hand, stresses a style of helping by soothing the patient's distress and stabilizing her emotional equilibrium. In this, the therapist functions as a consultant, taking a calm and open but more impersonal approach to the patient's problems.

The patient's interpretation of her role was reflected in J-II, *patient agency vs. patient passivity.* The style of getting help entailed in *patient agency* is a very active pursuit of personal care from the therapist. The patient had a lively and urgent sense of her needs and sought to provoke the therapist's engagement with them. *Patient passivity,* on the other hand, emphasizes the patient's helplessness. Her very impotence and inertness seem a plea for the therapist's active intervention.

The interpretation each participant gives to his role is represented almost exclusively in his own experience of therapy, without saliently involving any experience for the other. These interpretations, however, do not occur in a vacuum, since each participant has perceptions of the other to which his own approach is presumably adapted. Moreover, it would be wrong to assume that patients' and therapists' presentational styles are merely reflections of their own personality characteristics. It seems quite possible that a therapist's interpretation of his role may vary from patient to patient, or even from time to time with the same patient. It is similarly possible to imagine a patient approaching her task of getting help in different ways with different therapists. There is some evidence to indicate that the presentational styles of the patient and the therapist are each responsive to characteristics of both the patient and the therapist, but the proportion of variance attributable to these sources has not yet been determined.

The other five dimensions are each jointly defined by experiences of both patient and therapist. We have called them relational processes, representing emergent interactive properties of the therapeutic dyad. Each dimension is an independent strand in the fabric of conjoint experience that constitutes the phenomenal interior of the relationship. Although the nature of these dimensions is influenced by tasks specific to psychotherapy, the dimensions take their form around issues that are implicit in the interpersonal involvement that develops in intensive interaction. The interpersonal involvement has its roots in the role system that defines the social or institutional basis of the relationship, but it both fleshes out and transcends the normative framework of the role system. This occurs because the participants in a relationship confront each other as persons, not merely as functionaries of a system. They have particular characteristics, such as age and sex and appearance, to which they are bound to react in some fashion, although these characteristics may be irrelevant to the performance of their roles. They also have needs and impulses whose expression must be managed in the relationship. Moreover, each participant is a self—sensitive, feeling, choosing among available alternatives, and self-reflective. As selves, the participants are bound to take some account of each other, and to make some mutual adaptation. This "personal" level of relationship becomes all the more difficult to ignore the more intensive and sustained in time are the interactions of the participants. Thus, the remaining five dimensions of conjoint experience reflect not only the interactive functioning of the participants in their roles, but also their ways of being together as persons.

All of the conjoint dimensions showed a marked tendency toward bipolarity. Thus, the strand of relational experience defined by each may be traced along the line of opposition. In J-III (*productive rapport vs. unproductive contact*), the opposition was between a flowing rapport and a stagnant alienation in the involvement. In the former, the participants seemed to "click" and find each other "simpatico"; in the latter, they were stuck in a superficial contact and unable to "reach" one another. At issue here is the extent to which the partnership of the two persons is validated by their perceptions of each other's expressive conduct. Closely related to the issue of *partnership validity* is the degree of acceptance or rejection as peers that the persons who were patient and therapist experienced in the relationship. *Peer inclusion* was reflected in J-IV, where the null point represented a state of mutual personal openness, and the extreme implied peer exclusion in the form of *ambivalent nurturance-dependence*. A third strand was defined by an opposition between expectant faith and defensive mistrust in the relation of patient to therapist. At issue in J-V (*healing magic vs. uncomfortable involvement*) is the degree of *charismatic trust* developed in the interpersonal involvement. The strands of partnership validity, peer inclusion, and charismatic trust all center in the relation of self vis-à-vis self. From a psychoanalytic viewpoint, they might be described (respectively) in terms of object-perception, ego-identification, and superego-identification. In contrast to these, the last two strands of relationship focus on the deployment and management of erotic and aggressive impulses. An opposition between sublimated and unsublimated libidinous feeling, in the forms of affection and desire, characterized the relational strand defined by J-VI (*sympathetic warmth vs. conflictual erotization*). Another opposition between externalized sublimated aggression in the form of task collaboration, and projected aggression in the form of mutual threat, characterized J-VII (*therapeutic alliance vs. defensive impasse*).

J-VI entails the *erotic orientation*, and J-VII the *aggressive orientation*, of the therapeutic relationship.

The five strands of relational process are defined by the contrast of opposites. That contrast is in each case a contrast between a consonant pattern and a conflictual pattern of interpersonal involvement. Our discussion thus far has focused on these patterns in the context of the dimensions they define. To get a better sense of the range of conjoint experience in the therapeutic relationship, however, it seems wise to discuss the consonant patterns together, and then to compare the conflictual patterns as a group.

### Consonant Patterns of Involvement

The consonant patterns of relational process represent ways in which therapy seemed to be going well. Our data do not permit us to make judgments of final outcomes, but they do show patterns of apparently helpful process. The consonant patterns were *productive rapport,* "mutual personal openness" (the null point of J-IV), *healing magic, sympathetic warmth,* and *therapeutic alliance.* Clinical observers would probably agree that each of these should foster the attainment of therapeutic goals. In what follows, we shall try to formulate the manner in which each might prove effective.

*Productive rapport* is partially defined by a sense of therapeutic progress. The movement experienced here derives from the effectiveness of the interpersonal involvement as a vehicle for the constructive motivation of the participants. Good role performance is enhanced by the emotional validity of the patient-therapist pair as a work partnership. Although this may not be curative in itself, it provides a facilitative context for the realization of more specific therapeutic aims.

The potential helpfulness of "mutual personal openness" inheres in a person-to-person encounter that augments the patient's adult social effectiveness and her sense of worth as a mature human being. This encounter is characterized by the honesty of both participants in recognizing their immediate wants and feelings, and by their honesty in expressing these so that they are meaningfully present for the other person. The recognition and statement of one's wishes in a direct and comprehensible way leads at best to their reasonable satisfaction, and at the least makes possible their rational evaluation and disposition. Personal openness provides an opportunity for experiencing the remedial and growthful influence of the other person's perception of, and response to, one's own behavior. Through this the patient can better judge the impact her behavior makes on others, and in learning to "take the role of the other" may gain a more objective self-image. By acting in a similarly open fashion, the therapist offers both an instructive model and a convincing reinforcement to the patient, furthering her education in adult relationships.

*Healing magic,* on the other hand, inheres in the achievement of an experience that duplicates, for the patient, a childhood state of real or wished-for help from a powerful caring parent. The roots of this duplication, or rather of this fulfillment, are unconscious and probably must be so for the healing magic to have efficacy. This state is experienced as present and *sui generis,* and although it emanates largely from the patient herself, it is nevertheless experienced as due exclusively to the therapist's caring and strength. It may be viewed not only as a positive transference, but as a factor that may inhibit painful feelings by eliciting an incompatible emotional response.

A different approach to providing help modeled on benign parental influence is represented by *sympathetic warmth.* Unlike *healing magic,* however, *sympathetic warmth* emanates largely from the therapist, and makes considerably less impact on the patient's experience. The potential value of this therapeutic pattern stems from the fact that it prevents the development of a more disturbing process of erotization in the relationship.

Finally, *therapeutic alliance* represents a process in which the patient's emotional problems and conflicts may be resolved through a deepened and more compassionate understanding of her past experiences and present life situation. It is the *modus operandi* of intensive analytic therapy, which aims to achieve freedom from regressive trends and renewed personal growth through emotionally significant insight. *Therapeutic alliance, healing magic,* and "mutual personal openness" seem to be the consonant patterns that most directly embody specific forms of recognized therapeutic activity.

### Conflictual Patterns of Involvement

Patterns of dissonance or conflict in relational process were also present in the conjoint dimensions. These were *unproductive contact, ambivalent nurturance-dependence, uncomfortable involvement, conflictual erotization,* and *defensive impasse.* Psychologically, each may be viewed as a threatening fantasy that has begun to take shape jointly in both participants, evoking anxiety and mobilizing defensive reactions to prevent its realization. Like hidden shoals, these fantasized possibilities imperil the course that patient and therapist must navigate together. They constitute risks of potentially harmful involvement inherent in intensive personal relationships.

In *unproductive contact,* distancing defenses and depressive affect appear as reactions against loss of individual identity through being engulfed and overwhelmed by the other. There is a joint fantasy about and fear of a self-extinguishing absorption into a primordial symbiotic union. Defense against this danger takes the form of an emotionally self-insulating retreat from response to what is experienced as encroaching pressure from the other person. Laing (1965) has provided a vivid clinical portrayal of the dynamic processes underlying this schizoid development.

In contrast to this, *ambivalent nurturance-dependence* seems a mutual defensive reaction against a felt threat of object-loss and isolation. Here we discern a joint fantasy about and fear of rejection and abandonment. The anxiety aroused by this fantasy is countered with an attitude of passive dependence by the patient, and an attitude of active nurturance by the therapist. Rigid adherence to this pattern appears as a desperate effort to avoid the mutually felt danger of abandonment, yet the underlying wish to reject or to escape from the other lends an ambivalent quality to both the therapist's giving and the patient's helplessness. Instead of retreating as in *unproductive contact,* the participants in *ambivalent nurturance-dependence* cling to each other through a ritualized exaggeration of their therapeutic roles.

*Uncomfortable involvement* reflects a joint fantasy about and fear of personal exploitation. Each participant seems to struggle against a sense of being seduced and captivated by the other, as if he might fall under a spell cast by the other person and be used in a fashion contrary to his interests or welfare. Protection is sought in a defensive pattern of wariness, uneasy vigilance, and mistrust. Unlike the mutual retreat through a turning off of emotional responsiveness that was seen in *unproductive contact,* however, the participants in *uncomfortable involvement* were clearly aroused to each other's presence.

*Conflictual erotization* shows a mutual defensive reaction against what is felt by both to be a threatened outbreak of, or loss of control over, sexual impulses. It would be misleading to suggest that the physical intimacy imagined here was solely or even primarily a version of emotionally mature love-making. The arousal of incorporative and eliminative bodily need sensations along with the sexual impulses implies that the fantasized intimacy has important roots in regressive psychosexual motives. Moreover, the extent of conscious distress evoked in this pattern seems to indicate that the erotic impulses were not only socially unacceptable in the context of psychotherapy, but would have been ego-alien to the participants even in more permissive circumstances. The fact remains, however, that in an intense dyadic relationship each person may come to regard the other as a potential sexual object. The privacy and propinquity of the office setting, plus the emotionally intimate nature of the therapeutic involvement, probably tend to make the felt potential for physical intimacy all the more real.

*Defensive impasse* is a mutual reaction against an imagined outbreak of, or loss of control over, aggressive impulses. There is a joint fantasy about and fear of harming or damaging each other, not only emotionally (e.g., through competition) but physically. Unlike the fantasy in *conflictual erotization,* the expectation of damaging aggression was not experienced as a self-originating impulse. In *defensive impasse,* the source of aggression was perceived by both patient and therapist to be in the other participant. In normal social intercourse, the ability of the participants to control erotic and aggressive impulses is taken for granted. This trust may be effectively undermined in situations of emotional stress, however. *Defensive impasse* and *conflictual erotization* represent such moments in the therapeutic process.

The conflictual patterns in the conjoint experiential process, if extensively developed, might well become serious pitfalls in the psychotherapeutic relationship. It is unclear at this point, however, whether conflict is wholly avoidable in psychotherapy, or whether it is even desirable that it be minimized. The psychoanalytic concept of the "transference neurosis" suggests that the really long-range efficacy of psychotherapy hinges precisely upon the development of the patient's core conflictual tendencies *within* the patient-therapist interaction, and their ultimate resolution in the crucible of the analytic relationship. Possible resolutions of the conflictual patterns described are considered in Part V.

In this chapter, we have presented findings responsive to the question, "How do the experiences of individuals participating in therapeutic dyads fit together?" We have gained a dyadic perspective by focusing on the experiences of both participants simultaneously, and have indeed found coherent patterns that meaningfully integrate those experiences. We have noted dimensions of presentational style (role interpretation) and relational process. The latter reflected joint resolution of such problematic issues as partnership validity, peer inclusion, charismatic trust, erotic orientation, and aggressive orientation. Although these conjoint dimensions were shaped by the exigencies of the clinical situation, examination of their content suggests their relevance for intensive personal relationships (e.g., marriage) whose interest extends beyond the bounds of psychotherapy.

# Chapter 12

# Types of Psychotherapeutic Relationships and their Correlates

The analysis of types of psychotherapeutic relationships carries the complex methodological design of this study to completion. In Chapter 2 we likened this multi-level, hierarchical design to a musical system: the items of the questionnaires were compared to musical notes or tones; the item clusters defining the facet factors were compared to chords; the global experience dimensions derived from the facet factors were compared to melodic themes; and the separate patient and therapist experience-types were likened to solo compositions constructed from these themes. Finally, the dimensions of conjoint experience were compared to patterns of harmony and counterpoint, and the conjoint experience-types to be presented here were likened to the duets that patient-therapist pairs played out together.

In this chapter, the initial focus is on the analysis of total patterns of experience characterizing psychotherapeutic relationships. Total patterns of experience were represented by the profile of scores for each patient-therapist pair on the seven conjoint dimensions. The empirical derivation of relationship types was based on an analysis of profile similarities (see Chapter 4). The second part of this chapter considers the personal and social characteristics of the people in each relationship type, in conjunction with the findings reported in Chapters 8 and 10. The integration of these findings permits us to probe beyond the descriptive question, "Who has what type of experience?", into the causal question, "How do the differential characteristics of people influence their therapeutic experience?"

## CONJOINT EXPERIENCE-TYPES

The cluster analysis of profiles of conjoint experience revealed two relationship types, permitting the classification of 23 of the 28 patient-therapist pairs in our sample. For each cluster, a composite profile was obtained that defined the distinctive total pattern of conjoint experience. The composite profile was inspected to determine the dimensions that organized the cluster, i.e., the dimensions that were consistently high or low for the patient-therapist pairs included in it. The two relationship types were thus identified as:

J-A:  Collaborative progress
J-B:  Dependency impasse.

### J-A: Collaborative Progress

The composite profile of type J-A was organized around J-VII+, *therapeutic alliance,* and J-IV−, "mutual personal openness" (low *ambivalent nurturance-dependence*). This pattern of experience distinguished a group of psychotherapeutic relationships marked by effective collaboration between the participants, along with a shared sense of movement toward their therapeutic goal. There was a distinctly democratic atmosphere in relationships of this type. Despite their differentiated roles, patients and therapists maintained a personal involvement of mutual respect and honesty. Seventeen of the 23 classifiable relationships belonged to type J-A. Thus, nearly three-fourths of the classified patient-therapist pairs were involved in relationships in which psychotherapy appeared to be going well.

### J-B: Dependency Impasse

A second group of relationships was characterized by a pattern of experience that showed therapeutic movement at a standstill while patients passively, submissively, and fearfully sought *and* resisted direction from their therapists. The composite profile for this group was organized around: J-IV+, *ambivalent nurturance-dependence;* J-III−, *unproductive contact;* J-II−, *patient passivity;* J-VII−, *defensive impasse;* and J-VI+, *sympathetic warmth.* A static quality of relationship was particularly evident; the prevailing mood was one of depression, frustration, and withdrawal. Patients were highly resistive to influence from their therapists, yet at the same time felt powerless and incapable of changing on their own. Therapists were alternately directively nurturant, in an effort to meet the apparent needs of their patients, and passively resigned to failure. The patients' dependency on their therapists emphasized the personal inequality of the participants. An authoritarian, but stagnant, atmosphere characterized this group of relationships. Six of the 23 classifiable patient-therapist pairs belonged to type J-B. Thus, about one-fourth of the classified relationships were involved in a therapeutic experience that appeared to be going poorly.

The two relationship types, *collaborative progress* and *dependency impasse,* are in effect a pair of polar opposites. In the former, the participants function effectively in their respective roles while maintaining a personal involvement of equality and openness. In the latter, the participants cling to their different roles, avoid any real personal contact, and generate an unequal and defensive relationship.

## CORRELATES OF CONJOINT EXPERIENCE-TYPES

How do these two experience-types relate to the individual characteristics of patients and therapists? Are certain types of conjoint experience restricted to patients and therapists who have specific personal or social characteristics? Tables 63 and 64 present the data pertinent to this issue, the former showing the patient characteristics and the latter the therapist characteristics associated with each relationship type. The internal classification of the characteristics surveyed is the same as was presented in Tables 41 and 42, and 54 and 55, with the number of participants in each experience-type for each classification shown in the adjacent columns.

Four patient characteristics and one therapist characteristic distinguished patient-therapist pairs who experienced *collaborative progress.* Patients in such relationships were most frequently between 20 and 26 years of age, single, not mothers, and had at least some college education. These patients also tended to be the oldest children in their families. Their characteristics are those that are often used clinically as signs of good prognosis for psychotherapy—they are young, single, well educated, and self-supporting. Perhaps one reason for these women to be good candidates for therapy is the freedom they have to invest affectively in the therapeutic relationship. Without children or husbands, and being too old to lean on parents without guilt, they may be more disposed to make their therapists influential figures in their emotional lives. Perhaps another reason for these young women to progress well in therapy is their ability to attract significant emotional responses from their therapists.

The therapist characteristic that distinguished relationships of *collaborative progress* was small family size. Therapists in such relationships were most frequently either only children or from two-child families. They also tended *not* to be parents. Our impression is that these therapists are disposed to form concentrated rather than diffuse emo-

TABLE 63

### Number of Profiles of Each Conjoint Type in Each of the Patient Background Groups

| Patient Background Groups | Conjoint Experience-Types | | |
|---|---|---|---|
| | A | B | % [a] |
| **Age** | | | |
| 20-26 | 12 | 1 | 56 |
| 27-36 | 3 | 2 | 22 |
| 37-60 | 2 | 3 | 22 |
| **Marital Status** | | | |
| Single | 11 | 1 | 52 |
| Married | 2 | 3 | 22 |
| Formerly married | 4 | 2 | 26 |
| **Parental Status** | | | |
| No children | 12 | 1 | 57 |
| Children | 5 | 5 | 43 |
| **Employment** | | | |
| Employed | 17 | 4 | 91 |
| Not employed | 0 | 2 | 9 |
| **Social class of origin** | | | |
| Upper middle and middle | 5 | 1 | 26 |
| Lower middle | 2 | 2 | 17 |
| Upper lower | 8 | 3 | 48 |
| Lower and lower lower | 2 | 0 | 9 |
| **Education** | | | |
| High school graduate or less | 4 | 5 | 39 |
| Some college | 7 | 1 | 35 |
| College graduate or more | 6 | 0 | 26 |
| **Religion** | | | |
| Protestant | 8 | 2 | 43 |
| Catholic | 7 | 3 | 43 |
| Jewish | 1 | 1 | 9 |
| Other or none | 1 | 0 | 4 |
| **Family size** | | | |
| Only child | 2 | 1 | 13 |
| One sib | 3 | 1 | 17 |
| 2-3 sibs | 7 | 2 | 39 |
| 4 or more sibs | 5 | 2 | 30 |
| **Birth order** | | | |
| Oldest | 10 | 2 | 52 |
| Middle | 5 | 1 | 26 |
| Youngest | 2 | 3 | 22 |

## TABLE 63 (continued)

| Patient Background Groups | Conjoint Experience-Types | | |
|---|---|---|---|
| | A | B | % [a] |
| **Age at family disruption** | | | |
| under 5 | 4 | 0 | 17 |
| 6-10 | 3 | 1 | 17 |
| 11-15 | 0 | 0 | 0 |
| 16+, or never | 10 | 5 | 65 |
| **Diagnosis** | | | |
| Depressive reaction | 7 | 3 | 43 |
| Anxiety reaction | 3 | 0 | 13 |
| Personality disorder | 3 | 3 | 26 |
| Schizophrenia | 4 | 0 | 17 |
| **Previous therapy** | | | |
| Yes | 8 | 3 | 48 |
| No | 9 | 3 | 52 |
| **Weeks of current therapy** | | | |
| 1-26 weeks | 8 | 3 | 48 |
| 27-52 weeks | 2 | 3 | 22 |
| 53 or more weeks | 7 | 0 | 30 |
| **Number of dyads** | 17 | 6 | |

[a] % based on 23 classifiable dyads.

tional involvements, and are sufficiently free of dependents in their personal lives to form such involvements with their patients. If the therapist's emotional attachment to his patient is not neurotic, then it need not be considered a countertransference and may in fact facilitate the progress of therapy.

Type J-B, *dependency impasse,* was distinguished by four patient characteristics and two therapist characteristics. Patients involved in this relationship type were most frequently 27 years of age or older, married or formerly married, mothers, and had only a high school education or less. They also tended to be later-born children. These traits are just the opposite of those that marked patients in relationship type J-A, and the interpretation offered there presumably applies in the reverse direction. Thus, these patients are by and large less free to form, and less likely to attract, intense emotional involvements in psychotherapy.

The two therapist characteristics associated with *dependency impasse* were family size and professional experience. Therapists involved in type J-B relationships were most frequently from families of three or more children, and had less than six years of experience in therapeutic

## TABLE 64

### Number of Profiles of Each Conjoint Type in Each of the Therapist Background Groups

| Therapist Background Groups | Conjoint Experience-Types | | % [a] |
| | A | B | |
|---|---|---|---|
| **Age** | | | |
| 29-35 | 12 | 4 | 70 |
| 36 or over | 5 | 2 | 30 |
| **Marital status** | | | |
| Single | 3 | 1 | 17 |
| Married | 12 | 3 | 65 |
| Formerly married | 2 | 2 | 17 |
| **Parental status** | | | |
| No children | 11 | 2 | 57 |
| Children | 6 | 4 | 43 |
| **Social class of origin** | | | |
| Upper middle and middle | 13 | 4 | 74 |
| Lower middle and upper lower | 4 | 2 | 26 |
| **Religion** | | | |
| Protestant | 2 | 0 | 9 |
| Catholic | 1 | 0 | 4 |
| Jewish | 12 | 3 | 65 |
| Other or none | 2 | 3 | 22 |
| **Sex** | | | |
| Male | 13 | 4 | 74 |
| Female | 4 | 2 | 26 |
| **Family size** | | | |
| Only child | 2 | 0 | 9 |
| One sib | 8 | 1 | 39 |
| Two or more sibs | 7 | 5 | 52 |
| **Birth order** | | | |
| Oldest | 11 | 4 | 65 |
| Middle | 1 | 1 | 9 |
| Youngest | 5 | 1 | 26 |
| **Profession** | | | |
| Psychiatry | 4 | 2 | 26 |
| Psychology | 9 | 3 | 52 |
| Social work | 4 | 1 | 22 |
| **Years of experience** | | | |
| 0-5 years | 8 | 5 | 57 |
| 6 or more years | 9 | 1 | 43 |
| **Personal psychotherapy** | | | |
| Yes | 13 | 5 | 78 |
| No | 4 | 1 | 22 |
| **Number of dyads** | 17 | 6 | |

[a] % based on 23 classifiable dyads.

practice. They also tended to be parents. Again, these characteristics suggest an interpretation that is the reverse of the one offered for type J-A. These therapists are probably disposed to form diffuse rather than concentrated emotional involvements, and seem to have more of such involvements in their private lives. Their relative inexperience as therapists may be the differentiating factor, however, since there are a number of therapists with extensive past and present familial involvements among the type J-A relationships.

## PREDICTORS OF CONJOINT EXPERIENCE-TYPES

As in Chapters 8 and 10, our interest in the characteristics of patients and therapists here also extends to their predictive utility vis-à-vis the conjoint experience-types. The form the question takes in this context is: What type of conjoint experience is likely to be found in patient-therapist pairs comprising persons of given characteristics? That is, to what extent can we predict the relationship type from a knowledge of who the patient and the therapist in the dyad are to be? The data on which answers to this question are based have been presented in Tables 63 and 64. As in previous chapters, the analysis consisted in the computation of the percentage of cases in each experience-type for each subclass of a background characteristic. In general, the most likely conjoint experience-type was *collaborative progress* (74%), and only characteristics that improve the base-rate prediction will be noted below.

Patient-therapist pairs were most likely to have a conjoint experience of *collaborative progress* when the patient was diagnosed as an anxiety reaction or schizophrenic (100%), had at least some college education (93%), was between 20 and 26 years old (92%), was single (92%), had no children (92%), and came from a disrupted family background (88%). Type J-A was also most likely when the therapist had six or more years of experience in practice (90%), was an only child or had one sibling (91%), and had no children (85%). These findings suggest that *collaborative progress* is most likely to occur in combinations where the patient has considerable anxiety and personal need available for investment in a relationship, and nowhere to channel it but therapy. The therapist, on his part, is disposed to form, available for, and experienced in handling, emotionally intense relationships. We may also note that therapeutic relationships after their first year were very likely (100%) to involve the conjoint experience of *collaborative progress*.

Dyads were most likely to have a conjoint experience of *dependency impasse* when the patient was not employed (100%), was between 37 and 60 years old (60%), was married (60%), had children (55%), had been the youngest child in her family (60%), and had only a high school education or less (56%). The only therapist characteristic that predicted this relationship type was the therapist's claim of no religious affiliation (60%). Although these percentages do not seem high, they must be evaluated against a base-rate prediction for *dependency impasse* of 26%. The findings indicate that older, less well educated women, who are settled firmly into the traditional role of housewife-mother, are the people most likely to become involved in this static, authoritarian pattern of conjoint experience. It may be that persons with these characteristics tend to expect a traditional doctor-patient relationship in psychotherapy, in which they are supposed to "follow the doctor's orders." It is also clear that these patients have many significant emotional investments in their lives, in which context psychotherapy is likely to have a comparatively peripheral place. Thus, they seem both ill-adapted by previous experience to the independent role required of the patient, and unprepared to invest the kind of emotional energy associated with personal change in psychotherapy. Regardless of patient characteristics, however, therapeutic relationships in their second six months are likely (60%) to involve the conjoint experience of *dependency impasse.*

## PERSONAL CHARACTERISTICS AND TYPES OF THERAPEUTIC EXPERIENCE: AN INTERPRETIVE SYNTHESIS

Two questions have consistently been the focus of this research. The first was: What are the varieties of experience patients and therapists have in psychotherapy? The second, aimed at uncovering some determinants of the first, was: Who has which type of experience? In this section, we draw together the consistent findings and major interpretive themes that emerged from our analyses.

Efforts to answer the first question led to the delineation of four patient experience-types, two therapist experience-types, and two conjoint experience-types. The patient types were *helpful experience, stressful experience, dependent experience,* and *counter-dependent experience.* The first pair (*helpful/stressful*) was interpreted as a reflection of the reduction or mobilization of anxiety in the patient during therapy; the second pair (*dependent/counter-dependent*) appeared to reflect the patient's acquiescence to, or resistance against, the therapist's influence. The therapist types were *helping experience* and *stressful experience,* contrasting a situation in which the therapist was able to balance emotional responsiveness with professional objectivity, and a situation in which he felt a painful lack of such balance in the relationship. Finally, the relationship types were *collaborative progress* and *dependency impasse*. As their names suggest, these were interpreted as a contrast between effective therapeutic task performance in a personally open relationship, and a static involvement between a dominant the.apist and a submissive patient.

In attempting to answer the second question, we investigated the personal and social characteristics associated with the different types of therapeutic experience. The patient characteristics most consistently influencing therapeutic experience were age, marital status, parental status, education, and number of siblings. These characteristics distinguished patients who were young, single, had no children, and had a higher education, from those who were older, married, and mothers, with less education. They also distinguished between patients who came from smaller or larger families. The therapist characteristics most consistently influencing therapeutic experience were sex, profession, parental status, and number of siblings. Type of therapeutic experience was also a function of the duration of the current relationship.

In elucidating the connections between the personal and social characteristics of the participants, and the types of therapeutic experience they had, a number of interpretive themes were proposed. These were derived, in each instance, by comparing the various characteristics that were associated with a given type of experience, and inferring the common threads of meaning that seemed to link them together. The interpretive significance attributed to any particular personal or social characteristic was dependent on the context provided by other characteristics and by the distinctive context of the experience-type. Thus, a specific characteristic that was associated with more than one experience-type, such as age or family size, might contribute to the definition of different themes.

The interpretive themes were conceptualized as patient traits, therapist traits, and relational traits. Seven themes were defined as patient traits:

1. The disposition to seek a few intense emotional involvements vs. the disposition to seek more diffuse emotional involvements. This was related principally to the size of the patient's childhood family.
2. Availability or unavailability for intense emotional involvement in therapy, as a function of the number of other current emotional involvements. This was related to the patient's age, marital status, and parental status.
3. Attractiveness as an object of emotional involvement (especially to the therapist). This was a function of the patient's age, education, parental status, and birth order.
4. The disposition to seek a passive-dependent role in relationships

vs. the disposition to seek an equal role in relationships, through assertiveness if necessary. This trait was related to the family size, birth order, and age of the patient.

5. An interpersonally responsive (anaclitic) emotional orientation vs. an interpersonally unresponsive (narcissistic) emotional orientation. This was related to the patient's diagnosis, family size, birth order, and socioeconomic background.

6. A disposition to express anxiety in interpersonal relationships. This was related principally to the patient's diagnostic classification.

7. A readiness to appreciate the helpfulness of the therapist, as a result of previous experiences of disruption in important intimate relationships. This was related to family break-up in childhood and to divorce.

Eight themes were defined as traits in the interpretation of therapists' personal and social characteristics. These were:

1. The disposition to seek a few intense emotional involvements vs. the disposition to seek more diffuse emotional involvements. As with patients, this was related principally to the number of siblings in the therapist's childhood family.

2. Availability or unavailability for intense emotional involvement in therapy, as a function the number of other current emotional involvements. This was related principally to the parental status of therapists.

3. Attractiveness as an object of emotional involvement to the patient. This was related to the therapist's social class of origin, and to whether he was an only child.

4. The disposition to seek a directive role in relationships vs. the disposition to seek an equal role in relationships. For therapists, this was related to family size and to parental status.

5. An attitude of nurturant commitment to helping others. This was a function of the therapist's sex, profession, age, and parental status.

6. A readiness to respond at a sexual level (given a heterosexual context). This was related principally to the sex of the therapist.

7. Comfort vs. discomfort in emotionally intense relationships. This was principally a function of the amount of the therapist's professional experience.

8. An attitude of emotional reserve or control. This was related to amount of professional experience, and to whether the therapist was an only child.

One relational trait that emerged as an interpretive theme was the mutual personal adaptation of the patient and therapist to each other. This was principally a function of the duration of the current therapeutic relationship.

The different traits we have proposed seem to fall into several categories as theoretical constructs. A number of traits have been described as *dispositions* or goal-directed tendencies (motives). Other traits have been described as *response sets* or reaction tendencies (attitudes). Another type of concept invoked was that of the *life space* or psychological world of the participant, with reference to the importance of psychotherapy as a part of that subjective world. Finally, a fourth type of psychological construct used was the *social stimulus value* of the participant, the kind of environmental press he presents as an elicitor or inhibitor of the other person's responses.

About half the traits attributed to patients and to therapists as interpretive themes were identical or highly similar. This consistency was based more on the similarity of the characteristics involved (e.g., family size) than on any *a priori* conceptual scheme. It suggests to us that an important part of what patients and therapists contribute to the therapeutic process depends on traits they have as *persons,* rather than on their traits as performers of patient and therapist *roles.* It also implies that these personal traits have relevance beyond the clinical psychotherapeutic situation, in the more general domain of interpersonal relations.

A meaningful synthesis of interpretive themes, and of patterns of therapeutic experience, can be obtained by searching out the consistencies among patient, therapist, and relationship experience-types. Of the sixteen possible combinations of patient, therapist, and relationship experience-types ($4 \times 2 \times 2$), significant findings were observed for the following five:

1.  P-A, patient *helpful experience;* T-A, therapist *helping experience;* J-A, conjoint *collaborative progress*—This consistently positive therapeutic experience occurred especially *when the patient was likely to be an attractive object of emotional involvement to the therapist, when the therapist was disposed to seek a few intense emotional involvements, when the therapist had an attitude of nurturant commitment to helping others, and when the patient was ready to appreciate the helpfulness of the therapist.* The key elements here are clearly the therapist's emotional investment in the patient and her ability to attract it, and the therapist's commitment to being helpful and the patient's readiness to be appreciatively responsive to this help.

2.  P-B, patient *stressful experience;* T-B, therapist *stressful experience;* J-A, conjoint *collaborative progress*—This intriguing com-

bination is one in which the patient and the therapist each individually experienced distress, whereas the therapeutic relationship appeared to be progressing effectively. In contrast to the smooth going of the preceding combination, this gives evidence of being rough going for the participants—yet going nevertheless. It occurred more frequently *when the patient was available for intense emotional involvement in therapy, and when the patient was likely to be an attractive object of emotional involvement to the therapist.* Both of these are patient traits, but they imply an intensity of emotional involvement on the parts of both patient and therapist.

3.  P-B, patient *stressful experience;* T-B, therapist *stressful experience;* J-B, conjoint *dependency impasse*—This consistently negative therapeutic experience occurred more frequently *when the patient was not disposed to express anxiety overtly in interpersonal relationships, and when the patient tended to have an interpersonally unresponsive (narcissistic) emotional orientation.* In contrast to the preceding combination, the patient here was able to invest little affect in the relationship.

4.  P-C, patient *dependent experience;* T-A, therapist *helping experience;* J-B, conjoint *dependency impasse*—This combination presents a situation in which the patient felt dependent on the therapist, the therapist experienced himself as helpful, but the relationship remained at a standstill. This occurred especially *when the patient was unavailable for intense emotional involvement in therapy, when the patient was unlikely to be an attractive object of emotional involvement to the therapist, when the patient was disposed to seek relatively diffuse emotional involvements, and when the therapist was disposed to seek a directive role in relationships.* The key elements in this pattern are the low levels of emotional involvement on the part of both participants, and the therapist's disposition to take a directive role, not matched by a complementary disposition in the patient.

5.  P-C, patient *dependent experience;* T-A, therapist *helping experience;* J-A, conjoint *collaborative progress*—The patient and therapist experience-types in this and in the preceding combination are the same, but the relationship gives evidence of therapeutic movement rather than stagnation. This pattern was observed more often *when the patient was disposed to seek a passive dependent role in relationships.* There were no marked deterrents to intense emotional involvement, and the basis of the patient's dependency was probably family socialization resulting in nurturance-seeking, rather than a generational attitude of submissiveness to authority.

The foregoing findings leave a strong impression about the effect of certain patient and therapist traits on the course of psychotherapeutic experience. The evidence on which it is based is not complete enough to consider this impression a firm conclusion; it is offered as a clinically meaningful and empirically based hypothesis that seems to merit further study.

Our main impression is that intensity of emotional involvement in the relationship, particularly but not exclusively on the therapist's part, generates therapeutic movement. When this is accompanied by an attitude of helpfulness in the therapist, and appreciativeness in the patient, anxiety for both tends to be minimized. When, on the other hand, these attitudes are not present, and involvement is made even more emotionally intense through the responsiveness and attractiveness of the patient, both participants tend to experience a heightening of anxiety as an accompaniment to the therapeutic movement. Particularly low levels of emotional involvement in the relationship, as a function of unavailability or of a disposition to diffuse rather than to concentrate one's involvements, leads to a therapeutically static situation. One can almost think of the therapeutic relationship as a vehicle of a given inertial mass, which can be moved at a rate that is proportional to the amount of emotional energy applied to it. The attitudes of helpfulness and appreciativeness in therapist and patient function as shock absorbers to make the ride more comfortable. Therapy can be a jarring experience for the riders and still make effective progress. The minimal energy investment needed to produce movement in the therapeutic relationship would seem to be the problematic feelings that the patient brings to therapy, and her emotional responsiveness to the therapist's influence.

The tendency of psychotherapy to evolve as a dependent involvement seems to be a function of the dispositions of patient and therapist to seek passive and directive roles in their relationships. When dependency develops, it is often but not necessarily associated with a static situation. Some conditions that predispose a patient toward dependency also predispose to a low intensity of emotional involvement; others do not.

If the intensity of emotional involvement is a central factor in the generation of therapeutic movement, it is also clear that many variables affect that intensity. Various patient and therapist characteristics dispose the participants to make therapy a more or less intense experience. Other characteristics of patient or therapist stimulate the other participant to a more or less intense emotional response. Still other personal-social characteristics affect the kind of opportunity for emotional involvement that therapy provides in the lives of patient and therapist.

Part V

# The Functioning of the Psychotherapist: Some Implications for Clinical Practice

*Chapter 13*

# The Therapist as an Instrument of Observation

When the psychotherapist enters into a professional relationship, he undertakes a two-fold responsibility. He undertakes to make himself fully and accurately aware of his patient's condition. This requires that he be sensitive to, and knowledgeable about, her psychological state. Even more strongly, the psychotherapist commits himself to having a beneficial impact on his patient—both in what he prescribes for, and in how he treats, her condition.

This definition of his professional obligations stresses the psychotherapist's performance, his instrumentality rather than his peronality. The therapist is, in effect, both an instrument of observation and an instrument of treatment. Although his qualities as a person do have a demonstrable impact on therapy, his responsibilities as a professional therapist focus on what he does—on how, and on how well, he *uses* himself—not on who he is.

What is the therapist's observational task? What assets may he rely on in seeking to know his patient's psychological state? What liabilities must he allow for, and seek to correct? In this chapter, we shall attempt to determine from the data that we have gathered how well the therapist functions as an instrument of observation; and in the next how well he functions as an instrument of treatment. Our aim in this final section is not merely to judge, but, where possible, also to offer suggestions for improving the functioning of the psychotherapist.

## MODES OF OBSERVATION

Laymen often attribute rather unusual powers of perception to the psychotherapist, powers that border on the fabled "x-ray vision." Therapists are expected to be able to see through or into people, to discern their secrets and their heart's desire, in a way that others cannot. The psychotherapist must, of course, be skillful in gleaning important and reliable evidence about a patient's psychological state through direct personal contact with the patient, but the kinds of information to which the therapist has access are not different from those available to laymen. Generally, two modes of observation are distinguished in the process of gaining direct knowledge of others. These modes may be called *object perception* and *empathic induction.*

Object perception, as we use the term, involves the formation of a consciously held, "factual" image of the other.[1] This image is formed by focusing attention on the immediate sensory (e.g., visual and auditory) evidence one has concerning the other person, ratified by a more or less cursory interpretive judgment of that evidence. The criteria of good object perception are clarity and precision; the result, an "objective" awareness of the other.

Empathic induction, on the other hand, involves a "feeling" that one gets in the other's presence—a feeling that may be elaborated as a fantasy about the other, or that may be experienced as free-floating in the "atmosphere" of the relationship. The feeling results from a sensori-motor accommodation to subtle changes in the other's expressive behavior, to cues that are "given" and "given off" by the other in relating to one (see, e.g., Goffman, 1963). Information derived by this mode of observation is sometimes labelled "intuitive," as contrasted to "objective" perception, because there is no self-evident sensory reference to the other person. To use this intuitive or empathic mode accurately, the perceiver must be able to take his own idiosyncratic tendencies into account and to distinguish these from the effects that the other produces in him. The criteria of good empathic induction are responsiveness and sensitivity; the result, an intuitive or subjective awareness of the other.

The psychotherapist's task as an instrument of observation requires alert and self-conscious monitoring of both object perception and empathic induction. As an object perceiver, the therapist pays attention to what his patient says and does, or fails to say and do, in their sessions. He consciously scans the verbal and the nonverbal cues that his patient emits, to determine the latent intent and meaning of her communications. But the therapist must also rely on his "third ear," his empathic sense, as a guide to what his patient is really experiencing. This latter mode, for example, is stressed in classical psychoanalysis, despite the fact that it is often regarded as a rational therapeutic procedure. Freud's

---

[1] The self can also be experienced as an "object," and thus object perception applies to internal as well as external phenomena.

(1912b) technical recommendations for the conduct of psychoanalysis emphasize an unfocused "evenly hovering attention" in the therapist, coupled with free scope for the therapist's "unconscious memory." In a vividly graphic description of empathic induction, Freud states that the analyst:

. . . must bend his own unconscious like a receptive organ towards the emerging unconscious of the patient, be as the receiver of the telephone to the disc. As the receiver transmutes the electric vibrations induced by the sound waves back again into sound waves, so is the physician's unconscious mind able to reconstruct the patient's unconscious, which has directed his associations, from the communications derived from it. (Freud, 1912b; p. 328.)

This analogic reference to "vibrations" for describing empathic induction curiously enough recurs in the language of contemporary psychedelic culture, along with the related notion of "tuning in."

Evaluation of the psychotherapist's functioning as an observer entails a number of methodological problems. The salient issue regarding object perception is the therapist's accuracy in observing his patient. Against what independent, objective standard are the therapist's observations to be judged? In principle, there are two possibilities. One is the consensus of a set of non-participant observers, should their own perceptions be sufficiently convergent to permit the formulation of a meaningful average. The alternative possibility for a standard of what the patient is really like is the patient's own self-perception. Lack of relevant data in our study simply forecloses recourse to the first possibility. Even were such data available, however, it would be arguable whether the perspective of non-participants would in itself constitute a privileged standard of reality, especially concerning the patient's *experience*.

Our study does permit us to use the patient's self-perception as a standard for testing the therapist's observations, but not without facing questions concerning selection and distortion in the patient's reports. The concept of unconscious defense leads one to ask how accurate the patient is able to be in observing herself: is she not likely to provide a less trustworthy picture of herself than her therapist can? Further, the concept of response bias leads one to ask how fair the patient is willing to be in reporting her self-perceptions: will she not present a more selectively favorable picture of herself than her therapist would? Although in ordinary situations it is customary to give the benefit of the doubt to the person whose experience and behavior are in question, the conventional wisdom in psychotherapy reverses this presumption. Because of the patient's "repressions," "selective inattention," or "conditions of worth," it is often assumed that the therapist is better able than the patient to know and to tell what she is really experiencing. Given this state of affairs, disagreements between patient and therapist about the patient's experience and behavior may be attributed *either* to the therapist's inaccuracy (his error and selective bias) *or* to limitations in the patient's testimony—or to both!

This dilemma, however, need only be faced when disagreements arise. Agreement between patient and therapist (which is what we hope to find) makes the dilemma irrelevant. Our evaluation of object perception, therefore, simply involved the assessment of correspondences between the therapist's report of the patient's behavior and experience, and the patient's self-report. Since there were many identical or highly similar items concerning the patient's experience and behavior in both the patient and the therapist forms of the TSR, it should be possible to obtain an estimate of the therapist's functioning as an object perceiver. Operationally, this entailed an examination of correlations [2] between patients and therapists for 89 items pertaining to patients' dialogue, aims, behavior, feelings, and session development. These correlations, computed across cases for the 28 matched patient-therapist pairs, are responsive to the following question: If a therapist's average rating of his patient on an item was high compared to ratings by other therapists, was his patient's average rating of herself on that item also high as compared with the self-ratings of other patients?

By contrast, the salient issue regarding empathic induction is the sensitivity of the therapist's experience to changes in the experience of the patient. This issue implies a different analysis from that pursued with respect to object perception. There it was relevant to examine only the correspondence between the therapist's impression of a specific behavior or experience and the patient's reported impression of the same. To study empathic induction, however, we must examine the articulation of the total range of patient experiences with *each* specific aspect of therapist experience. Thus, we shall have to determine the correlations of all therapist experiences, within and across facets, with all patient experiences. To make this a manageable task, and to enhance the clinical relevance of the analysis, we shall compute these correlations (for the 28 matched patient-therapist pairs) using scores on the 43 therapist facet factors and the 45 patient facet factors.[3] This analysis is subject to many of the same methodological qualifications noted about object perception.

[2] Statistical evaluation of accuracy in interpersonal perception has many technical methodological problems (e.g., the base rate of responses). Since accuracy *per se* was a subordinate issue in the context of our study, we have elected to use an unmodified correlational approach to its analysis.

[3] See Chapter 4 and Appendices F and G for descriptions of the patient and therapist facet factors.

It does, however, provide a unique opportunity to make an empirical determination of the ways that a therapist may use his own experience as a guide to awareness of his patient's state.

## OBSERVING THE PATIENT

### Dialogue

Psychotherapy is basically a conversation, a form of interaction in which most overt behavior consists of the dialogue between patient and therapist. Initiative in this dialogue rests mainly with the patient. What is discussed during sessions is thus a particularly salient aspect of the patient's involvement. How good an observer of this aspect of patient involvement is the therapist, in the modes of object perception and empathic induction?

Regarding object perception, the question turns on how well the therapists' observations of dialogue match those of their patients. Significant and substantial correlations between patients' and therapists' reports were found for 11 of the 18 dialogue items. Assuming the patients' reports as a standard of comparison, therapists' perceptions of dialogue were most reliable in the following areas: childhood experiences with family members $(r=.86^4)$; sexual feelings and experiences $(r=.76)$; relations with spouse or boyfriend $(r=.73)$; current relations with parents or sibs $(r=.73)$; feelings toward the therapist, or as a patient $(r=.72)$; and physical health or symptoms $(r=.72)$. Other topics for which significant agreement was found were: domestic concerns $(r=.68)$; work or school $(r=.67)$; dreams and fantasy $(r=.62)$; hopes or goals for the future $(r=.61)$; and feelings of being close to or needing others $(r=.57)$. Therapists' object perceptions of dialogue thus appear to be reasonably accurate in most areas of discussion. There were exceptions, however; very little correspondence was found on feelings and attitudes toward self $(r=.01)$; fears, inadequacies, and successes in getting along $(r=.12)$; and social activities or relationships $(r=.14)$.[5]

Empathic induction was assessed by examining the correlations between patient experiences and the therapists' facet factors for dialogue. Table 65 presents the significant findings of this analysis. One of the five therapist facet factors (T-1, talking about *anger, intimacy, and competence in personal relationships*) had no significant correlates

---

[4] For correlations with $N = 28$, $p \leq .05$ when $r = .37$ or more, and $p \leq .01$ when $r = .48$ or more.

[5] Nonsignificant correlations were also found for the following topics: recreations and hobbies $(r = .30)$; strange or unusual ideas and experiences $(r = .28)$; childhood experiences in school and with friends $(r = .24)$.

among any patient facet factors. It also seems particularly interesting that therapists' perceptions of talking about *heterosexual concerns* was a significant empathic indicator of the patients' sense of *doing well and making progress.* In addition, the therapists' observation of talking about *social and vocational concerns* may provide a clue to the patients' perception of the therapist as relating with *active criticism* and as not feeling *effective*—both of which are important reflections about the therapist that do not appear to match with any self-related object perceptions in the therapist. On the whole, Table 65 indicates that even from so simple a facet of therapy as dialogue, therapists might become aware of 15 distinct patient experiences.

### Patient Aims

The therapists' object perceptions of patient aims fell disappointingly short of the level attained for dialogue. Only two of the ten comparable items in the patient and therapist TSRs showed significant correlations: the patient's desire to find out more about the therapist as a person ($r=.61$), and her hope to get the therapist to take her side ($r=.53$).[6] Evidently this is one area in which therapists ought not to place too much confidence in their direct impressions of the patient's psychological state.

The correlations indicative of empathic induction are presented in Table 66. All four therapist facet factors in this area had some significant correlates. Among the more interesting was the therapists' view of the patient as seeking to *provoke the therapist,* which corresponded with the patients' view of the therapist as feeling *embarrassed and tense,* and of themselves as not getting *insight and rapport* in their sessions. Perhaps therapists also ought to take warning from the fact that their view of the patient as wanting to *gain insight* showed a greater correspondence to patients' wish to *win the therapist's respect* than to their wish to *get help from the therapist.* The import of these findings is that therapists must take special care in assessing their patients' motivations.

### Patient Behavior

Poor object perception, in the form of little consensus between patients and therapists, was also found regarding judgments of how the patient acted in relating to the therapist during sessions. Only 2 of 16 items concerning patient behavior showed significant correlations. These were the patient acting in an independent or uninfluenced manner ($r=.50$), and in a distant or reserved manner ($r=.40$). Two other

---

[6] Other correlations ranged from .25 to —.29.

TABLE 65

### Therapists' Views of Dialogue: Correlations With Patients' Experiences

| *Therapist Experience* | *Patient Experience* |
|---|---|
| Therapist views patient as talking about: | |
| T-2 *heterosexual concerns* | P-44 patient *doing well and making progress* (.51)[*][a] |
| | P-13 therapist not feeling *ineffective* (.39) |
| | P-6 patient feeling *good* (.37) |
| T-3 *familial and therapeutic concerns* | P-1 patient talking about *anger and family relations* (.52)[*] |
| | P-3 patient not talking about *social reality and "outer" concerns* (.50)[*] |
| | P-6 patient not feeling *good* (.40) |
| | P-9 patient feeling *embarrassing sexual arousal* (.39) |
| T-4 *social and vocational concerns* | P-2 patient talking about *career concerns vs. domestic concerns* (.55)[*] |
| | P-31 therapist relating with *active criticism vs. affective involvement* (.52)[*] |
| | P-12 therapist not feeling *effective* (.40) |
| | P-30 therapist relating *independently vs. persuasibly* (.38) |
| | P-5 patient not talking about *identity and competence in heterosexual relationships* (.38) |
| T-5 *somatic and domestic concerns* | P-2 patient talking about *domestic concerns vs. career concerns* (.57)[*] |
| | P-17 therapist not feeling *"turned off"* (.47) |
| | P-42 patient not *looking forward to sessions* (.43) |
| | P-22 patient relating with *independent activity vs. emotional involvement* (.38) |
| | P-18 therapist not feeling *invested* (.38) |

[a] Parenthetical entries are product moment correlation coefficients; $N = 28$.

[*] Indicates correlations that are significant beyond the .01 level; all other listed correlations are significant at the .05 level.

TABLE 66

Therapists' Views of Patients' Aims: Correlations With
Patients' Experiences

| Therapist Experience | Patient Experience |
|---|---|
| Therapist views patient as wanting to: | |
| T-34 *work at problem vs. gain sympathy* | P-42 patient *looking forward to sessions* (.39)[a] |
| | P-11 patient feeling *bodily need sensations* (.39) |
| T-35 *gain support and relief* | P-14 therapist feeling *displeased* (.42) |
| | P-7 patient feeling *bad* (.42) |
| T-36 *provoke the therapist* | P-19 therapist feeling *embarrassed and tense* (.56)* |
| | P-40 patient not getting *insight and rapport* (.47) |
| T-37 *gain insight vs. obstruct therapy* | P-35 patient wanting to *win the therapist's respect* (.39) |
| | P-21 patient relating *assertively vs. collaboratively* (.37) |

[a] See notes to Table 65.

items fell barely short of significance: the patient being talkative but unemotional ($r = .37$), and critical or sarcastic ($r = .35$). The clearest agreement thus seems to concern behavior that is inconsistent with the patient role.

This impression is reinforced by the correlations among facet factors in the analysis made of empathic induction (see Table 67). Here we see that the therapists' view of the patient as relating with *hostile withdrawal* corresponded with the patients' view of themselves as relating with *aloofness*—and of their therapists as relating with *aloofness!* On a more positive note, the therapists' view of the patient as relating with *enthusiastic acceptance* appeared as a good empathic indicator of patients' relating *collaboratively,* getting *insight and rapport,* and having a sense of *doing well and making progress.*

### Patient Feelings

Therapists may be able to place a little more confidence in their observations of patient feelings. Object perception was slightly better in this area than it was for patient aims and behavior, but was still not up to the level attained for dialogue. Significant correlations were found

TABLE 67

**Therapists' Views of Patients' Behaviors: Correlations With Patients' Experiences**

| *Therapist Experience* | *Patient Experience* |
|---|---|
| Therapist views patient as relating with: | |
| T-24 *mutuality vs. unresponsive activity* | P-42 patient *looking forward to sessions* (.43)[a] |
| | P-2 patient talking about *career concerns vs. domestic concerns* (.43) |
| | P-35 patient not wanting to *win the therapist's respect* (.38) |
| | P-8 patient feeling *flirtatious* (.38) |
| T-25 *enthusiastic acceptance vs. ambivalent involvement* | P-21 patient relating *collaboratively vs. assertively* (.58)* |
| | P-40 patient getting *insight and rapport* (.50)* |
| | P-44 patient *doing well and making progress* (.46) |
| | P-7 patient not feeling *bad* (.40) |
| | P-43 patient *communicating effectively* (.39) |
| | P-23 patient not relating with *passive compliance* (.38) |
| T-26 *passive dependence* | P-32 therapist relating with *attentive compliance* (.38) |
| T-27 *hostile withdrawal* | P-25 patient relating with *aloofness* (.49)* |
| | P-27 therapist relating with *aloofness* (.39) |

[a] See notes to Table 65.

for 12 of the 40 feeling items that occurred in both forms of the TSR. The most substantial of these were for feeling playful ($r = .72$), bored ($r = .62$), cheerful ($r = .59$), satisfied ($r = .58$), and optimistic ($r = .58$). Other significant correlations were for feeling relieved ($r = .56$), angry ($r = .54$), embarrassed ($r = .51$), relaxed ($r = .45$), triumphant ($r = .45$), effective ($r = .39$), and sad ($r = .39$).[7] This array includes a variety of positive and negative emotional states, but perhaps most notably absent are the feelings tense ($r = .24$) and anxious ($r = -.14$).

[7] The remaining correlations ranged from .35 to —.15.

TABLE 68

## Therapists' Views of Patients' Feelings: Correlations With Patients' Experiences

| Therapist Experience | Patient Experience |
|---|---|
| Therapist views patient as feeling: | |
| T-6   *good* | P-44 patient *doing well and making progress* (.62) * [a] |
| | P-6   patient feeling *good* (.59) * |
| | P-35 patient wanting to *win the therapist's respect* (.46) |
| | P-21 patient relating *collaboratively vs. assertively* (.44) |
| | P-23 patient not relating with *passive compliance* (.43) |
| | P-16 therapist feeling *pleased* (.42) |
| T-7   *trusting warmth* | P-19 therapist feeling *embarrassed and tense* (.48) * |
| | P-8   patient feeling *flirtatious* (.40) |
| T-9   *anxious* | P-2   patient talking about *domestic concerns vs. career concerns* (.52) * |
| | P-30 therapist relating *persuasibly vs. independently* (.50) * |
| | P-23 patient relating with *passive compliance* (.39) |
| | P-13 therapist not feeling *ineffective* (.39) |
| T-10 *mistrustful* | P-24 patient relating with *restrained emotion vs. enthusiastic acceptance* (.42) |
| T-11 *relaxed vs. embarrassed* | P-41 patient getting *relief and control* (.54) * |
| | P-35 patient wanting to *win the therapist's respect* (.53) * |
| | P-43 patient *communicating effectively* (.53) * |
| | P-44 patient *doing well and making progress* (.53) * |
| | P-6   patient feeling *good* (.51) * |
| | P-40 patient getting *insight and rapport* (.49) * |
| | P-24 patient relating with *enthusiastic acceptance vs. restrained emotion* (.46) |
| | P-16 therapist feeling *pleased* (.43) |

**TABLE 68** (continued)

| Therapist Experience | Patient Experience |
|---|---|
| T-12 *angry and guilty* | P-25 patient relating with *aloofness* (.46) |
| | P-9 patient feeling *embarrassing sexual arousal* (.42) |
| | P-43 patient not *communicating effectively* (.42) |
| | P-7 patient feeling *bad* (.40) |
| | P-27 therapist relating with *aloofness* (.39) |
| | P-20 therapist feeling *depressed and irritable* (.37) |
| T-13 *depressed* | P-44 patient not *doing well and making progress* (.49) * |
| | P-42 patient not *looking forward to sessions* (.48) * |
| | P-40 patient not getting *insight and rapport* (.44) |
| | P-41 patient not getting *relief and control* (.38) |
| T-14 *flirtatious* | P-19 therapist feeling *embarrassed and tense* (.54) * |
| | P-16 therapist not feeling *pleased* (.40) |
| | P-29 therapist relating with *helpful strictness vs. indulgent acceptance* (.40) |
| | P-21 patient relating *collaboratively vs. assertively* (.38) |

ᵃ See notes to Table 65.

The analysis of observation in the mode of empathic induction (shown in Table 68) indicates that therapists' perceptions of patients as feeling *anxious* corresponded to patients' perceptions of themselves as talking about *domestic concerns,* and of their therapists as relating *persuasibly,* rather than to any patient feelings. Since anxiety is such an important concept in psychotherapy, these findings are somewhat disquieting. As an aid to therapists, we should note that patients' feeling *bad,* which included anxiety and related dysphoric states, was significantly correlated with therapists' views of the patient as wanting to *gain support and relief,* as feeling *angry and guilty,* as relating with *ambivalent involvement*— and with therapists' views of themselves as not feeling *good!* [8]

[8] See Tables 66, 68, 67, and 72, respectively.

In general, all but one of the nine therapist facet factors concerning patient feelings showed significant correlates among patient experiences (T-8, viewing the patient as feeling *inferior,* was the exception). The therapists' view of patients' feeling *good* proved an accurate indicator of the patients' sense of *doing well and making progress* and feeling *good.* So, too, did the therapists' view of patients' feeling *relaxed vs. embarrassed.* One of the more intriguing findings about the therapist as an instrument of empathic induction also occurs in this area: therapists' views of the patient as feeling *trusting warmth* and *flirtatious* were both most saliently correlated with patients' perceptions of the therapist as feeling *embarrassed and tense.* On the therapists' behalf, we should note that another salient correlate of their patients' view of them as *embarrassed and tense* was their own sense of feeling *uneasy intimacy*—a sign of self-awareness among therapists, or at least of accurate object perception among their patients.

### Session Development

Therapists may be reassured of their functioning as object perceivers where their patients' contributions to the successful implementation of sessions is concerned. Five session development items focused on the patient's participation, and four of these showed significant correlations between patients and therapists. These were: eagerness in coming to sessions ($r=.57$); freedom and spontaneity of expression ($r=.54$); clarity of focus on concerns ($r=.54$); and level of emotional and psychological functioning ($r=.54$). There was less agreement on the degree of progress made by the patient in sessions ($r=.23$)—and less agreement, too, in the patients' and therapists' global evaluations of their common sessions ($r=.20$).

Among the therapist facet factors for session development, two were focused on the patient's participation (see Table 69). Therapists should note that their view of the patient as *making therapeutic progress* is likely to be very misleading if taken at face value. That view appears to be most responsive to patients' *looking forward to sessions,* that is, to patients' eagerness or motivation. When an indicator of patients' experienced benefit from therapy is wanted, therapists would do far better to consult their perceptions of the patient as *communicating effectively.* The latter not only reflected the accurate object perception remarked above (P-43, *communicating effectively*), but corresponded in addition to the patients' sense of getting *insight and rapport,* getting *relief and control,* finding the therapist *understanding and helpful,* and *doing well and making progress.*

TABLE 69

**Therapists' Views of Session Development: Correlations With Patients' Experiences**

| *Therapist Experience* | *Patient Experience* |
|---|---|
| Therapist views: | |
| T-41 patient as *making therapeutic progress* | P-30 therapist relating *independently vs. persuasibly* (.48) * [a] |
| | P-42 patient *looking forward to sessions* (.45) |
| | P-17 therapist feeling *"turned off"* (.40) |
| | P-2 patient talking about *career concerns vs. domestic concerns* (.38) |
| T-42 patient as *communicating effectively* | P-43 patient *communicating effectively* (.59) * |
| | P-40 patient getting *insight and rapport* (.58) * |
| | P-26 patient relating with *warmth vs. ambivalence* (.47) |
| | P-21 patient relating *collaboratively vs. assertively* (.46) |
| | P-13 therapist not feeling *ineffective* (.42) |
| | P-45 therapist *understanding and helpful* (.41) |
| | P-44 patient *doing well and making progress* (.41) |
| | P-6 patient feeling *good* (.40) |
| | P-41 patient getting *relief and control* (.39) |
| | P-10 patient feeling *trusting warmth vs. "turned off"* (.38) |
| T-43 himself as *motivated and understanding* | P-42 patient *looking forward to sessions* (.45) |
| | P-32 therapist not relating with *attentive compliance* (.44) |
| | P-43 patient *communicating effectively* (.41) |
| | P-10 patient feeling *trusting warmth vs. "turned off"* (.39) |

[a] See notes to Table 65.

The analyses we have just reviewed suggest that the therapist's observations of the patient are rather more sensitive as indices of empathic induction than they are accurate as object perceptions, at least where the standard of object perception is taken to be patients' self-reports. Before making further comments or recommendations about the therapist as an instrument of observation, however, there is another question we should consider. So far the patient has been taken as the target person. What, if anything, can the therapist know about his patient's experience through observing *his own* intentions, behavior, and feelings?

## SELF-OBSERVATION

Ordinarily, self-observation is thought to be only a more or less adequate means for deriving information about one's own psychological state. If the concept of empathic induction is valid, however—as we believe it is—then self-observation should also reflect alterations in the expressive behavior of others, and through these the changing psychological states of others. The expression of such changes is typically subtle and fleeting, and characteristically eludes the conscious scan of object perception. Empathic induction, by contrast, arises largely from the preconscious sensorimotor accommodations that we continuously make in response to others who compose our current social stimulus field. In continually adapting to others, we not only affect those others in turn [9] but also produce further reactions within ourselves. These secondary accommodations, arising from changes in our intuitive "feeling" for the situation, can in principle tell us much that may not be reflected in our object perception. The problem in using this information is discriminating one's own adaptational biases from the effects that others produce.

The findings that we shall report provide persuasive evidence that therapists' self-observations do in fact have significant, and sometimes substantial, correlations with their patients' psychological states. The following tables specify the nature of these intersubjective correlations, and thus offer therapists help in interpreting how they may use their own self-perceptions to gain information about the concurrent experiences of their patients.

### Therapist Goals

One area of therapists' self-report surveyed by the TSR was that of goals or intentions. These reflect how the therapists hoped to affect

---

[9] This mutuality of adaptation in social relations suggests a multidirectionality of cause-effect sequences; which, however, need not preclude a predominant causal influence for one of the parties involved.

TABLE 70

**Therapists' Goals: Correlations With Patients' Experiences**

| *Therapist Experience* | *Patient Experience* |
|---|---|
| Therapist views himself as aiming to provide: | |
| T-38 *experiential insight vs. emotional stability* | P-35 patient not wanting to *win the therapist's respect* (.41) [a] |
| | P-18 therapist feeling *invested* (.39) |
| | P-29 therapist relating with *helpful strictness vs. indulgent acceptance* (.39) |
| | P-22 patient relating with *emotional involvement vs. independent activity* (.38) |
| T-39 *active supportive relationship* | P-43 patient *communicating effectively* (.42) |
| | P-4 patient not talking about *fantasy and "inner" concerns* (.39) |
| | P-9 patient not feeling *embarrassing sexual arousal* (.37) |
| | P-34 patient not wanting to *get a rise out of the therapist* (.37) |

[a] See notes to Table 65.

their patients during therapy sessions. Our analysis of therapists' goals yielded two facet factors, which are shown with their correlates among patient experiences in Table 70. Here we see that when therapists reported attempting to stimulate *experiential insight,* their patients tended to view themselves as relating with *emotional involvement* without wanting to curry favor (P-35), and also tended to see the therapist as feeling *invested* while treating them with *helpful strictness.* This particular goal among therapists was the obverse of another intention, that of fostering *emotional stability* in the patient. When the latter was prominent in the therapists' experience, patients tended to seek to *win the therapist's respect,* but to relate with *independent activity* rather than emotional involvement. It might also be valuable for therapists to know that their attempts at fostering *emotional stability* sometimes caused them to be seen by their patients as offering *indulgent acceptance* without feeling very *invested.*

The second facet factor of therapist goals, providing an *active supportive relationship,* can tell the therapist much that may not be obvious about his patient—when this particular goal seems notably absent in his experience! That absence corresponds to patients' views of themselves as not *communicating effectively,* as being absorbed with *fantasy and "inner" concerns,* as feeling *embarrassing sexual arousal,* and as wishing to *get a rise out of the therapist.* Insofar as the patient is not communicating effectively, the therapist may need to place even more reliance on empathic indicators than usual, and thus this correlation may be particularly useful.

### Therapist Behavior

Therapists' perceptions of how they relate to their patients are delineated in the four facet factors shown in Table 71. Several of these seem to reflect patterns of symmetrical participation, from the evidence

## TABLE 71

### Therapists' Behaviors: Correlations With Patients' Experiences

| *Therapist Experience* | *Patient Experience* |
| --- | --- |
| Therapist views himself as relating: | |
| T-29 with *impassive control* | P-27 therapist relating with *aloofness* (.44) [a] |
| | P-30 therapist relating *independently vs. persuasibly* (.43) |
| | P-13 therapist feeling *ineffective* (.39) |
| | P-25 patient relating with *aloofness* (.38) |
| | P-43 patient not *communicating effectively* (.38) |
| T-30 with *attentive compliance vs. collaborative intervention* | P-35 patient wanting to *win the therapist's respect* (.39) |
| T-31 *frankly vs. supportively* | P-1 patient talking about *anger and family relations* (.44) |
| T-32 with *affective involvement vs. unresponsive activity* | P-42 patient *looking forward to sessions* (.40) |
| | P-43 patient *communicating effectively* (.38) |
| | P-5 patient talking about *identity and competence in heterosexual relationships* (.38) |

[a] See notes to Table 65.

of patients' concurrent perceptions. Thus, when therapists viewed themselves as relating with *impassive control,* patients viewed them as relating *independently* and with *aloofness,* but also saw themselves as relating with *aloofness* and as not *communicating effectively.* On the other hand, when therapists viewed themselves as relating with *affective involvement,* patients saw themselves as *looking forward to sessions, communicating effectively,* and as talking about the often rather involving subject of *heterosexual relations.* The same sort of symmetry seems to exist between the therapists' reports of themselves as relating with *attentive compliance* and their patients' experience of wanting to *win the therapist's respect.* Here they both show a particular solicitousness toward each other.

### Therapist Feelings

The therapist's feeling states are most directly related to the concept of empathic induction, and Table 72 shows how much those feelings reflect about (and are reflected in) the experiences of patients—rather than merely being private subjective states. The therapist's feeling *good,* for example, reflected not only his own sense of well-being but also a rather multi-faceted and positive state of involvement in the patient. Conversely, the therapist's feeling *resigned* corresponded to the report from patients of not *doing well,* not getting *insight and rapport,* and not *looking forward to sessions.* When therapists found themselves feeling *uneasy intimacy,* patients viewed them as feeling *embarrassed and tense* and not feeling *effective.* Again, when therapists feel a *sense of failure,* they can expect that their patients may instead take them to be feeling *displeased,* and as emphasizing this disdain or rejection by relating with *aloofness.* Finally, therapists may find it useful to note that when they are feeling *disturbing sexual arousal* in therapy, their patients tend to see them as feeling *depressed and irritable*—but report wanting, provocatively, to *get a rise out of the therapist.* The therapist who feels *disturbing sexual arousal* thus may not be the hapless victim of countertransference, but he is also not communicating.

### Session Development

One of the three session development factors derived from the therapist form of the TSR reflected the therapist's contribution to successful implementation of therapy sessions (see Table 69). In that one, therapists viewed themselves as *motivated and understanding* (T-43). When therapists' experiences focused on this dimension, patients reported themselves to be *looking forward to sessions,* to be feeling *trusting warmth,* and to be *communicating effectively.* Therapist motivation and

TABLE 72

## Therapists' Feelings: Correlations With Patients' Experiences

| Therapist Experience | Patient Experience |
| --- | --- |

Therapist views himself as feeling:

T-15 *good*

P-35 patient wanting to *win the therapist's respect* (.48) * [a]

P-21 patient relating *collaboratively vs. assertively* (.44)

P-7  patient not feeling *bad* (.41)

P-43 patient *communicating effectively* (.40)

P-22 patient relating with *independent activity vs. emotional involvement* (.39)

P-44 patient *doing well and making progress* (.39)

P-23 patient not relating with *passive compliance* (.38)

T-16 *uneasy intimacy*

P-19 therapist feeling *embarrassed and tense* (.59) *

P-12 therapist not feeling *effective* (.44)

T-17 *disturbing sexual arousal*

P-20 therapist feeling *depressed and irritable* (.61) *

P-34 patient wanting to *get a rise out of the therapist* (.44)

P-25 patient relating with *aloofness* (.40)

T-18 *withdrawn vs. involved*

P-32 therapist relating with *attentive compliance* (.38)

T-19 *intent vs. calm*

P-18 therapist feeling *invested* (.48) *

P-28 therapist relating with *forceful direction vs. collaboration* (.47) *

P-35 patient not wanting to *win the therapist's respect* (.40)

T-20 *sense of failure*

P-14 therapist feeling *displeased* (.49) *

P-27 therapist relating with *aloofness* (.39)

T-21 *distress*

P-24 patient relating with *restrained emotion vs. enthusiastic acceptance* (.39)

T-22 *resigned*

P-44 patient not *doing well and making progress* (.59) *

P-42 patient not *looking forward to sessions* (.44)

P-40 patient not getting *insight and rapport* (.43)

[a] See notes to Table 65.

patient motivation thus seem to correspond, as do patient openness and therapist understanding. It would be most interesting to know which causes which, or whether each is simply supportive of the other.

## CONCLUSIONS

Our analyses of the psychotherapist as an instrument of observation have yielded results that are both disappointing and surprising. The main disappointment is that therapists' object perceptions of patients are not very accurate, or at least are not very accurate as guides to what patients report about themselves. Two aspects of patient participation that proved exceptions to this conclusion were dialogue and session development; in both, therapists were reliable observers. On the other hand, the main surprise in our findings is the degree of sensitivity shown by therapists in empathic induction. Not a few of the dimensions of therapist experience had numerous correlates among dimensions of patient experience, both where the patient and where the therapist himself was the target of observation. Among the most sensitive empathic indicators in the therapists' experiences, judging by the number of significant correlates, were the therapists' view of their patients as *communicating effectively* (Table 69), and of themselves as feeling *good* (Table 72).

Noteworthy, too, was the fact that several dimensions of patient experience were especially effective as stimuli to empathic induction in the therapists (that is, had numerous significant correlates among therapist experience dimensions). These were patients' talking about *domestic concerns vs. career concerns* (P-2), wanting to *win the therapist's respect* (P-35), relating *collaboratively vs. assertively* (P-21) or with *passive compliance* (P-23), feeling *good* (P-6), getting *insight and rapport* (P-40), *looking forward to sessions* (P-42), and their sense that they were *doing well and making progress* (P-44). These were the aspects of patients' self-experience that made the greatest impact on the experiences of their therapists.

The main import of these assessments of the therapist as an instrument of observation is that he ought not to be too quick to trust his own direct impressions of his patient's psychological state—but not too slow in learning to use indirect or intuitive signs toward that end. Direct object perception is often misleading regarding the patient's experience, whereas emergent features of his own concurrent experience can in certain instances be quite valid as empathic indicators. The findings reported in this chapter should help to specify what those instances are.

*Chapter 14*

# The Therapist as an Instrument of Treatment

The professional obligation of the psychotherapist is not only to diagnose, to understand, or to empathize with his patient's problems; he must also treat them effectively. Ideally, the things he says and the actions he takes or recommends to his patient are all calculated—with due deliberation or with spontaneous craft—to produce a beneficial impact. This is the therapist's function as an instrument of treatment.

What does our study permit us to say about, and to, the therapist in this respect? Do the results on which we have labored so long imply anything of practical value for his work? The pragmatic test of knowledge, after all, is one's ability to perform in the area of inquiry. It is not the only test of knowledge, certainly not the most elegant; but perhaps it is well suited to a study of a practical art like psychotherapy. Two questions that a therapist might ask concerning his functioning as an instrument of treatment are: How does this study help to evaluate the hopefully beneficial impact of interventions? And—where those interventions are unproductive—what kinds of tactics does this study suggest to improve their effectiveness?

It should be clear from the outset that we cannot and will not try to propose technical rules for the conduct of psychotherapy. As scientists, we can only advise the therapist of the conditions in which he works, and as fellow therapists we can only share our ideas about possible strategies for dealing with those conditions. The facts that we work from are statistical estimates, trends, and patterns. Therapists should be aware of these facts as they consider their options and implement their plans, but they must also recognize that—in the very nature of the case—these estimates, trends, and patterns do not uniformly fit all of the observations on which they are based. Even with the sample of patients and therapists actually studied, a technical rule of conduct based on statistical findings would be wrongly applied in *some* cases; and the uncertainty surrounding the application of such a rule is further compounded in dealing with cases not included in the original sample. The guidelines that we offer, therefore, ought to be used in the same way that one uses weather forecasts. A forecast may state that, for a certain time in a given region, there is an 80% likelihood of rain. Yet, it either will or will not rain where you are, and you must choose between carrying an umbrella or not. The forecast is a contingency to be weighed in the decision, but the choice must be based ultimately on the expected costs and benefits of alternative actions. Research can advise the therapist of probabilities, but cannot relieve him of responsibility for exercising judgment.

The disparity between what practice requires and what research offers is evident, too, in the attitude of mind that each fosters. Research breeds an orientation that may be called *cognitive modesty,* an orientation that says "Assume nothing." Rational doubt is its modality. Practice, on the other hand, demands an attitude of mind that may be called *cognitive confidence.* To act effectively one must act surely, as if he knew what he was doing. The therapist who is mindful of research, and the researcher who is also a therapist, must find some way to embrace these antithetical attitudes. Perhaps the way to do this is to think of cognitive confidence and cognitive modesty as a dialectical pair, as necessary virtues that limit each other. The resulting synthesis is an attitude of *calculated risk:* knowing as much as one can, guessing as best he can what he does not know, and acting as surely as he can when the time for action comes. The caution in this is that sureness must come from the need of action, not from the need of ego, if the ever-present complementary need to learn more is not to be blunted.

Our questions about the functioning of the psychotherapist may be taken up again with this caveat in mind. How shall the therapist know when his interventions are beneficial? How can his unproductive interventions be made more beneficial? This is what concerns the therapist as an instrument of treatment. To answer these questions, however, some criterion of benefit must first be established. The evaluation of treatment benefit is customarily based on assessments of treatment outcome, at the time of termination and at subsequent intervals. We have no data of this sort available to our study; thus we have no way of telling whether therapy has been effective in the long run, and no way to advise the therapist which of his interventions produce the best final result. We do, however, have another kind of data that may prove useful in clinical practice: *evaluations by both patients and therapists of the treatment process.* Thus, if we cannot tell how well therapy has worked, we can nevertheless observe how well it seems to be working. Therapy may be progressing well or poorly. Good progress is experienced by the participants in therapy as *movement,* lack of progress as *impasse.* Evaluation of movement or impasse clearly is different from the judgment of success or failure, and the relation of process evaluation to outcome evaluation cannot be specified until appropriate data are obtained. For the present, we shall assume that sufficient therapeutic movement will in fact culminate in success, and that continuing therapeutic impasse will lead to failure.

## SIGNS OF THERAPEUTIC MOVEMENT

Evidence of experienced movement and impasse exists in our data at each level of analysis. Various items in the Therapy Session Reports bear directly on this issue. Patients were asked to evaluate each session as a total experience, to assess their own progress, and to report on the specific satisfactions they obtained. Therapists were also asked for their global evaluations of the session, and for their judgments of the progress their patients made. Other items in both patient and therapist forms of the TSR provided additional indirect evidence of therapeutic movement, e.g., ratings of the therapist's helpfulness in the session.

Among facet factors, at the second level of analysis, these items were highly intercorrelated within the patients' perspective and the therapists' perspective, but were only moderately correlated between the two perspectives. Analysis of the patients' TSRs produced a dimension called *doing well and making progress* (P-44 in Appendix F), defined by items reflecting felt progress in treatment, global session evaluation, and current level of functioning. The two dimensions of patient satisfaction, *insight and rapport* and *relief and control,* were shown in subsequent analyses to be closely related to P-44. Separate analysis of the therapists' TSRs yielded a dimension that was called *making therapeutic progress* (T-41 in Appendix G). The items reflected in this dimension focused on therapists' judgments of their patients' motivation and progress, of their own helpfulness toward their patients, and of the overall quality of the session.

Divergence in the meaning of therapeutic progress to patients and therapists emerged more clearly in the global and the conjoint factor analyses. The various signs of movement in the patients' experience were all saliently loaded on the global dimension called *therapeutic satisfaction* (P-I in Chapter 7), which in turn was most salient on the conjoint dimension of *healing magic* (J-V in Chapter 11). Movement in the patients' experience thus seems to reflect a very immediate sense of benefit, and to be highly influenced by the charismatic quality of the therapeutic relationship.

By contrast, the principal sign of movement in the therapists' experience found its context in the global dimension called *depressive stasis vs. effective movement* (T-I in Chapter 9), which in its turn contributed to the definition of two conjoint factors. One was *productive rapport vs. unproductive contact* (J-III), reflecting the degree of rapport and flow in personal communication between therapist and patient. The other, *therapeutic alliance vs. defensive impasse* (J-VII), reflected the extent of effective collaboration between the participants. Movement in the former case was a result of the compatibility of patient and therapist as persons; in the latter case, it resulted from the complementarity of their role performance.

The divergence in meaning between therapist and patient criteria of progress makes it important for the therapist to be aware of both. The therapists' sense of movement appeared in the context of other indications of progress, and may prove a better predictor of ultimate success or failure than the patients' sense of movement. But movement is only one element in the formula that was proposed for therapeutic success. Our assumption was that success would result from *sufficient* movement, which requires a continued commitment to treatment from the participants. Continuance is generally the patient's option, and it seems reasonable to suppose that motivation and commitment to therapy are sustained by her feeling of immediate benefit. Since the therapists' sense of movement was not significantly correlated with that of patients, therapists cannot simply rely on their object perceptions of progress as a guide to their patients' experience.

When the therapist feels that progress is being made in treatment, he is also likely to view his patient as wanting to *work at problems,* as relating with *mutuality* and *communicating effectively* with him, and he feels himself to be *motivated and understanding.* When the therapist feels that no progress is being made, he is likely to view his patient as concentrating on *somatic and domestic concerns,* as wanting to *gain sympathy,* as feeling *depressed,* as relating with *unresponsive activity,* and as not *communicating effectively.* These are the aspects of his own experience that correlate with the therapist's perception of movement.

To achieve a clear appreciation of movement in his patient's experience, however, the therapist must disregard his own object perception and focus on the empathic indicators of patient progress in his experience. Thus, when the patient feels that she is *doing well and making progress* (P-44), the therapist is likely to perceive her as speaking about *heterosexual concerns,* as feeling *relaxed* and *good,* as relating to him with *enthusiastic acceptance,* and as *communicating effectively.* He is also likely to find that he is feeling *good.* On the other hand, when the patient senses that she is doing poorly and getting nowhere in treatment, the therapist is likely to perceive her as feeling *depressed* and *embarrassed,* as relating to him with *ambivalent involvement,* as not *communicating effectively*—and is likely to find himself feeling *resigned.* These are the several signs by which the therapist may recognize his patient's experience of movement and impasse.

A few aspects of therapist experience correlate fairly well with both the patients' and therapists' sense of progress, most notably his view of the patient as *communicating effectively* (additional evidence on this indicator may be found in Orlinsky and Howard, 1968). When the therapist perceives his patient as feeling *depressed,* and himself as feeling *resigned,* it is likely that neither of them has very much sense of movement.

## COPING WITH THERAPEUTIC IMPASSES

An impasse in the therapeutic relationship occurs when there is little or no discernible movement over an extended period of time. Extricating himself and his patient from such an impasse in their relationship is probably the most difficult task a therapist must perform, if only because he himself is part of the problem. Several types of impasse were revealed in the present study among those dimensions of conjoint experience that were called conflictual patterns of involvement (see Chapter 11). The two main instances of therapeutic impasse were called *unproductive contact* (J-III-) and *defensive impasse* (J-VII-), but three other dimensions also represent impasses or impasse-prone states. *Ambivalent nurturance-dependence* (J-IV) displayed a strong hierarchical polarization of the therapeutic relationship that tended to be static, and that clustered with J-III- and J-VII- in the experience-type defined as *dependency impasse* (J-B in Chapter 12). *Uncomfortable involvement* (J-V-) reflected a heightened state of mutual mistrust between patient and therapist; and *conflictual erotization* (J-VI-) reflected a breakdown of communication over problems of impulse control. The dynamics of these conflictual patterns of involvement were discussed in Chapter 11; here we shall consider some ways of dealing with them that we think may be helpful.

The main clues to strategies for coping with impasse exist in the bipolarity of the dimensions of conjoint experience. The opposition of polar patterns affords us an understanding of the positive direction toward which to move in order to reduce the presence of impasse in therapeutic experience. Additional clues for coping with impasse exist in the relation of patient and therapist background characteristics to the different experiential patterns. These may be used to avoid the assignment of patients whose characteristics are predictive of conflict and impasse to therapists whose characteristics predict the same. By the same token, it permits the assignment or transfer of such patients to therapists whose characteristics have the effect of minimizing the particular conflict or impasse to which the patient is prone.

### Unproductive Contact

From the therapist's viewpoint, *unproductive contact* is probably the most wearisome and frustrating of impasses. There is a failure to make effective personal contact through the medium of patient and therapist roles. At a manifest level, the problematic element is the poor fit between the expectations that each has about the kind of person the other should be, and the kind of person that the other is in fact perceived to be. At a latent level, however, the impasse seems to reflect a mutual defensive reaction against loss of identity through being emotionally overwhelmed or consumed by the demands of the other person.

*Unproductive contact* is more saliently defined by the patient's experience, and seems to be more responsive to the patient's personal and social characteristics than to the therapist's. The type of patient who is particularly prone to this impasse is 37 to 60 years of age, a housewife and mother, diagnosed as a personality disorder, whose family was disrupted later in childhood, and who has attained no more than a secondary education.

What are the moves that a therapist can make to resolve an impasse of this type? Short of transferring the patient to the kind of therapist whose personal and social characteristics predispose strongly toward the opposite pattern (i.e., *productive rapport*), our findings suggest two possible expedients. One is simply to wait it out, since this impasse occurs with disproportionate frequency in the second six months of treatment (sessions 26 to 52) and rather infrequently thereafter. The reversal that appears to take place with time, however, may very well be due to selective termination by cases of *unproductive contact* before the second year. Waiting with fervent expectation for an end to frustration thus may not be a viable alternative. A second course that might be attempted by the therapist is an effective demonstration of firmness in relating to the patient: a show of strength coupled with a consistent respect for his own and his patient's ego boundaries, to convince them both that they can remain distinct and separate selves despite the fact that the therapist is interested in and responsive to the patient's inner life. If the therapist can succeed in producing this effect, the patient should then be able to permit herself greater involvement with her feelings and fantasies, and thus be able to make them more accessible to the therapist's influence. The means for producing this effect must depend largely on the prior beliefs and attitudes of the individual patient, and on the situational opportunities that arise.

If the effect cannot be produced and the passage of time fails to end the impasse, the responsible professional might recommend that his patient transfer to a different therapist. In the sample that we have studied, therapists who were least likely to become involved in the experience of *unproductive contact* were psychiatric social workers, were between 29 and 35 years of age, were not parents, were of working-class origin, and came from families of three or more children. On the other hand, therapists who were only children and who were parents were most likely to become involved in relationships of *unproductive contact,* and colleagues with these characteristics might consider avoiding the type of patient who is prone to this impasse. In general, therapists of all descriptions were least likely to develop an *unproductive contact* with patients who were 20 to 26 years of age, were single and childless, were the youngest members of their families, had experienced familial disruption in early childhood, had no religious affiliation, and had been diagnosed as schizophrenic.

### Defensive Impasse

In this pattern of involvement, effective collaboration between patient and therapist is precluded by a sense of mutual threat—although the threat the patient feels emanating from the therapist is rather more frightening to her than she is to him. The most salient element in *defensive impasse* is the patient's experience of the therapist as an attacking rather than a helpful figure. In contrast, the therapist views himself as a detached, essentially passive figure confronting an assertive, obstructive patient. A heightened sense of the aggressive potential inherent in the relationship, and the vulnerability to attack that intimate exposure to one another makes possible, gives this impasse its particular flavor.

In attempting to resolve a *defensive impasse,* and to transform it into a *therapeutic alliance,* the therapist is probably best advised to focus upon his patient's perception of him. He must recognize her obstructive assertiveness for the defense that it is, and move positively to assuage his patient's fear of him by dealing with it openly but with warmth and gentleness. In other words, he must abandon his own defensive posture, master his own sense of vulnerability, and resume his therapeutic vocation of rendering empathic help and understanding to his patient. The patient is already convinced of the therapist's power to affect her; she must also become convinced of his sensitive and adept commitment to affect her beneficially. Our experience suggests that the classical Rogerian technique of nondirectively reflecting the patient's feelings is a good way to accomplish this. It seems likely that the therapist's explicit recognition and supportive response to the patient's fear of him, rather than to her obstructive defensiveness, would in itself help the patient to see him as an empathic, effective figure with whom she can safely carry on the intimate and often painful self-exploration that psychotherapy entails.

The patients in our sample who were most prone to involvement in *defensive impasse* were older housewives (i.e., over 37 years of age, married, and not employed), claimed no religious affiliation, and tended to be in the second six months of treatment. In order to pair such patients with therapists who would be least likely to be involved in this pattern, one should seek a male therapist who is 29 to 35 years of age, married, a parent, a youngest child, from a two-child family, Jewish, and a psychologist or psychiatric social worker. Therapists with these characteristics may be more sensitive in dyadic relationships, especially with respect to the feelings of the junior partner, and may be less inclined to retire into a neutral, passive attitude. The therapists in our sample who were most prone to *defensive impasse,* and who therefore might wish to exercise care with the type of patient described above, tended to be single, only children or the middle child among three or more siblings, and psychiatrists. For all therapists, the impasse was least likely with patients between 27 and 36 years of age. The pattern of background characteristics, however, and the structure of the experience, suggest to us that the therapist's response to the patient's fear of him may be the most crucial element in sustaining or resolving a *defensive impasse.*

### Ambivalent Nurturance-Dependence

*Ambivalent nurturance-dependence* was defined more saliently by the therapist's experience than by the patient's, but the personal and social characteristics associated with it were almost exclusively those of the patient. The pattern might be described as the therapist's experience of a patient who is prone to form a self-rejecting dependent attachment. The response of the therapist, however, is not warmly nurturant, as one might expect, but an impersonally active one dictated by his sense of the patient's need and fragility. This, together with the patient's sense of unworthiness and the therapist's inner sense of frustration, defines the peculiar quality of the impasse.

Although the therapist is overtly active in this pattern, his activity is divorced from his real sense of frustration and failure. It is more an effort to sustain the precarious existence of a fragile object—as if the patient were a kind of Humpty Dumpty whose balance he must preserve—than an expression of his honest response to a fellow human being. In this sense, even though he does not withdraw or retreat from the patient, *ambivalent nurturance-dependence* can be seen as a significant failure of responsiveness on the therapist's part.

The reparative tactic suggested by the structure of this dimension is an attitude of confident frankness toward the patient. Such personal openness would imply the therapist's unwillingness to regard the patient as less than a valued fellow human, despite the patient's self-presentation as a helpless and unworthy creature. The therapist should avoid being trapped by the patient's passive dependence into doing things for her or to her, since this type of person feels too unworthy to accept anything that might be done in any event. The unwary or inexperienced therapist may be tempted to escalate the extent of his helpful activity only to meet with more frustration, for the more generous his help is the more undeserving of it the patient is likely to feel. The therapist's emphasis should be more on being with the patient as an equal than on doing for her out of charity. If he follows and expresses the thread of his own feeling with her, he has a chance to establish a more effective relationship, or at least to relieve his own feelings of frustration and failure. He is likely to find that he has a keener appreciation and warmer acceptance of her claim to exist as a person than the patient herself does, even though his appraisal of her is qualified by a realistic acknowledgment of her limitations. The patient will change her self-rejection and passive dependent behavior—will, in effect, do more for herself—once she begins to feel that she has some basic worth as a person.

The type of patient who was most likely to be involved in a relationship of *ambivalent nurturance-dependence* tended to be between 27 and 36 years of age, from a lower-class social background, the youngest child in her family, and to have had no more than a high school education. These characteristics reflect low status positions that may have contributed to the patient's lack of self-esteem. Among the therapists that we have studied, psychiatric social workers were the least likely to fall into this pattern. So, too, were patients who were middle children, had experienced familial disruption in childhood, were college graduates, and were diagnosed as anxiety reactions or schizophrenics.

### Uncomfortable Involvement

The impasse implicit in this conflictual pattern is suggested mainly by a notable deficit in the patient's sense of therapeutic progress. As the opposite pole to *healing magic, uncomfortable involvement* represents the therapeutic relationship at its furthest remove from the positive charismatic transference that sometimes makes therapy a cure by faith.

Here, the innocent trust necessary for the investment of charismatic power in the therapist has been replaced by the suspicion of exploitation that each participant feels toward the other.

The internal evidence seems too slight for us to make strong recommendations concerning the reversal of this pattern. It is clear, however, that the therapist's uneasy reserve in relating to his mistrustful patient is not an effective recourse. Perhaps his most promising approach would be to work through his own sense of unsafety, toward the more open ·commitment of self that is evident in the animated responsiveness of his engagement in *healing magic*.

Patients in our sample who were most prone to the experience of *uncomfortable involvement* were Jewish, and were diagnosed as personality disorders. The therapists most prone to this impasse were Catholic. Intuitively, one might guess that such persons are poorly matched; but the reasons for this are still unclear. To forestall the development of *uncomfortable involvement* for these patients, it would be desirable to pair them with therapists who are women, are divorced or widowed, and were middle children in their families. The type of patient who was least likely to develop this impasse—and, by the same token, most likely to experience *healing magic*—was an only child, had suffered familial disruption in early childhood, claimed no formal religious affiliation, and was diagnosed as an anxiety reaction or schizophrenic. Perhaps people with these characteristics are too much in need of a parent-figure in whom to believe to afford the luxury of great circumspection in psychotherapy.

### Conflictual Erotization

This impasse involves a classical pattern of resistance, described in psychoanalytic writings, in which the patient's stream of associations runs dry. The surface of the relationship is marked by painful silences, attempts to conceal inner distress, and a mutual hostile withdrawal. Beneath the surface, a mutual sense of sexual arousal and attraction gives the relationship an intense affective charge. Each partner fears to lose control over this impulse, and inhibits spontaneous communication with the other lest such initiative betray his real concern.

The major problem for the therapist in coping with *conflictual erotization* is to re-establish the rapport and flow of communication. He must find a way to overcome his own defensiveness and to return once more to helping the patient deal with her feelings. Perhaps the therapist will be helped by the assurance that his plight is neither uncommon among psychotherapists nor without parallel in the patient's concurrent experience. In fact, his own erotic arousal seems to be a sensitive indicator of, and a response to, rather similar feelings emergent in the patient's experience. If the therapist is sufficiently self-confident, he can risk re-opening contact with the patient, sharing his awareness in such a way as to reassure and affirm the patient in her feelings. The structure of the experience suggests that responsibility for taking the initiative should lie with the therapist. As further reassurance to the therapist, we note that the contrary of *conflictual erotization* is more closely associated with *dependency impasse* (experience-type J-B) than is this far less comfortable but more highly energized conflictual pattern.

This impasse, like several of the others, was most likely to occur during the second six months of treatment. The patients in our sample who were most prone to *conflictual erotization* were from middle-class or higher social backgrounds, and had experienced familial disruption in early childhood. The most susceptible therapists were Catholic, and psychologists—but the sex of the therapist made no apparent difference. Therapists who were parents, and psychiatric social workers, were the least likely to become enmeshed in this conflictual pattern, perhaps because they could more readily mobilize the *sympathetic warmth* required to offset it. A number of distinctive characteristics were found among patients who were unlikely to be involved in *conflictual erotization:* they were over 36 years of age, were mothers, were divorced or widowed, had one sibling, came from lower-middle-class backgrounds, were Jewish, and were diagnosed as schizophrenic. In general, they seem to be people whose need for support is more salient or more readily mobilized than their sexual feelings, as well as people more likely to elicit nurturant than erotic responses from their therapists.

## CONCLUSIONS

We have considered the functioning of the psychotherapist as an instrument of observation and as an instrument of treatment. We have done so "from the inside," as it were, with the peculiar advantages and limitations that arise from using patients' and therapists' experiences as our base. Now, insofar as it is possible to separate the two functions, we might sum up by saying that the psychotherapist's responsiveness in treatment is both more adequate and more essential than is his perceptiveness. His failures in object perception were found to be the rule rather than the exception, but somehow these failures must not be crucial. His failures of responsiveness, on the other hand, although often attributable to the difficulties and obstacles presented by patients, tended to stall the progress of treatment.

The advice that we have to offer the psychotherapist about his function as an instrument of treatment can be put in the words that E. M. Forster chose as the motto for his novel, *Howard's End:* "Only connect." The therapist must connect in two ways. He must stay responsive to his own experience—to the spontaneous flow of impulse, feeling, and fantasy that gives him a sense of his personal position in the therapeutic involvement. He must also remain in touch with that parallel thread of aliveness and continuity in the patient's experience, no matter what unexpected turns it takes or frightening places it leads, and no matter how the patient tries to protect it and conceal it from him. Obviously the latter is by no means always a simple task, but those who are called to the vocation of psychotherapy are usually people who have a talent for—and find a satisfying challenge in—making the difficult human connection. The heroes of the psychotherapeutic profession tend to be just those therapists who succeed in making the most difficult sorts of connection, e.g., those who, like Sullivan and Fromm-Reichman, chose to work with the hospitalized schizophrenic.

There are patients who will test each therapist beyond his capacity to respond effectively. Some types of patient will "turn him off," and he will "turn off" some types of patient. There are also times in treatment when an effective connection is more difficult to maintain. We all have our limits as therapists. We also have some resources for getting around them, however, chiefly by calling on others for help. Personal therapy and supervisory consultation are traditional resources for the psychotherapist. Bringing another therapist into the treatment situation as a consultant to the relationship is another resource. Working with a co-therapist is yet another. Using sound or video recordings, therapists—or patients and therapists together—may try to provide their own consultation. Even the Therapy Session Report questionnaires seem to have a consultative potential. Other aids to enlarging the responsiveness of the therapist exist or, with sufficient ingenuity, can be devised.

By keeping in touch with the pulse of his own and his patient's experience, the therapist makes the vital connection that permits therapy to happen. He functions as a medium through which the response of each becomes available to the other. This does not mean that the therapist must interpret the patient's experience, nor that he must always disclose his own experience to the patient—although timely interpretation and timely disclosure can work to enlarge and strengthen the vital experiential bond. Even when the therapist is not engaged in exploring and explicating his own or his patient's experience, he must act in a way that is implicitly responsive to both. The therapist's responsibility *is* his responsiveness to his patient and to himself—a responsiveness that serves to connect the experiences of each to the other. That is the challenge to the psychotherapist as an instrument of treatment, as we see it.

# References

Auerbach, A. H.; & Luborsky, L. Accuracy of judgments of psychotherapy and the nature of the "good hour." In J. M. Shlien (Ed.), *Research in psychotherapy*, Vol. 3. Washington, D.C.: American Psychological Association, 1968.

Bandura, A.; & Walters, R. H. *Social learning and personality development.* New York: Holt, Rinehart and Winston, 1963.

Bergin, A. E.; & Garfield, S. L. (Eds.). *Handbook of psychotherapy and behavior change: an empirical analysis.* New York: John Wiley, 1971.

Blau, P. *Exchange and power in social life.* New York: John Wiley, 1964.

Campbell, D. T.; & Stanley, J. C. *Experimental and quasi-experimental designs for research.* Chicago: Rand McNally, 1966.

Chassan, J. B. *Research design in clinical psychology and psychiatry.* New York: Appleton-Century-Crofts, 1967.

Deutsch, H. *The psychology of women,* Vol. II. New York: Grune and Stratton, 1945.

Erikson, E. The nature of clinical evidence. *Daedalus,* 1958, *87,* 65-87.

Feifel, H.; & Eells, J. Patients and therapists assess the same psychotherapy. *Journal of consulting psychology,* 1963, *27,* 310-318.

Ford, D. H.; & Urban, H. B. *Systems of psychotherapy.* New York: John Wiley, 1963.

Freud, S. The dynamics of the transference (1912a). *The collected papers of Sigmund Freud,* Vol. II. London: Hogarth Press, 1953.

Freud, S. Recommendations for physicians on the psychoanalytic method of treatment (1912b). *The collected papers of Sigmund Freud,* Vol. II. London: Hogarth Press, 1953.

Freud, S. Further recommendations in the technique of psychoanalysis: observations on transference-love (1915). *The collected papers of Sigmund Freud,* Vol. II. London: Hogarth Press, 1953.

Goffman, E. *Asylums: essays on the social situations of mental patients and other inmates.* Garden City, N.Y.: Doubleday Anchor, 1961.

Goffman, E. *Behavior in public places.* New York: Free Press, 1963.

Goldman, R. K.; & Mendelsohn, G. A. Psychotherapeutic change and social adjustment: A report of a national survey of psychotherapists. *Journal of Abnormal Psychology,* 1969, *74,* 164-172.

Goldstein, A. P.; Heller, K.; & Sechrest, L. B. *Psychotherapy and the psychology of behavior change.* New York: John Wiley, 1966.

Henry, W. E.; Sims, J. H.; & Spray, S. L. *The fifth profession.* San Francisco: Jossey-Bass, 1971.

Homans, G. C. *Social behavior.* New York: Harcourt, Brace and World, 1961.

Howard, K. I. Differentiation of individuals as a function of repeated testing. *Educational and Psychological Measurement,* 1964, *24,* 875-894.

Howard, K. I.; & Diesenhaus, H. I. Direction of measurement and profile similarity. *Multivariate Behavioral Research,* 1967, *2,* 225-238.

Howard, K. I.; & Gordon, R. A. An empirical note on the "number of factors" problem in factor analysis. *Psychological Reports,* 1963, *12,* 247-250.

Howard, K. I.; & Orlinsky, D. E. Psychotherapeutic processes. In *Annual review of psychology,* Vol. 23. Palo Alto: Annual Reviews, Inc., 1972.

Kadushin, C. *Why people go to psychiatrists.* New York: Atherton, 1969.

Kamin, I.; & Caughlan, J. Subjective experiences of outpatient psychotherapy. *American Journal of Psychotherapy,* 1963, *17,* 660-668.

Kaplan, A. *The conduct of inquiry.* San Francisco: Chandler, 1964.

Laing, R. D. *The divided self.* Baltimore: Penguin Books, 1965.

Laing, R. D. *The politics of experience.* London: Penguin Books, 1967.

Lennard, H. L.; & Burnstein, A. *The anatomy of psychotherapy: systems of communication and expectation.* New York: Columbia University Press, 1960.

MacKinnon, W. J. Compact table of twelve probability levels of the symmetrical binomial cumulative distribution for sample sizes to 1,000. *Journal of the American Statistical Association,* 1959, *54,* 164-172.

Matarazzo, J. D.; Wiens, A. N.; Matarazzo, R. G.; & Saslow, G. Speech and silence behavior in clinical psychotherapy and its laboratory correlates. In J. M. Shlien (Ed.), *Research in psychotherapy,* Vol. 3. Washington, D.C.: American Psychological Association, 1968.

McQuitty, L. L. Capabilities and improvements of linkage analysis as a clustering method. *Educational and Psychological Measurement,* 1964, *24,* 441-456.

Mead, G. H. *The social psychology of George Herbert Mead* (A. Strauss, Ed.). Chicago: University of Chicago Press, 1956.

Meltzoff, J.; & Kornreich, M. *Research in psychotherapy.* New York: Atherton, 1970.

Mendelsohn, G. A.; & Geller, M. H. Structure of client attitudes toward counseling and their relation to client-counselor similarity. *Journal of Consulting Psychology,* 1965, *29,* 63-72.

Meyer, H. J.; Borgatta, E. F.; & Fanshel, D. A study of the interview process: the caseworker-client relationship. *Genetic Psychology Monographs,* 1964, *69,* 247-295.

Orlinsky, D. E. The modalities of interpersonal style: a neglected component of social interaction. *Research Report, 2:8.* Chicago: Institute for Juvenile Research, 1965.

Orlinsky, D. E.; & Howard, K. I. *Therapy Session Report,* Forms P and T. Chicago: Institute for Juvenile Research, 1966.

Orlinsky, D. E.; & Howard, K. I. Communication rapport and patient "progress." *Psychotherapy: Theory, Research and Practice*, 1968, *5*, 131-136.

Polya, G. *Patterns of plausible inference*. Princeton: Princeton University Press, 1954.

Roff, M.; & Ricks, D. F. (Eds.). *Life history research in psychopathology*. Minneapolis: The University of Minnesota Press, 1972.

Ryan, W. (Ed.) *Distress in the city*. Cleveland: Case Western Reserve University Press, 1969.

Schneider, D. *American kinship: a cultural account*. Englewood Cliffs, N.J.: Prentice-Hall, 1968.

Snyder, W. U. *The psychotherapy relationship*. New York: Macmillan, 1961.

Strupp, H. H.; Wallach, M.; & Wogan, M. Psychotherapy experience in retrospect: questionnaire survey of former patients and their therapists. *Psychological Monographs*, 1964, *78*:11.

Szasz, T. S. *Law, liberty and psychiatry*. New York: Macmillan, 1963.

Tellegen, A. Direction of measurement: a source of misinterpretation. *Psychological Bulletin*, 1965, *63*, 233-243.

Tower, L. E. Countertransference. *Journal of the American Psychoanalytic Association*, 1956, *4*, 224-255.

Weber, M. *The theory of social and economic organization* (T. Parsons, Ed.). New York: Free Press, 1964.

Witkin, H. A.; Dyk, R. B.; Faterson, H. F.; Goodenough, D. R.; & Karp, S. A. *Psychological differentiation: studies of development*. New York: John Wiley, 1962.

# Appendices

*Appendix A*

# Information on the Research Program of the Katharine Wright Mental Health Clinic

### The Research Program

A program of research has been established at the Katharine Wright Mental Health Clinic as a supplement to its treatment program. The aim of the research program is to increase scientific understanding of what happens during psychotherapy. This program is a part of the regular Clinic routine, and all patients at the Clinic are asked to join us in it.

### What it Involves

Your part in the research program will involve *about 15 minutes* each evening you come here. *After each therapy session,* you will go to the Clinic Research Room where you will be given a booklet containing some questions. There will be a Research Assistant in the room to help you with any matters that come up as you fill out the booklet.

### What Kind of Questions

The questions contained in the booklet are about what happened in the session you will have just finished. These questions are designed to make your description of your session simple and quick. As mentioned, it should take about 15 minutes to fill out the booklet. Probably, as you become familiar with the questions in the booklet, the time needed for answering them will be even less.

231

### Confidentiality

The answers that you give will be kept in strict professional confidence. No one on the Staff of the Clinic, including your therapist, will see your answers or be able to identify you personally. Your answers will be transferred to IBM cards and analyzed by electronic computers at a research center that is separate from this Clinic. Every precaution will be taken to protect your privacy.

### What it is For

While the main purpose of this program is for the long range benefits that greater knowledge will bring, we think that you will find participating in it both interesting and potentially helpful. Remember to schedule a little extra time for yourself after each therapy session.

*Appendix B*

# Patient Therapy Session Report

You are being asked to take part in a study of what happens during therapy sessions. After each session, you will be given this booklet, which contains a number of questions about the session you have just finished. The questions are designed to make your description of your session simple and quick. Once you have become familiar with the questions through regular use, answering them will take only a few minutes of your time.

There will be many people participating in this project. The personal reactions of individuals are not being studied. Rather, the study seeks to determine the *typical* or average kinds of events that take place in therapy.

Because your honest responses are so important, your answers will be kept confidential. Every resource has been used to guarantee complete anonymity for the participants in this study. However, we do need a method of keeping all of the reports from each person together. Consequently, we are asking you to put your initials and the date of each session at the bottom of this cover sheet. This sheet will be removed and destroyed as soon as an appropriate code number is entered on the other sheets.

The knowledge gained from this research will deepen our understanding of the psychotherapeutic process. We want to thank you for your contribution to this effort.

*Initials* _____

*Today's date* _____

*Be sure to answer each question.*

**233**

1. *How do you feel about the therapy session which you have just completed?*

   (Check the statement which best applies.)

   _____ 1. This was one of the best sessions we have had.

   _____ 2. This was a really good session.

   _____ 3. This was a pretty good session.

   _____ 4. This was a fair session.

   _____ 5. This was a pretty poor session.

   _____ 6. This was a really poor session.

## SESSION CONTENT AREA THEMES

*What did you talk about during this session?*
(Check as many of the answers below as apply to this session.)
*During this session,* I *talked about:*

_____ 2. social activities and relationships, friends and acquaintances.
_____ 3. work, supervisors, associates on the job (or at school).
_____ 4. recreations, hobbies, interests.
_____ 5. domestic and household responsibilities, concerns, and activities (finances, children, etc.).
_____ 6. relationship with spouse, boyfriend, or girlfriend.
_____ 7. current relations with parents, brothers, or sisters.
_____ 8. childhood experiences with family members, and feelings about them.
_____ 9. childhood experiences in school, with friends and with other kids.
_____10. feelings and attitudes toward myself.
_____11. body functions, health, physical symptoms.
_____12. inadequacies, fears, or successes in getting along personally and socially.
_____13. sexual feelings and experiences.
_____14. angry and aggressive feelings and experiences.
_____15. feelings about being close to or needing someone.
_____16. dreams, fantasies.
_____17. plans, hopes, and goals for the future.
_____18. strange or unusual ideas, feelings, or experiences.
_____19. therapy, the therapist, being a patient.
          other: _____

# PURPOSES OF THERAPY SESSION

*What did you want or hope to get out of this therapy session?*
(Check as many of the answers below as apply.)

*This session, I hoped (or wanted) to:*

_____20. get relief from nervousness and bad feelings.

_____21. get a chance to let go and get things off my chest.

_____22. get a better understanding of my feelings and behavior.

_____23. show my therapist that I know what is going on, too.

_____24. get some reassurance about how I'm doing.

_____25. let my therapist see how I've improved.

_____26. work out a problem that I have.

_____27. get advice on how to deal with my life and with other people.

_____28. get my therapist to like me better as a person.

_____29. get my therapist to leave me alone for a while.

_____30. get my therapist to take my side.

_____31. find out more about my therapist as a person.

_____32. get even with my therapist for the way I've been treated.

_____33. work together with my therapist on a person-to-person basis.

_____34. get help in talking about what is really troubling me.

_____35. talk and just get the session over with.

_____36. get better self-control over my moods and over the things I do.

_____37. get an emotional response from my therapist.

_____38. get straight on which things I feel and think are real and which are mostly in my mind.

_____39. get my therapist to say what he (she) really thinks.

           other: _____

## BEHAVIOR IN THERAPY SESSION

*How did you act toward your therapist during this session?*
(Try to check only one set of words for each item; but, if the way you acted changed during this session, check as many sets of words as are necessary.)

*Item I. During this session, I was mainly:*

_____40. taking the lead: having my own ideas: bringing up things to talk about

_____41. following: receptive: waiting for direction from my therapist

_____42. working together: joining in: cooperating

_____43. distant: reserved: holding back

*Item II. During this session, I was mainly:*

_____44. determined: not giving in: firm

_____45. agreeing: going along with: changing my mind

_____46. able to compromise: sharing: "give and take"

_____47. independent: uninfluenced: making up my own mind

*Item III. During this session, I was mainly:*

_____48. friendly: warm: respectful

_____49. critical: negative: sarcastic

_____50. respectful but critical: both positive and negative: "mixed feelings"

_____51. neutral: impartial: neither positive nor negative

*Item IV. During this session, I was mainly:*

_____52. excited: emotional: actively involved

_____53. feeling deeply: moved but controlled: stirred up but quiet

_____54. talkative: businesslike: active but not stirred up

_____55. quiet: inactive: unemotional

---

| | | | | |
|---|---|---|---|---|
| 67_____ | 70_____ | 72_____ | 75_____ | 80_____ |
| 68  2 | 71_____ | 73_____ | 76_____ | |
| 69  1 | | 74_____ | 77_____ | |
| | | | 78_____ | |
| | | | 79_____ | |

## FEELINGS IN THERAPY SESSION

*How did you feel during this session?*
(Check as many as apply.)

| | | |
|---|---|---|
| _____ 1. tense | _____16. satisfied | _____31. suspicious |
| _____ 2. anxious | _____17. cheerful | _____32. hurt |
| _____ 3. worried | _____18. optimistic | _____33. rejected |
| _____ 4. calm | _____19. shy | _____34. trusting |
| _____ 5. relaxed | _____20. embarrassed | _____35. secure |
| _____ 6. relieved | _____21. guilty | _____36. accepted |
| _____ 7. inadequate | _____22. confident | _____37. tired |
| _____ 8. inferior | _____23. playful | _____38. dull |
| _____ 9. helpless | _____24. likeable | _____39. energetic |
| _____10. effective | _____25. bored | _____40. alert |
| _____11. superior | _____26. irritable | _____41. hungry |
| _____12. triumphant | _____27. angry | _____42. thirsty |
| _____13. frustrated | _____28. interested | _____43. sexually aroused |
| _____14. sad | _____29. sympathetic | _____44. need to relieve bladder |
| _____15. discouraged | _____30. tender | _____45. need to relieve bowels |
| | | _____other:_____ |
| | | _____ |
| | | _____ |

## DEVELOPMENT OF THERAPY SESSION

Think of the session which you have just completed. Read each of the following questions, and *circle* the number of the answer which best describes the *way you felt about this session. Be sure to answer each question.*

46. *To what extent were you looking forward to coming to this session?*
    1. I was very much looking forward to coming to this session; could hardly wait to get here.
    2. I was somewhat looking forward to coming to this session; was glad to get here.
    3. I was not anticipating this session one way or the other; it was scheduled and I didn't think much about it.
    4. I felt somewhat unwilling to come to this session; there were other things I would have liked to do.
    5. I felt very unwilling to come to this session; I thought about not coming this time.
    6. I felt I didn't want to come to this session; I had to make myself come here.

47. *How freely were you able to talk with your therapist during this session?*
    1. I had a great deal of difficulty talking to my therapist; it was very hard for me to express myself.
    2. I had considerable difficulty talking with my therapist, but I was able to discuss some things with him (her).
    3. I had occasional difficulty in talking to my therapist, but for the most part I was able to express myself freely.
    4. I didn't have any difficulty in talking with my therapist this session.

48. *How clearly did you know what you wanted to talk about during this session?*
    1. I knew clearly what I wanted to talk about this session.
    2. I knew pretty much what I wanted to talk about this session, but sometimes I lost track.
    3. I had some difficulty this session in finding the things I wanted to talk about; at times I didn't have any thoughts or know what to say.
    4. I had a great deal of difficulty in knowing what to talk about; either my mind was blank or the things I thought of didn't seem right.

49. *How well did your therapist seem to understand how you were feeling and what was really on your mind during this session?*
    1. My therapist seemed to understand very well how I was feeling and what was on my mind during this session.
    2. My therapist understood pretty well how I was feeling and what was on my mind, but there were some things that I couldn't seem to get across to him (her).
    3. I didn't think that my therapist understood too well how I was feeling and what was on my mind during this session.
    4. My therapist seemed to misunderstand how I was feeling and what was on my mind during this session.

50. *Do you feel that what your therapist said and did this session was helpful to you?*
    1. The things that my therapist said and did this session were very helpful to me.
    2. The things that my therapist said and did this session were pretty helpful to me.
    3. The things that my therapist said and did this session were somewhat helpful to me.
    4. The things that my therapist said and did this session were only slightly or not at all helpful to me.
    5. I feel that the things my therapist said and did this session may have made me worse off than I was.

51.  *Do you feel that you made progress in this session in dealing with the problems for which you are in therapy?*

1.  I made a considerable amount of progress in dealing with my problems during this session.
2.  I made some progress in this session in dealing with my problems.
3.  I really didn't get anywhere in this session in dealing with my problems.
4.  In some ways my problems got worse during this session.

52.  *How well do you feel that you are getting along, emotionally and psychologically, at this time?*

1.  I am getting along quite well; much the way I would like to.
2.  I am getting along pretty well; have my ups and downs.
3.  I am getting along fairly well; manage to keep going with some effort.
4.  I am getting along fairly poorly; life gets pretty rough for me at times.
5.  I am getting along quite poorly; I feel that I can barely manage to deal with things.

## SATISFACTIONS IN THERAPY SESSION

*What do you feel that you got out of this session?*
(For each item, *circle* one of the following numbers:

            1—very much;
            2—moderately;
            3—slightly or not at all.)

*During this session, I feel that I got:*

| | | | | |
|---|---|---|---|---|
| 53. | relief from the tension I was under. | 1 | 2 | 3 |
| 54. | better insight and self-understanding. | 1 | 2 | 3 |
| 55. | reassurance and encouragement about how I'm doing. | 1 | 2 | 3 |
| 56. | better ability to feel my feelings, to be what I really am. | 1 | 2 | 3 |
| 57. | ideas for new or better ways of dealing with people. | 1 | 2 | 3 |
| 58. | a sense of having an honest person-to-person relationship with my therapist, of working together. | 1 | 2 | 3 |
| 59. | help in being able to talk about what was troubling to me and really important. | 1 | 2 | 3 |
| 60. | a better ability to tell which of the things I felt and thought were real and which were mostly in my own mind. | 1 | 2 | 3 |
| 61. | better self-control over my moods and actions. | 1 | 2 | 3 |
| | other:_____ | | | |

62. *To what extent are you looking forward to your next session?*

1. I am looking forward to my next session very much; I wish it were sooner.
2. I am looking forward to my next session pretty much; will be ready for it when it comes.
3. I am not looking forward to my next session one way or the other; it is scheduled and so far as I know I'll be there.
4. I am definitely not looking forward to my next session; I'm not so sure I will want to come.

| | | | | |
|---|---|---|---|---|
| 67_____ | 70_____ | 72_____ | 75_____ | 80_____ |
| 68 _2_ | 71_____ | 73_____ | 76_____ | |
| 69 _2_ | | 74_____ | 77_____ | |
| | | | 78_____ | |
| | | | 79_____ | |

# BEHAVIOR IN THERAPY SESSION

*How did your therapist act toward you during this session?*
(Try to check only one set of words for each item; but if there were changes in the way your therapist acted, check as many sets of words as are necessary.)

*Item I. During this session,* my therapist *was mainly:*

_____ 1. leading: directing: bringing things up to talk about
_____ 2. attentive: waiting for me to lead: following
_____ 3. joining in: working together: cooperating
_____ 4. distant: reserved: holding back

*Item II. During this session,* my therapist *was mainly:*

_____ 5. insistent: demanding: firm
_____ 6. agreeing: going along with: doing what I wanted
_____ 7. democratic: open minded: willing to compromise
_____ 8. independent: uninfluenced: making up his own mind

*Item III. During this session,* my therapist *was mainly:*

_____ 9. friendly: helpful: on my side
_____10. critical: negative: sarcastic
_____11. strict but fair: helpful but critical
_____12. neutral: impartial: impersonal

*Item IV. During this session,* my therapist *was mainly:*

_____13. intense: enthusiastic: excited
_____14. moved but controlled: stirred: involved
_____15. businesslike: active but uninvolved: brisk
_____16. uninvolved: quiet: inactive

## FEELINGS IN THERAPY SESSION

*How did your therapist seem to feel during this session?*
(Check as many as apply.)

| | | |
|---|---|---|
| ____17. calm | ____32. bored | ____47. energetic |
| ____18. confident | ____33. irritable | ____48. alert |
| ____19. effective | ____34. angry | ____49. tired |
| ____20. tense | ____35. satisfied | ____50. dull |
| ____21. apprehensive | ____36. cheerful | ____other:_____ |
| ____22. inadequate | ____37. optimistic | |
| ____23. involved | ____38. frustrated | |
| ____24. close | ____39. depressed | |
| ____25. intimate | ____40. discouraged | |
| ____26. preoccupied | ____41. pleased | |
| ____27. detached | ____42. attracted | |
| ____28. withdrawn | ____43. playful | |
| ____29. interested | ____44. disappointed | |
| ____30. sympathetic | ____45. repelled | |
| ____31. tender | ____46. embarrassed | |

| | | | | |
|---|---|---|---|---|
| 67____ | 70____ | 72____ | 75____ | 80____ |
| 68 2 | 71____ | 73____ | 76____ | |
| 69 3 | | 74____ | 77____ | |
| | | | 78____ | |
| | | | 79____ | |

*Appendix C*

# Therapist Therapy Session Report

This booklet contains a set of checklists to be filled out immediately after your therapy session. The items in it are designed to make your report of what has taken place in the therapy session meaningful, simple, and quick. As you become familiar with the questions through regular use, answering them will take only a few minutes of your time.

As you know, the focus of this research is on the encounter between patients and therapists in their therapy sessions. The study is not concerned with the experiences of individuals. Every resource has been used to guarantee complete anonymity for the participants. However, we do need a method for keeping the reports of each patient-therapist pair together. To do this, we are asking you to write the patient's name and the date of each session in the spaces provided below. This cover sheet will be removed and destroyed as soon as the appropriate numerical code is entered on the other sheets, so that no record with either your name or the patient's will be used.

We appreciate your participation and will be pleased to receive any further help you can give in the way of suggestions and comments.

*Patient's name* _____

*Today's date* _____

*Be sure to answer each question.*

1. *How do you feel about the session which you have just completed?* (Check the statement which best applies.)

_____ 1. This was one of the best sessions we have had.
_____ 2. This was a really good session.
_____ 3. This was a pretty good session.
_____ 4. This was a fair session.
_____ 5. This was a pretty poor session.
_____ 6. This was a really poor session.

## SESSION CONTENT AREA THEMES

*What did your patient talk about during this session?*
(Check as many as apply.)
*During this session, my patient talked about:*

_____ 2. social activities and relationships, friends and acquaintances.

_____ 3. work, supervisors, associates on the job (or at school).

_____ 4. recreations, hobbies, interests.

_____ 5. domestic and household responsibilities, concerns, and activities (finances, children, etc.).

_____ 6. relationship with spouse, boyfriend, or girlfriend.

_____ 7. current relations with parents, brothers, or sisters.

_____ 8. childhood experiences with family members, and feelings about them.

_____ 9. childhood experiences in school, with friends and with other kids.

_____10. feelings and attitudes toward self.

_____11. body functions, health, and physical symptoms.

_____12. inadequacies, fears, or successes in getting along personally and socially.

_____13. sexual feelings and experiences.

_____14. angry and aggressive feelings and experiences.

_____15. feelings about being close to or needing someone.

_____16. dreams, fantasies.

_____17. plans, hopes, and goals for the future.

_____18. strange or unusual ideas, feelings, or experiences.

_____19. therapy, the therapist, being a patient.

other:_____

_____

# PATIENT'S AIMS IN THERAPY SESSION

*What did your patient seem to want out of this session?*
(Check as many as apply.)

*During this session, my patient's behavior seemed aimed at:*

_____20. avoiding anxiety through defensive behavior and security operations.

_____21. getting relief by giving vent to suppressed or pent up feelings.

_____22. gaining insight and better self-understanding.

_____23. competing with the therapist.

_____24. gaining attention, approval, sympathy, or affection.

_____25. working through or resolving a recognized emotional conflict.

_____26. getting "expert" advice, opinion, etc., on some problem.

_____27. seductive provocation of the therapist.

_____28. withdrawal or evasion of contact with the therapist.

_____29. winning the therapist as an ally in a dispute or conflict.

_____30. gaining knowledge of the therapist's personal life.

_____31. revenge on or punishment of the therapist.

_____32. testing the limits of the therapist and the therapy relationship.

_____33. getting respite or relief from external involvements and pressure.

_____34. filling time to get through the therapy session.

_____35. provocation of the therapist to criticism or anger.

_____36. getting oriented to therapy and to being a patient.

other: _____

_____

## BEHAVIOR IN THERAPY SESSION

*How did your patient act toward you during this session?*
(Try to check only one set of words for each item; but, if there were changes in the way your patient acted, check as many as you feel are necessary.)

*Item I. During this session,* my patient *was predominantly:*

_____37.  purposeful: taking the lead: initiating topics

_____38.  responsive: waiting for direction: receptive

_____39.  cooperating: joining in: working together

_____40.  distant: withdrawing from interaction: remote

*Item II. During this session,* my patient *was predominantly:*

_____41.  insistent: controlling: unyielding

_____42.  agreeing: submissive: giving in

_____43.  mutually influencing: sharing: "give and take"

_____44.  independent: making up own mind: uninfluenced

*Item III. During this session,* my patient *was predominantly:*

_____45.  friendly: warm: engaging

_____46.  critical: negative: hostile

_____47.  conflicted: ambivalent: "mixed feelings"

_____48.  neutral: impersonal: impartial

*Item IV. During this session,* my patient *was predominantly:*

_____49.  animated: enthusiastic: excited

_____50.  deeply feeling: moved but expressively controlled: stirred

_____51.  businesslike: brisk: active but uninvolved emotionally

_____52.  impassive: unmoved: restrained

---

| 67_____ | 70_____ | 72_____ | 75_____ | 80_____ |
|---------|---------|---------|---------|---------|
| 68 1    | 71_____ | 73_____ | 76_____ |         |
| 69 1    |         | 74_____ | 77_____ |         |
|         |         |         | 78_____ |         |
|         |         |         | 79_____ |         |

## FEELINGS IN THERAPY SESSION

*How did your patient seem to feel during this session?*
(*Check* those feelings which seemed distinctly present. If you think your patient had a feeling without being directly aware or conscious of it, *circle* that feeling.)

| | | |
|---|---|---|
| _____ 1. tense | _____16. satisfied | _____31. suspicious |
| _____ 2. anxious | _____17. cheerful | _____32. hurt |
| _____ 3. worried | _____18. optimistic | _____33. rejected |
| _____ 4. calm | _____19. shy | _____34. trusting |
| _____ 5. relaxed | _____20. embarrassed | _____35. secure |
| _____ 6. relieved | _____21. guilty | _____36. accepted |
| _____ 7. inadequate | _____22. confident | _____37. tired |
| _____ 8. inferior | _____23. playful | _____38. dull |
| _____ 9. helpless | _____24. likeable | _____39. energetic |
| _____10. effective | _____25. bored | _____40. alert |
| _____11. superior | _____26. irritable | _____other:_____ |
| _____12. triumphant | _____27. angry | _____ |
| _____13. frustrated | _____28. interested | _____ |
| _____14. sad | _____29. sympathetic | |
| _____15. discouraged | _____30. tender | |

## DEVELOPMENT OF THERAPY SESSION

Think of the session which you have just completed. Read each of the following questions, and *circle* the number of the answer which best describes the *way you felt about this session. Be sure to answer each question.*

41. *To what extent were you looking forward to seeing your patient this session?*
    1. I was quite interested in seeing my patient this session, and found myself looking forward to it.
    2. I was not anticipating this session in particular, but found myself pleased to see the patient when the time came.
    3. I wasn't looking forward one way or the other to seeing the patient this session; I was neutral in my feelings about it.
    4. I was definitely not looking forward to seeing the patient this session, and anticipated a trying or unpleasant experience.

42. *How well motivated for coming to therapy was your patient this session?*
    1. My patient was strongly motivated in coming to therapy this session, and had been looking forward to it.
    2. My patient showed positive motivation for therapy once here, but didn't seem to have anticipated coming in particular.
    3. My patient was not positively motivated for therapy this session; seemed to come just to keep the scheduled appointment.
    4. My patient was definitely not motivated for therapy this session, and expressed clear resistance to being here.

43. *How freely did your patient express herself (himself) in this session?*
    1. My patient was for the most part unable to communicate with me effectively; was silent, withdrawn, or not coherent.
    2. My patient had considerable difficulty in expressing herself (himself), but managed to overcome it sufficiently for some communication with me.
    3. My patient had occasional difficulty in communicating with me, but for the most part expressed herself (himself) adequately.
    4. My patient was free in communicating with me; talked expressively and coherently.

44. *To what extent did your patient bring out the thoughts and feelings which really seemed to concern her (him) during this session?*
    1. My patient was for the most part unable to bring out the thoughts and feelings which really concerned her (him).
    2. My patient had considerable difficulty bringing out these concerns, and was able to deal with them only to a limited degree.
    3. My patient had some difficulty in bringing out her (his) real thoughts and feelings, but was able to deal with them to a considerable extent.
    4. My patient had little or no difficulty in bringing out her (his) real thoughts and feelings and dealing with them.

45. *To what extent did you feel in rapport or empathically "in touch" with what your patient was experiencing during this session?*
    1. I felt in touch with my patient's feelings and experiences nearly all of this session.
    2. I felt mostly in touch with what my patient was experiencing during this session, but occasionally lost empathic contact with her (him).
    3. I could recognize but only occasionally empathize with what my patient was experiencing during this session.
    4. I nearly always felt out of direct, empathic touch with my patient's experiences and feelings during this session.

46. *How well do you feel you understood the meaning of what your patient said and did during this session (in whatever conceptual terms you find most useful for describing personality)?*
    1. I understood the meaning of almost all that my patient said and did during this session.
    2. I understood a good deal of what my patient said and did, but remain uncertain about the meaning of important aspects of her (his) behavior.
    3. I understood some, but generally felt unclear about the meaning of a good deal of what my patient said and did during this session.
    4. I understood little or none of the meaning of what my patient said and did during this session.

47. *How helpful do you feel that you were to your patient during this session?*

    1. What I did this session seemed to be of considerable help to my patient.
    2. What I did this session seemed pretty helpful to my patient.
    3. What I did this session seemed somewhat helpful to my patient.
    4. What I did this session seemed only slightly if at all helpful to my patient.
    5. What I did this session may have been more disturbing than helpful to my patient.

48. *To what extent did your patient seem to make progress during this session in dealing with the problems for which she (he) is in therapy?*

    1. My patient seemed to make considerable progress in dealing with her (his) problems during this session.
    2. My patient made some progress in this session in dealing with her (his) problems, but not very much.
    3. My patient really didn't get anywhere this session in dealing with the problems for which she (he) is in treatment.
    4. My patient seemed to lose ground therapeutically during this session; to slip back to a more pathological level of functioning.

49. *At what level of effectiveness and integration (emotionally and psychologically) did your patient seem to be during this session?*

    1. My patient was functioning quite well, emotionally and psychologically, during this session; seemed in very good condition.
    2. My patient was functioning fairly well during this session, but still showed some distinct impairment in effectiveness and integration.
    3. My patient was functioning with limited effectiveness and integration; her (his) problems constitute a significant impairment emotionally and psychologically.
    4. My patient was functioning fairly poorly during this session; seemed considerably impaired in effectiveness and integration, but able to get by.
    5. My patient was functioning quite poorly during this session; level of adjustment seemed very marginal.

## GOALS IN THERAPY SESSION

*In what direction were you working with your patient during this session?*
(For each item, *circle* one of the following numbers:

> 1—if very much;
> 2—if moderately;
> 3—if little, or not at all.)

*During this session, I was working toward:*

| | | | | |
|---|---|---|---|---|
| 50. | relieving my patient's tension and anxiety. | 1 | 2 | 3 |
| 51. | increasing my patient's insight and self-understanding. | 1 | 2 | 3 |
| 52. | supporting my patient's self-esteem. | 1 | 2 | 3 |
| 53. | moving my patient closer to experiencing her (his) real feelings, what she (he) really is. | 1 | 2 | 3 |
| 54. | helping my patient learn new or better ways of dealing with people and problems. | 1 | 2 | 3 |
| 55. | supporting my patient's defenses. | 1 | 2 | 3 |
| 56. | engaging my patient in an honest person-to-person relationship, working together authentically. | 1 | 2 | 3 |
| 57. | helping my patient overcome her (his) resistance and defenses in order to get to what was of real concern to her (him). | 1 | 2 | 3 |
| 58. | orienting my patient more effectively to interpersonal reality in order to discriminate and control autistic tendencies. | 1 | 2 | 3 |
| 59. | helping my patient gain better control over her (his) moods or impulses. | 1 | 2 | 3 |
| | other:_____ | | | |

_____

| 67_____ | 70_____ | 72_____ | 75_____ | 80_____ |
|---|---|---|---|---|
| 68  1 | 71_____ | 73_____ | 76_____ | |
| 69  2 | | 74_____ | 77_____ | |
| | | | 78_____ | |
| | | | 79_____ | |

## BEHAVIOR IN THERAPY SESSION

*How did you act toward your patient during this session?*
(Try to check only one set of words for each item; but, if there were changes in the way you acted, check as many as you feel are necessary.)

*Item I.    During this session, I was predominantly:*

_____ 1. structuring: intervening: initiating topics

_____ 2. receptive: attentive: responsive

_____ 3. interacting: joining in: working together

_____ 4. reserved: distant: remote

*Item II.    During this session, I was predominantly:*

_____ 5. determined: insistent: firm

_____ 6. agreeing: complying: going along with

_____ 7. mutually influencing: sharing: "give and take"

_____ 8. independent: uninfluenced: self-determining

*Item III.   During this session, I was predominantly:*

_____ 9. supportive: empathic: friendly

_____10. reproving: correcting: critical

_____11. supportive but critical: correcting but friendly

_____12. neutral: impartial: impersonal

*Item IV.   During this session, I was predominantly:*

_____13. animated: enthusiastic: excited

_____14. moved but expressively controlled: emotionally responsive: stirred

_____15. businesslike: active but uninvolved affectively

_____16. inactive: restrained: unmoved

## FEELINGS IN THERAPY SESSION

*How did* you *feel during this session?*
(Check as many as apply.)

| | | | |
|---|---|---|---|
| ____17. calm | ____32. bored | ____47. energetic | |
| ____18. confident | ____33. irritable | ____48. alert | |
| ____19. effective | ____34. angry | ____49. tired | |
| ____20. tense | ____35. satisfied | ____50. dull | |
| ____21. apprehensive | ____36. cheerful | ____51. hungry | |
| ____22. inadequate | ____37. optimistic | ____52. thirsty | |
| | | ____53. sexually aroused | |
| ____23. involved | ____38. frustrated | ____54. need to relieve bladder | |
| ____24. close | ____39. depressed | | |
| ____25. intimate | ____40. discouraged | ____55. need to relieve bowels | |
| ____26. preoccupied | ____41. pleased | ____other:_____ | |
| ____27. detached | ____42. attracted | _____ | |
| ____28. withdrawn | ____43. playful | _____ | |
| ____29. interested | ____44. disappointed | | |
| ____30. sympathetic | ____45. repelled | | |
| ____31. tender | ____46. embarrassed | | |

---

| | | | | |
|---|---|---|---|---|
| 67____ | 70____ | 72____ | 75____ | 80____ |
| 68 $\underline{1}$ | 71____ | 73____ | 76____ | |
| 69 $\underline{3}$ | | 74____ | 77____ | |
| | | | 78____ | |
| | | | 79____ | |

## Appendix D

# Patient Background

Please fill in the following information.

*Personal Background*

1,2. Age:_____years

3. Sex: 1_____Female
       2_____Male

4. Education:
   1_____Grammer school or less
   2_____Some high school
   3_____Completed high school
   4_____Some college
   5_____Completed college
   6_____Graduate school

5. Occupation—Are you employed? _____

6. If "yes," what is your job?

   _____

7. Marital Status:
   1_____Single
   2_____Engaged
   3_____First marriage
   4_____Second or more marriage
   5_____Separated
   6_____Divorced
   7_____Widowed

8. If married, what is your husband's (wife's) job?

   _____

9. How many children do you have?
   1_____None
   2_____One
   3_____Two
   4_____Three or more

*Family Background*

10. How many *older* brothers did you have?_____

11. How many *older* sisters did you have?_____

12. How many *younger* brothers did you have?_____

13. How many *younger* sisters did you have?_____

14. What is the marital status of your parents?
    1_____Living together
    2_____Separated
    3_____Divorced
    4_____One parent widowed
    5_____Both deceased

15. If your parental home was broken while you were growing up (by separation, divorce, or death) how old were you at the time when this first happened? _____

16. What is (or was) your father's occupation? _____

_____

*Cultural Background*

17. Racial background:
    1_____White
    2_____Negro
    3_____Other

18. What is your father's nationality background? _____

_____

19. What is your mother's nationality background? _____

_____

20. What is your religious background?
    1_____Protestant
    2_____Roman Catholic
    3_____Jewish
    4_____Other
    5_____None
    6_____Mixed

21. How big is your "home town" (the place where you grew up)?
    1_____Large city (over 1,000,000)
    2_____City (under 1,000,000)
    3_____Suburb
    4_____Town
    5_____Rural

*Psychotherapy Background*

22. Have you ever had psychotherapy before?
    1_____Yes
    2_____No

    If "yes,"

23,4 (a) How long a time were you in therapy? _____months

25,6 (b) On the average, how many times a month did you meet with your therapist? _____sessions a month

Identification _____

Today's date _____

| 66 9 | 70_____ | 72_____ | 75_____ | 80_____ |
| 67_____ | 71_____ | 73_____ | 76_____ | |
| 68 2 | | 74_____ | 77_____ | |
| 69 9 | | | 78_____ | |
| | | | 79_____ | |

# Appendix E

# Therapist Background

As a coordinate part of the program of therapy research being conducted at this clinic, we are making a survey of all therapists. Please fill in the following information and return this form to Mr. Miller. Thank you for your cooperation.

Name:_____

*Professional Background*

1. Profession:
   1____Psychiatrist
   2____Psychologist
   3____Psychiatric social
        worker
   4____Other (specify)
        _____

2,3. How many years of experience have you had as a psychotherapist?
     ____years

Which of the following people or schools of thought have significantly influenced your approach to psychotherapy? (Check as many as apply.)

4. ____Freud
5. ____Sullivan
6. ____Adler
7. ____Rank
8. ____Jung
9. ____Rogers

10. ____Existentialism
11. ____Other (Specify)_____
        _____
        _____
        _____

12. Have you had personal therapy?
    1____Yes
    2____No

*Personal Data*

13,14. Age:____years

15. Sex: 1____Male
         2____Female

16. Marital status:
    1____Single
    2____Engaged
    3____First marriage
    4____Second or more
         marriage
    5____Separated
    6____Divorced
    7____Widowed

17. Do you have any children?
    1_____Yes
    2_____No

*Cultural Background*

18. What is your father's nationality background?

    _____

19. What is your mother's nationality background?

    _____

20. What is your religious background?
    1_____Protestant
    2_____Roman Catholic
    3_____Jewish
    4_____Other
    5_____None

21. Racial background:
    1_____White
    2_____Negro
    3_____Other

22. How large is your "home town" (the place where you grew up)?
    1_____Large city (over 1,000,000)
    2_____City (under 1,000,000)
    3_____Suburb
    4_____Town
    5_____Rural

*Family Background*

23. What is (or was) your father's occupation? _____

    _____

24. How many *older* brothers did you have ? _____

25. How many *older* sisters did you have? _____

26. How many *younger* brothers did you have? _____

27. How many *younger* sisters did you have? _____

| 67_____ | 70_____ | 72_____ | 75_____ | 80_____ |
| 68  9 | 71_____ | 73_____ | 76_____ | |
| 69  9 | | 74_____ | 77_____ | |
| | | | 78_____ | |
| | | | 79_____ | |

# Appendix F

# Salient Items[1] for Each Patient Facet-Factor

**Dialogue—"What did you talk about during this session?"**

P-1  *Anger and Family Relations*
   8. Childhood experiences with family members, and feelings about them.
   14. Angry and aggressive feelings and experiences.
   7. Current relations with parents, brothers, or sisters.
   10. Feelings and attitudes toward myself.

P-2  *Domestic Concerns vs. Career Concerns*
   5. Domestic and household responsibilities, concerns, and activities (finances, children, etc.).
   3. *Not* work, supervisors, associates on the job (or at school).

P-3  *Social Reality and "Outer" Concerns*
   4. Recreation, hobbies, interests.
   17. Plans, hopes, and goals for the future.

P-4  *Fantasy and "Inner" Concerns*
   16. Dreams, fantasies.
   18. Strange or unusual ideas, feelings, or experiences.

P-5  *Identity and Competence in Heterosexual Relationships*
   6. Relationship with spouse, boyfriend, or girlfriend.
   13. Sexual feelings and experiences.
   12. Inadequacies, fears, or successes in getting along personally and socially.
   15. Feelings about being close to or needing someone.
   19. Therapy, the therapist, being a patient.

[1] Items are listed in descending order of loadings; significant non-salient loadings are listed in parentheses when used to interpret the meaning of a facet-factor.

## Patient Feeling Process—"How did you feel during this session?"

P-6 *Good*
   22. Confident
   35. Secure
   16. Satisfied
   17. Cheerful
   5. Relaxed
   10. Effective
   6. Relieved
   40. Alert
   4. Calm
   34. Trusting
   18. Optimistic
   36. Accepted
   28. Interested
   39. Energetic
   24. Likeable
   12. Triumphant

P-7 *Bad*
   8. Inferior
   32. Hurt
   3. Worried
   2. Anxious
   9. Helpless
   15. Discouraged
   1. Tense
   33. Rejected
   7. Inadequate

   37. Tired
   27. Angry
   21. Guilty
   13. Frustrated
   14. Sad
   31. Suspicious
   26. Irritable

P-8 *Flirtatious*
   11. Superior
   23. Playful
   29. Sympathetic
   38. Dull

P-9 *Embarrassing Sexual Arousal*
   43. Sexually aroused
   20. Embarrassed
   19. Shy

P-10 *Trusting Warmth vs. "Turned Off"*
   36. (Accepted)
   30. Tender
   25. *Not* bored
   34. (Trusting)

P-11 *Bodily Need Sensations*
   41. Hungry
   44. Bladder pressure
   45. Bowel pressure

## Therapist Feeling Process—"How did your therapist seem to feel during this session?"

P-12 *Effective*
   19. Effective
   18. Confident
   17. Calm
   47. Energetic
   48. Alert
   37. Optimistic
   29. Interested
   30. Sympathetic

P-13 *Ineffective*
   22. Inadequate
   50. Dull
   40. Discouraged

   43. Playful
   26. Preoccupied

P-14 *Displeased*
   44. Disappointed
   45. Repelled
   34. Angry

P-15 *Uneasy Intimacy*
   31. Tender
   25. Intimate
   21. Apprehensive
   24. Close
   49. Tired

P-16 *Pleased*
    41. Pleased
    35. Satisfied
    36. Cheerful
    42. Attracted

P-17 *"Turned Off"*
    27. Detached
    28. Withdrawn
    32. Bored

P-18 *Invested*
    38. Frustrated
    23. Involved

P-19 *Embarrassed and Tense*
    46. Embarrassed
    20. Tense

P-20 *Depressed and Irritable*
    39. Depressed
    33. Irritable

## Patient Style of Relating—"How did you act toward your therapist during this session?"

P-21 *Collaboratively vs. Assertively*
    42. Working together: joining in: cooperating.
    46. Able to compromise: sharing: "give and take."
    44. *Not* determined: not giving in: firm.
    40. *Not* taking the lead: having my own ideas: bringing up things to talk about.

P-22 *Independent Activity vs. Emotional Involvement*
    54. Talkative: businesslike: active but not stirred up.
    52. *Not* excited: emotional: actively involved.

P-23 *Passive Compliance*
    45. Agreeing: going along with: changing my mind.
    41. Following: receptive: waiting for direction from my therapist.

P-24 *Restrained Emotion vs. Enthusiastic Acceptance*
    51. Neutral: impartial: neither positive nor negative.
    53. Feeling deeply: moved but controlled: stirred up but quiet.

P-25 *Aloofness*
    43. Distant: reserved: holding back.
    55. Quiet: inactive: unemotional.
    47. Independent: uninfluenced: making up my own mind.

P-26 *Ambivalence vs. Warmth*
    50. Respectful but critical: both positive and negative: "mixed feelings."
    48. *Not* friendly: warm: respectful.

## Therapist Style of Relating—"How did your therapist act toward you during this session?"

P-27 *Aloofness*
    16. Uninvolved: quiet: inactive.
    12. Neutral: impartial: impersonal.
    4. Distant: reserved: holding back.

P-28 *Forceful Direction vs. Collaboration*
    5. Insistent: demanding: firm.
   13. Intense: enthusiastic: excited.
    1. Leading: directing: bringing up things to talk about.
    3. (*Not* joining in: working together: cooperating.)

P-29 *Helpful Strictness vs. Indulgent Acceptance*
   11. Strict but fair: helpful but critical.
    9. *Not* friendly: helpful: on my side.

P-30 *Persuasibly vs. Independently*
    7. Democratic: open minded: willing to compromise.
    8. *Not* independent: uninfluenced: making up his own mind.

P-31 *Active Criticism vs. Affective Involvement*
   15. Businesslike: active but uninvolved: brisk.
   10. Critical: negative: sarcastic.
   14. *Not* moved but controlled: stirred: involved.

P-32 *Attentive Compliance*
    2. Attentive: waiting for me to lead: following.
    6. Agreeing: going along with: doing what I wanted.

## Patient Aims—"What did you want or hope to get out of this session?"

P-33 *Focus Collaboratively and Effectively on Problematic Issues*
   34. Get help in talking about what is really troubling me.
   33. Work together with my therapist on a person-to-person basis.
   39. Get my therapist to say what he (she) really thinks.
   38. Get straight on which things I feel and think are real and which are mostly in my mind.
   36. Get better self-control over my moods and over the things I do.
   26. Work out a problem that I have.

P-34 *Get a Rise out of the Therapist*
   32. Get even with my therapist for the way I've been treated.
   37. Get an emotional response from my therapist.

P-35 *Win the Therapist's Respect*
   25. Let my therapist see how I've improved.
   23. Show my therapist that I know what is going on, too.

P-36 *Get the Session Over With vs. Get Help From the Therapist*
   35. Talk and just get the session over with.
   27. *Not* get advice on how to deal with my life and with other people.
   20. *Not* get relief from nervousness and bad feelings.
   22. *Not* get a better understanding of my feelings and behavior.

P-37 *Get Lenient Acceptance*
   29. Get my therapist to leave me alone for a while.
   28. Get my therapist to like me better as a person.

P-38 *Find out More About the Therapist's Personal Life and Feelings*
>   31. Find out more about my therapist as a person.
>   24. Get some reassurance about how I'm doing.

P-39 *Get Support for Expressing Feelings*
>   30. Get my therapist to take my side.
>   21. Get a chance to let go and get things off my chest.

## Patient Satisfactions—"What do you feel that you got out of this session?"

P-40 *Insight and Rapport*
>   58. A sense of having an honest person-to-person relationship with my therapist, of working together.
>   59. Help in being able to talk about what was troubling me and really important.
>   54. Better insight and self-understanding.
>   56. Better ability to feel my feelings, to be what I really am.
>   57. Ideas for new or better ways of dealing with people.

P-41 *Relief and Control*
>   53. Relief from the tension I was under.
>   60. A better ability to tell which of the things I felt and thought were real and which were mostly in my mind.
>   61. Better self-control over my moods and actions.
>   55. Reassurance and encouragement about how I'm doing.

## Patient Session Development

P-42 *Looking Forward to Sessions*
>   46. To what extent were you looking forward to coming to this session?
>   62. To what extent are you looking forward to your next session?

P-43 *Communicating Effectively*
>   47. How freely were you able to talk with your therapist this session?
>   48. How clearly did you know what you wanted to talk about during this session?

P-44 *Doing Well and Making Progress*
>   51. Do you feel that you made progress in this session in dealing with the problems for which you are in therapy?
>   52. How well do you feel you are getting along, emotionally and psychologically, at this time?

P-45 *Understanding and Helpful*

49. How well did your therapist seem to understand how you were feeling and what was really on your mind during this session?
50. Do you feel that what your therapist said and did this session was helpful to you?
51. Do you feel that you made progress in this session in dealing with the problems for which you are in therapy?

# Salient Items[1] for Each Therapist Facet-Factor

**Dialogue—"What did your patient talk about during this session?"**

T-1    *Anger, Intimacy, and Competence in Personal Relationships*
     14.   Angry and aggressive feelings and experiences.
     12.   Inadequacies, fears, or successes in getting along personally and socially.
     15.   Feelings about being close to or needing someone.
     10.   Feelings and attitudes toward self.
     18.   Strange or unusual ideas, feelings, or experiences.

T-2    *Heterosexual Concerns*
     6.   Relationship with spouse, boyfriend, or girlfriend.
     13.   Sexual feelings and experiences.
     17.   Plans, hopes, and goals for the future.

T-3    *Familial and Therapeutic Concerns*
     8.   Childhood experiences with family members, and feelings about them.
     7.   Current relations with parents, brothers, or sisters.
     16.   Dreams, fantasies.
     19.   Therapy, the therapist, being a patient.

T-4    *Social and Vocational Concerns*
     2.   Social activities and relationships, friends and acquaintances.
     3.   Work, supervisors, associates on the job (or at school).
     9.   Childhood experiences in school, with friends and with other kids.
     4.   Recreation, hobbies, interests.

---

[1] Items are listed in descending order of loadings.

T-5  *Somatic and Domestic Concerns*
 11. Body functions, health, and physical symptoms.
  5. Domestic and household responsibilities, concerns, and activities (finances, children, etc.).

## Patient Feeling Process—"How did your patient seem to feel during this session?"

T-6  *Good*
 18. Optimistic
 10. Effective
 17. Cheerful
 22. Confident
 16. Satisfied
 11. Superior
 39. Energetic
 24. Likeable

T-7  *Trusting Warmth*
 35. Secure
 34. Trusting
 36. Accepted
 30. Tender
 28. Interested
 40. Alert

T-8  *Inferior*
 33. Rejected
  7. Inadequate
  8. Inferior
 32. Hurt

T-9  *Anxious*
  2. Anxious
 37. Tired
  3. Worried

T-10  *Mistrustful*
 31. Suspicious
 13. Frustrated
 26. Irritable

T-11  *Embarrassed vs. Relaxed*
 20. Embarrassed
 19. Shy
  1. Tense
  5. *Not* relaxed
  6. *Not* relieved

T-12  *Angry and Guilty*
 27. Angry
 21. Guilty

T-13  *Depressed*
 14. Sad
 25. Bored
 38. Dull
 15. Discouraged

T-14  *Flirtatious*
 23. Playful
 29. Sympathetic
  4. *Not* calm

## Therapist Feeling Process—"How did you feel during this session?"

T-15  *Good*
 36. Cheerful
 19. Effective
 37. Optimistic
 18. Confident
 41. Pleased
 30. Sympathetic

T-16  *Uneasy Intimacy*
 46. Embarrassed
 43. Playful
 25. Intimate
 42. Attracted
 35. Satisfied

T-17 *Disturbing Sexual Arousal*
    52. Thirsty
    33. Irritable
    53. Sexually aroused
    51. Hungry
    49. Tired

T-18 *Withdrawn vs. Involved*
    27. Detached
    50. Dull
    45. Repelled
    28. Withdrawn
    23. *Not* involved

T-19 *Intent vs. Calm*
    26. Preoccupied
    17. *Not* calm

T-20 *Sense of Failure*
    44. Disappointed

    22. Inadequate
    38. Frustrated
    21. Apprehensive

T-21 *Distress*
    59. Need to relieve bowels
    39. Depressed
    54. Need to relieve bladder
    34. Angry

T-22 *Resigned*
    32. Bored
    34. Discouraged

T-23 *Nurturant Warmth*
    31. Tender
    47. Energetic
    49. Alert
    24. Close

## Patient Style of Relating—"How did your patient act toward you during this session?"

T-24 *Unresponsive Activity vs. Mutuality*
    51. Businesslike: brisk: active but uninvolved emotionally.
    44. Independent: making up own mind: uninfluenced.
    43. *Not* mutually influencing: sharing: "give and take."

T-25 *Ambivalent Involvement vs. Enthusiastic Acceptance*
    47. Conflicted: ambivalent: "mixed feelings."
    49. *Not* animated: enthusiastic: excited.
    45. *Not* friendly: warm: engaging.
    50. Deeply feeling: moved but expressively controlled: stirred.

T-26 *Passive Dependence*
    48. Neutral: impersonal: impartial.
    42. Agreeing: submissive: giving in.
    38. Responsive: waiting for direction: receptive.

T-27 *Hostile Withdrawal*
    40. Distant: withdrawing from interaction: remote.
    46. Critical: negative: hostile.

T-28 *Assertion vs. Collaboration*
    37. Purposeful: taking the lead: initiating topics.
    39. *Not* cooperating: joining in: working together.
    52. *Not* impassive: unmoved: restrained.
    41. Insistent: controlling: unyielding.

## Therapist Style of Relating—"How did you act toward your patient during this session?"

T-29 *Impassive Control*
  12. Neutral: impartial: impersonal.
  10. Reproving: correcting: critical.
  16. Inactive: restrained: unmoved.
   5. Determined: insistent: firm.

T-30 *Attentive Compliance vs. Collaborative Intervention*
   2. Receptive: attentive: responsive.
   6. Agreeing: complying: going along with.
   3. Interacting: joining in: working together.
   1. *Not* structuring: intervening: initiating topics.
   7. *Not* mutually influencing: sharing: "give and take."

T-31 *Frankly vs. Supportively*
   9. *Not* supportive: empathic: friendly.
  11. Supportive but critical: correcting but friendly.
   4. Reserved: distant: remote.

T-32 *Affective Involvement vs. Unresponsive Activity*
  15. *Not* businesslike: brisk: active but uninvolved.
  14. Moved but expressively controlled: emotionally responsive: stirred.

T-33 *Animated Responsiveness vs. Independence*
  13. Animated: enthusiastic: excited.
   8. *Not* independent: making up my own mind: uninfluenced.

## Patient Aims—"What did your patient seem to want out of this session?"

T-34 *Work at Problems vs. Gain Sympathy*
  25. Working through or resolving a recognized emotional conflict.
  24. *Not* gaining attention, approval, sympathy, or affection.
  20. *Not* avoiding anxiety through defensive behavior and security operations.
  36. *Not* getting oriented to therapy and being a patient.

T-35 *Gain Support and Relief*
  29. Winning the therapist as an ally in a dispute or conflict.
  21. Getting relief by giving vent to suppressed or pent up feelings.
  34. Getting respite or relief from external involvements and pressures.
  26. Getting "expert" advice, opinion, etc., on some problem.

T-36 *Provoke the Therapist*
  30. Gaining knowledge of the therapist's personal life.
  31. Revenge on or punishment of the therapist.
  35. Provocation of the therapist to criticism or anger.

  27. Seductive provocation of the therapist.
  32. Testing the limits of the therapist and the therapy relationship.
  28. Withdrawal or evasion of contact with the therapist.

T-37 *Obstruct Therapy vs. Gain Insight*
  34. Filling time to get through the therapy session.
  23. Competing with the therapist.
  22. *Not* gaining insight and better self-understanding.

## Therapist Goals—"In what direction were you working with your patient during this session?"

T-38 *Emotional Stability vs. Experiential Insight*
  53. *Not* moving my patient closer to experiencing her (his) real feelings, what she (he) really is.
  51. *Not* increasing my patient's insight and self-understanding.
  55. Supporting my patient's defenses.
  50. Relieving my patient's tension and anxiety.
  59. Helping my patient gain better control over her (his) moods or impulses.

T-39 *Active Supportive Relationship*
  54. Helping my patient learn new or better ways of dealing with people and problems.
  52. Supporting my patient's self-esteem.
  56. Engaging my patient in an honest person-to-person relationship, working together authentically.

T-40 *Facilitation and Clarification*
  57. Helping my patient overcome her (his) resistance and defenses in order to get to what was of real concern to her (him).
  58. Orienting my patient more effectively to interpersonal reality in order to discriminate and control autistic tendencies.

## Therapist Session Development

T-41 *Making Therapeutic Progress*
  48. To what extent did your patient seem to make progress during this session in dealing with the problems for which she (he) is in therapy?
  47. How helpful do you feel that you were to your patient during this session?
  42. How well motivated for coming to therapy was your patient this session?
  1. How do you feel about the session which you have just completed?

T-42 *Communicating Effectively*

    44. To what extent did your patient bring out the thoughts and feelings which really seemed to concern her (him) during this session?

    43. How freely did your patient express herself (himself) in this session?

    45. To what extent did you feel in rapport or empathically "in touch" with what your patient was experiencing during this session?

T-43 *Motivated and Understanding*

    41. To what extent were you looking forward to seeing your patient this session?

    46. How well do you feel you understood the meaning of what your patient said and did during this session (in whatever conceptual terms you find most useful for describing personality)?

# Name Index

# Subject Index

277